Becoming an EX

Becoming an EX

The Process of Role Exit

Helen Rose Fuchs Ebaugh

With a Foreword by
Robert K. Merton

The University of Chicago Press
Chicago and London

Helen Rose Fuchs Ebaugh, professor and department chair of sociology at the University of Houston, is the author of *Out of the Cloister*.

The University of Chicago Press, Chicago 60637
The University of Chicago Press, Ltd., London

Published 1988
Printed in the United States of America

97 96 95 94 93 92 91 90 89 88 5 4 3 2 1

Library of Congress Cataloging-in-Publication Data

Ebaugh, Helen Rose Fuchs, 1942–
Becoming an ex.

Bibliography: p. 225.
Includes index.
1. Social role—United States. 2. Life change events—United States. 3. Identity (Psychology)—United States. I. Title. II. Title: Process of role exit.
HM131.E23 1988 305.3 87–25485
ISBN 0–226–18069–7
ISBN 0–226–18070–0 (pbk.)

To Sarah and Stephen
who have made my own role exit more meaningful

Contents

Foreword

This is an extraordinary book, both literally and figuratively. In part, it is out of the ordinary among recent sociological works in its sustained comparative focus on a single social process as it is played out in diverse social spheres. In another part, it is *extra ordinem,* out of a religious order. As readers of Professor Ebaugh's previous book, *Out of the Cloister,* know, and as readers of this one will soon learn for themselves, the author is herself an 'ex,' having left the life of a Catholic nun to become wife, mother, and professor of sociology.

I first came to know Professor Helen Rose Fuchs Ebaugh when, as Sister Helen Rose, clad in the traditional habit of the Sisters of Divine Providence, she enrolled for graduate study in the department of sociology at Columbia University. This was during the late 1960s and early 1970s, a time of turbulence at Columbia as at other universities and a time, too, after the Second Vatican Council, when religious orders were undergoing profound social change. A few years later, she had shed the habit, left the order, completed her dissertation on organizational dilemmas of religious orders, and married.

As Dr. Ebaugh put it in her earlier study, she found herself "collecting data as an insider and analyzing it as an outsider." The role of insider gave her sympathetic understanding and privileged access to basic field and documentary data about religious orders; the role of outsider helped provide her with a degree of interpretative distance and detachment. In that work, as in much of this one, she thus had access to two kinds of social knowledge: in the language made unforgettable by William James, "acquaintance with," a direct familiarity with phenomena often expressed in depictive representation, and "knowledge about," expressed in the more abstract formulations that do not all "resemble" what has been experienced.

Here, Professor Ebaugh takes up in focused, imaginative, methodical, and empirically grounded detail, a theoretical problem of social structure that I had raised some three decades ago but failed to pursue further: the dynamics and consequences of being an "ex-member" of a group or a former occupant of a social status. At once this raises the questions of how the "past history of statuses affects the present and future behavior of the individual" and how, in turn, it affects "the behavior of the repudiated membership group" toward the ex-member. Such questions move us from a static focus on the constraints and evocations of current social statuses to a dynamic focus on sequences of statuses. So far as I know, a comparative generic investigation of these questions has had to wait for this monograph, which provides a greatly enlarged sociological understanding of the process of "role exit" (as Zena Smith Blau first termed it).

This comparative study is based on qualitative focused interviews with a variety of "exes": ex-members of religious orders; divorced persons; mothers without custody of their children; former physicians, teachers, police officers, mental health workers, and air traffic controllers who had unexpectedly abandoned their occupations as well as retirees from such posts; ex-members of political groups; former prisoners and alcoholics; and transsexuals. The last of these exits from one role to another is perhaps the limiting case. In practically all societies, sex status is defined as ascribed and unchangeable. Yet, as Professor Ebaugh shows, the transsexual can achieve a great transformation, a composite personal and social redefinition of sex identity along with the public and private behaviors that go with it, all this rendered more malleable than ever before by the new surgical techniques designed to correct one of nature's anatomical "errors."

As the diverse array of role-exits signals, the study centers on voluntary rather than compelled exits from significant roles. Some attention is devoted to institutionalized status-sequences as these are typified, say, through the predictable, continuous movement from the status of medical student to intern, resident, and independent practitioner. But, to my mind, the distinctive contribution of the book resides in the sociological light it sheds on the unanticipated, often abrupt, and sometimes extreme *dis*continuities in roles, in the abandoning of once prized roles as physicians or nuns and in voluntary expatriation. From these pages, we learn that the recurrent social process of role-exit in diverse spheres of American social life varies within quite narrow bounds. These pages also provide what is by all odds the most thoroughgoing, empirically based analysis of anticipatory socialization to be found in the field.

Professor Ebaugh's book greatly advances our sociological understanding of role-exit as a major social process in the workings of social structures. Beyond that, its interplay of cogent ideas and vivid interview materials bids fair to maintain the interest of readers who don't give a tinker's damn about that noble accomplishment. This reader enjoyed it on both counts.

Robert K. Merton

Preface

The experience of being an ex of one kind or another is common to most people in modern society. While people who lived in earlier eras usually spent their entire lives in one marriage, one career, one religion, one geographical locality, most of us today make at least one major shift in an area of our lives that we consider central to who we are. Some of us negotiate several major role changes in the course of our lives, sometimes simultaneously. It is quite common, for example, for a major shift in career to reverberate in one's marriage and result in divorce, or for the death of a spouse to cause a major change in career.

In addition to learning how to be exes ourselves, and it is a learning process, we are constantly responding to exes among our families, friends, and acquaintances. Whether it be to ex-doctors, ex-career military people, ex-executives, divorced people, mothers without custody of children, ex-cons, ex-nuns, or retirees, responding to people who consider themselves exes in terms of their major self-identity is different from dealing with people for whom a past life is not especially salient. In fact, the phenomenon of being an ex is sociologically and psychologically intriguing since it implies that interaction is based not only on current role definitions but, more important, past identities that somehow linger on and define how people see and present themselves in their present identities.

For the past ten years I have been interested in the topic of role exit, both personally and professionally, and have been amazed and somewhat surprised at how little research exists on the topic. Having gone through a major role exit myself, I have been very sensitive to the shifts in self-identity that such an exit causes and to the reciprocal effects of the reactions of others to my being an ex. While there has been a plethora of books written in the past decade on life changes (e.g., Sheehy's *Passages,* 1976, and *Pathfinders,* 1981; Levinson's *Seasons of a Man's Life,* 1978; O'Neill's *Shifting Gears,* 1974; Goodman's *Turning Points,* 1979; Bridges's *Transitions,* 1980), none has dealt with what it means to exit a major role and learn to deal with a past identity.

My interest in the topic of role exit has a history that began at Columbia University in the early 1970s when I was a student of Robert K. Merton. One cannot study with Merton without being deeply immersed in the concept of role as central to social analysis. Merton's notion of "anticipatory socialization," that is, the adoption of values of a group to which one aspires but does not yet belong, suggested a process whereby one begins to make a role change before actually exiting a role. It became apparent to me, however, that the decision to exit a role involves much more than simply anticipating the requirements and values of a new role.

In 1970 and 1971, as part of my doctoral dissertation at Columbia, I conducted a study of religious orders of nuns in the Roman Catholic church, with emphasis on the growing numbers of ex-nuns in the United States. (This study resulted in my book, *Out of the Cloister: A Study of Organizational Dilemmas,* 1977.) I was an "insider" at the time, a Catholic nun affiliated with an order in the Southwest. Several prominent professors at Columbia were vitally interested in the changes occurring in the Catholic church, especially within convents, and they saw the convent as a laboratory for studying rapid social change and its impact, both institutionally and in the personal lives of the people involved. Several of these professors had tried to gain entrance into a religious order as researchers and had been met with closed doors and adamant refusals. Social research on the part of "outsiders" was still seen at that time as a threat to a cloistered, spiritually ordained institution. As an insider, I not only gained access but was welcomed as someone who might help religious orders understand what was happening.

Religious orders, under a mandate from the Second Vatican Council in Rome, were experiencing rapid and far-reaching changes structurally and, more important, in the basic belief and ideological systems that provided the rationale for celibate religious life. The Vatican Council in its official document, *Decree on the Appropriate Renewal of the Religious Life,* required each religious order to examine every aspect of its structure and life-style in the light of "changed conditions of the time" and, further, to effect any changes necessary to accommodate the religious life-style to the needs of the twentieth century.

Paradoxically, as religious orders updated and experienced change, the number of "defectors" who left American convents increased. In fact, in 1960 prior to the Second Vatican Council, there were 168,527 nuns in the United States. The number rose to 181,421 in 1966, after which there was a steady decline to an all-time low of 130,995 in 1976. The decline was due to two factors operating simultaneously: a marked decrease in the number of new recruits and a continuous increase in the numbers of nuns who were exiting.

The purpose of my research project in 1970 was twofold: (1) to study the relationship between change in religious orders and exit rates, and (2) to interview ex-nuns in order to understand why they left, factors that precipitated the exit, what the exiting process was like, and the experience of life as an ex-nun.

During the summer of 1971, I conducted intensive interviews with fifty-seven ex-nuns. In the course of interviewing, I became fascinated with the personal accounts of role exiting that I was hearing. Regardless of which order the interviewees had left, similar patterns and influences seemed to be operative. It also became obvious that there was a general process of exiting among these ex-nuns, demarcated by "stages" or sequential events. While the duration of these stages and the events that triggered them differed, their sequential ordering and the emotions and experiences at each stage were very similar. It was at this point that I began to conceptualize a general process of role exiting for ex-nuns.

In the course of analyzing data, I became one of my own statistics. I left the order I belonged to and became an ex-nun. How much my decision was influenced by what I was studying is hard to unravel. What is clear is that I gained enormous insight into the process of exiting from my own experience. In fact, there are nuances and depths of meaning that probably cannot be learned any other way. I lived what I had been studying, and it was only several years after I had exited that I was able to understand and integrate the pieces of the puzzle that I then began to label "role exit."

Shortly after I left the order, I met the man I later married. He had been officially divorced only ten days when I met him. He was still grieving over the "loss" of being an everyday father and facing the single, bachelor world again. The first year or so of our relationship, I was constantly struck by the similarity of his exit as a divorcé and my exit as an ex-nun. While we experienced events at different periods in the process, there were marked similarities between them. I was further intrigued with the idea of a general social process which could be identified as "role exit."

When a colleague invited me to write a chapter on the exit process for a book he was editing on self-identity, I developed a process or stage model of role exit, based on my ex-nun data (Ebaugh 1984). In the course of writing that chapter, I began to wonder how the model might apply to other kinds of voluntary exits, such as divorce, career changes, departures from ideological and sectarian groups, etc. Firsthand accounts from family members and friends made it clear that role exiting from any group that had central meaning in one's life was usually traumatic and painful. In the summer of 1983, I assembled a research group of graduate students to study the role-exit process across a variety of social roles. Our intention was to discover similarities and differences in the exiting process as experienced by people exiting all kinds of roles which they defined as central to their lives. We interviewed 106 individuals, including people who had experienced a variety of career changes (ex-doctors and dentists, ex-cops, ex-air traffic controllers, ex-teachers, ex-military men, ex-athletes, ex-professors), people who underwent major changes in familial roles (divorced people, widows, mothers without custody of their children), and people who exited highly stigmatized roles (ex-convicts, ex-prostitutes, ex-alcoholics). We conducted intensive, focused interviews with these individuals in order to find out what the exit process was like for them, what factors were prevalent at various points in the process, and how they dealt with being an ex once they left.

In the fall of 1984, I sent a prospectus of the book I planned to write to a number of publishers, and two of the editors wrote back and asked why I did not include in my sample the ultimate role exit—sex change. The idea intrigued me since we sociologists have traditionally considered sex as an ascribed status, determined at birth and not amenable to change. It happened that the psychiatrist in town who was commissioned to evaluate candidates for sex-change surgery is a close friend. He provided an entrée into a group of transsexuals who had recently undergone or were currently undergoing sex-change surgery. I conducted intensive interviews with ten transsexuals as well as several counselors who were conducting group therapy with them.

This book is the culmination and integration of the ten years of research efforts on role exits I have described. It is an attempt to develop a general theory of role exit as a social process based on empirical data.

Many people have contributed to this book in different ways. Robert K. Merton planted the seed for the concept of "role exit" while I was a student at Columbia University. He also spent time brainstorming with me in the early stage of the project and read the manuscript at a later stage. I am very honored that he agreed to write a foreword to the book.

A number of my colleagues in the sociology department at the University of Houston were enormously helpful. Janet Chafetz read several drafts of the book and spent many hours discussing ideas with me throughout the project. Her encouragement and challenge spurred me on at difficult moments in the process. Gary Dworkin read the manuscript and made helpful suggestions for revisions. Joseph Kotarba provided methodological assistance with the project. Russell Curtis took an interest in role exit as a topic and routinely suggested ideas and references for me to ponder and explore. The Center for Public Policy in the College of Social Sciences at the University of Houston provided financial support at various stages of the study. The University of Houston also awarded me a Faculty Development Leave as well as summer support during the data collection stages of the project. Mary Jo Duncan and Lonnie Anderson were superb in translating tapes and typing drafts of the manuscript to meet publisher deadlines.

Jill Alsup reviewed an early draft of the manuscript and provided immense encouragement as well as helpful suggestions for revisions. Peter Manning, as well as several anonymous reviewers, read several drafts of the book and challenged me to sharpen my conceptual focus, leave out redundancies, and relate my work to broader literatures.

Above all, I am grateful to all the people who were willing to share their exiting experiences and to the graduate students who helped me interview them: Stephanie Swanson, Pam Bentley, Conchita de la Garza, Deena Phillips, and Linda Cook. I also want to thank my parents and siblings who were not only accepting but very supportive throughout my own role exit. And to my husband, Albert, my stepsons, Nelson and James, and my own two children, Sarah and Stephen, I am thankful for constant and warm support in all my professional endeavors, especially in the writing of this book.

Becoming an EX

1
Defining the Issues

Most of us in today's world are exes in one way or another. We have exited a marriage, a career, a religious group, a meaningful voluntary organization, an institutional way of life, or perhaps a stigmatized role such as alcoholic or drug user. For some types of role exit society has coined a term to denote exiters: divorcé, retiree, recovered alcoholic, widow, alumnus. This is usually the case for exits that are common and have been occurring for a long time. Exits that have been around long enough to have been named are usually institutionalized in that they carry with them certain expectations, privileges, and status. In addition to these institutionalized exits, however, there are numerous exits that are simply referred to with the prefix, "ex": ex-doctor, ex-executive, ex-nun, ex-convict, ex-cult member, ex-athlete. The one thing all exes have in common is that they once identified with a social role which they no longer have.

The process of disengagement from a role that is central to one's self-identity and the reestablishment of an identity in a new role that takes into account one's ex-role constitutes the process I call role exit. While at first glance there may seem to be little in common between ex-nuns and transsexuals, ex-doctors and ex-convicts, or divorced people and ex-air traffic controllers, they have all experienced role exit. The purpose of this book is to explore the role-exit process as it is experienced by people who have left a wide array of roles. I argue throughout the book that role exit is a basic social process, as basic to the understanding of human social behavior as socialization, social interaction, or role conflict. Regardless of the types of roles being departed, there are underlying similarities and variables that make role exit unique and definable as a social process.

One of the reasons role exit has not yet found its way into the social science literature is because its widespread occurrence is a characteristic of only the past thirty years or so. Except at times of war or political upheavals, in earlier periods of history people were much less mobile in terms of role changes. They stayed in one marriage for a lifetime, prepared for one occupation which they followed regardless of how satisfied or dissatisfied they were, identified with the religion of their upbringing, stayed quite close to home geographically, and were not exposed to a variety of self-help groups that can become anchors for identity formation or transformation. In other words, role exit, while it did occur in cases of widowhood, unemployment, or ostracism from a group, was much less common than it is today.

In modern society, understanding role exit is every bit as important as learning how we become socialized into groups since most individuals in society experience several major role exits in the course of their lifetimes. Statistics on contemporary family trends are simply one indication of how widespread role exits are with regard to familial roles. The divorce rate today is almost three times what it was in the 1960s (Blumstein and Schwartz 1983). Demographers project that half of first marriages now taking place will end in divorce. Related to the rise in divorce rates is the increasing number of single-parent families, particularly female-headed households which rose from ten percent in 1960 to about fifteen percent in 1979 (Gross and Sussman 1982).

Behind these statistics are the personal lives of people who are experiencing the pains and sense of freedom associated with disengaging from and becoming an ex in relation to that role. Throughout this book I will present the lives of people we interviewed who had experienced role exit, many of whom were still establishing their identities as exes and learning to deal with their previous role identities.

Sociological Characteristics of the Ex-role

Being an ex is unique sociologically in that the expectations, norms, and identity of an ex-role relate not to what one is currently doing but rather to social expectations associated with the previous role. While statuses such as physician, wife, professor, and executive place one in the social structure on the basis of current occupancy, an ex-status derives meaning from contrast with the status previously held. What an ex-nun, ex-prostitute, ex-wife. ex-executive, and alumnus have in common is the fact that these individuals once occupied societally defined positions which they no longer occupy. While expectations regarding appropriate behavior on the part of various ex-statuses differ, there are characteristics of the ex-role that are generalizable beyond issues unique to the various roles exited.

Every ex has been involved in a process of disengagement and disidentification. Disengagement is the process of withdrawing from the normative expectations associated with a role, the process whereby an individual no longer accepts as appropriate the socially defined rights and obligations that accompany a given role in society. The individual removes him- or herself from those social expectations and no longer accepts them as relevant. Integrally involved in the process of disengagement are shifts in a person's role sets, in the collection of people occupying particular roles that are associated with an individual in a given social role. A wife, for example, is involved with an array of other people simply because of her role as wife. These include her husband, his family, his friends, their mutual friends, his business associates, neighbors, etc. In the process of disengagement, expectations of the wife shift on the part of these individuals. Usually, too, association with these people shifts in terms of either frequency or character.

Disengagement is a mutual process between the individual

and relevant role-set partners. As the person begins to remove him- or herself from the social expectations and associations with members of a previous role set, they in turn usually begin to withdraw from the exiting individual both emotionally and physically.

While disengagement refers to disassociation from the rights and obligations associated with a given role, disidentification refers to the process of ceasing to think of oneself in the former role. Disengagement leads to disidentification in the sense that individuals who withdraw from the social expectations of given roles begin to shift their identities in a new direction, that is, they begin to think of themselves apart from the people they were in the previous roles.

At the same time that exes are disengaging from previous roles and disidentifying with their normative expectations, they are in the process of learning new sets of role prescriptions. In one sense this is the process of role socialization, of internalizing the norms and expectations associated with a given social role. What makes exes different from others entering new roles is the fact that exes are unlearning normative expectations of previous roles at the same time that they are learning ones. This constitutes a process of resocialization to the extent that old sets of norms are given up and replaced by new sets of expectations.

Associated with socialization into a role is usually a shift of self-identity whereby the individual incorporates the social role into his or her perception of self. What characterizes the ex is the fact that the new identity incorporates vestiges and residuals of the previous role. To be a nonmember of a group is essentially different from being an ex-member in that nonmembers have never been part of the group. An individual has a self-identity that is formed as a result of numerous life experiences. For the ex-member a central experience is having been part of a previous group or social category. To become well integrated and a whole person, an ex must incorporate that past history into his or her current identity. Exes, therefore, share the fact that they must establish new identities that incorporate their past social status.

The process of role exiting involves tension between an individual's past, present, and future. Past identification with a social category or role lingers in one form or another throughout the lives of role exiters as they struggle to incorporate past identities into present conceptions of self. Exes tend to maintain role residual or some kind of "hangover identity" from a previous role as they move into new social roles. This role residual is part of self-identity and must be incorporated into current ideas of self.

Another characteristic that makes the ex-status unique are the images society holds of previous roles. People in society are conscious of ex-statuses and place an individual in a social structure not on the basis of current role occupancy alone but also on the basis of who the individual used to be. Life-cycle changes such as childhood, adolescence, and old age—those changes universally experienced by people—are usually not taken into account when considering ex-statuses. Rather, the unique statuses associated with occupation, life-style, marital status, or deviant roles tend to lead to societal stereotypes. Exes continually have to deal with society's reaction to their once having been part of a previous role set.

Role exit involves adjustment and adaptation, on the part not only of the individual making the change but also of significant others associated with the person. For example, mothers without custody have to deal with the reactions of their children as well as those of their own families of origin, who often look with horror on a woman who gives up custody of her children. Like divorcées, of which group she is also a part, she has to deal with former in-laws as well as an ex-spouse. One of the primary adjustments for transsexuals is dealing with significant others as they become aware of the sex change in the individual, including children, parents, and other relatives.

The ex also has unique relationships both with former group

members—individuals with whom one once shared a social status—and with fellow exes who were also part of the same social group. Having shared a previous social status establishes relationships with which nonmembers of the group do not have to deal. At the same time, exes have to deal with people who have never been part of the previous group. The attitudes of such people often involve ignorance, stereotypes, curiosity, and a lack of sensitivity to the nuances of a previous role. In a very real sense, exes from a specific social role constitute a marginal group and frequently develop a "marginal culture" (Stonequist 1937; Gist and Dworkin 1972) to support one another and cope with the labels and stereotypes of the broader society.

To be an ex, therefore, is sociologically unique. It differs significantly from never having been part of a previous social role. Likewise, the exiting process has unique characteristics that distinguish it from the process of socialization into new roles. Disengagement, disidentification, dealing with role residual, and being categorized as an ex-member of a group are a few of the elements that make role exit a unique social process.

Socialization and Role Exit

Role change, that is, entrances and exits from social roles, has been recognized by social scientists for many years. However, in terms of serious and systematic analysis, the emphasis has been placed on role entrances, especially in the socialization literature. Traditionally, especially since the work of Cooley, Mead, and W. I. Thomas, socialization has been a central focus for both sociologists and social psychologists. It is almost impossible to pick up an introductory book in either field without encountering a discussion of socialization.

While much of the early socialization literature focused on infant and childhood socialization, in the past few years adult socialization has become recognized as a neglected and important focus for study (see Brim and Wheeler 1966). A major impetus behind this trend are the contributions being made by scholars of the human life cycle, who are emphasizing socialization as a phenomenon of adolescence and adulthood roles as well as of childhood. Sociologists have recently become interested in age stratification (Riley, Johnson and Foner 1972; Foner 1974); the life cycle perspective (Elder 1975); career patterns (Rosenbaum 1983; Spilerman 1977; Kanter 1977a); mobility in adulthood (Featherman and Hauser 1978); the effects of life events (Brim and Ryff 1980; Hogan 1981); and developmental changes in the family (Elder 1980; Rubin 1979).

While numerous books have been written concerning role entrance, especially concerning socialization as the primary process of learning new roles, very little scholarly work exists on the exit dimension of role change, even though the concept is implicit in the idea of adult socialization, particularly when one takes into account discussions of "anticipatory socialization."

The idea of "anticipatory socialization," which has been in the sociological literature for several decades, is suggestive of several dimensions of the role-exit process. As originally formulated by Merton and Rossi (Merton and Rossi 1957; Merton 1957*a*), anticipatory socialization is the acquisition of values and orientations found in statuses and groups in which one is not yet engaged but which one is likely to enter. Internalizing group values prior to actually joining a new group serves two functions for the individual: it aids the individual's rise into that group in terms of motivation and ease of entrance, and it eases his or her adjustment after he or she has become part of it. By identifying with a group that one hopes to join, the person begins to be like members of the group in value orientation and normative expectations before actually entering the new role and assuming the rights and obligations associated with being a member.

When comparing the processes of socialization and role exit, fundamental questions arise. Is role exit simply socialization in reverse, that is, the mirror opposite of socialization, or is it a unique social process? Can we apply what we know about resocialization, anticipatory socialization, and adult socialization to understand role exit, or are these concepts insufficient for understanding the process? I argue throughout the book that role exit is unique and distinguishable from socialization, and that we know about socialization into roles is insufficient for an adequate understanding of role exit.

Role-exit theory views socialization as simply one aspect of the process. Looking ahead to the acquisition of a new role may or may not be important to a person exiting a role. In some cases, exiters have little or no idea of what they will do after a major role exit; they focus exclusively on getting out of undesirable present roles.

In addition, even for those exiters who do engage in anticipatory socialization, looking forward is simply one aspect of a much larger process of doubting, decision making, and disengaging from an array of obligations and expectations associated with a present role. The dynamics of disengagement are very different from the dynamics of learning and assimilating a new role.

The focus of socialization literature is primarily on the new role one is assimilating or to which one aspires. Disengagement from old roles is important only to the extent that it facilitates adaptation to a new role. The speedier and more completely such disengagement takes place, the greater the probability that socialization into a new role will "take" and be effective. Disengagement, therefore, is viewed as something that must be accomplished before socialization can be completed. The social dynamics of the disengagement process have never been central to socialization research.

Furthermore, nowhere in the social science literature on socialization is explicit emphasis placed on the impact of a "holdover" identity derived from an ex-status. Nor is there systematic attention placed on social reactions to an individual that are based on a previous role. The one exception might be labeling theory as applied to previous stigmatized roles, as in the case of the ex-con or ex-junkie. However, there has been no attempt to integrate these findings into a broader social process theory.

Merton (1957*a*) suggested the theoretical importance of the concept of ex-status when he observed that not only an individual's "current status but also his past history of statuses" affect the present and future behavior of the individual. However, with the exception of work done by researchers interested in studies of class mobility and the impact of past statuses on current class behavior, very little theoretical research has focused on ex-statuses and their impact on current identity.

Even though the difference between socialization and role-exit theories may be primarily one of focus and emphasis, this difference is significant with regard to the concepts, variables, and analyses that are generated to explain each process. It is important, therefore, for social scientists interested in explaining role exits to be well versed in the socialization literature; however, an adequate explanation of role exit must go beyond that.

Disengagement and Role Exit

Theories of disengagement have been developed by gerontologists and restricted almost exclusively to descriptions of the aging process. Cumming and Henry (1961) first introduced the concept of disengagement into the literature and defined it as "an inevitable mutual withdrawal or disengagement resulting in decreased interaction between the aging person and others in the social system he belongs to" (1961, 14). They distinguished three types of changes that accompany the process of disengagement in old age: (1) decreases in the number of people with whom the individual habitually interacts, as well as decreases in the amount of interaction with them; (2) qualitative changes in the interactions; and (3) decreased involvement with others linked to preoccupation with self. Most of the applications of disengagement theory have focused on life-cycle events and, most particularly, on the process of growing old. However, disengagement occurs any time a person withdraws from a group or social role. The types of changes described by Cumming and Henry as characterizing disengagement are equally applicable when individuals begin to disengage from groups of which they were members.

Disengagement has been viewed not only by gerontologists but by life-cycle theorists in general as a process of role loss and disidentification with a previous source of self-identity. It has been given a negative, perjorative connotation in the life-cycle literature, especially as it describes the aging process. However, as an analytical concept, disengagement is useful in describing a process that occurs frequently in the lives of most people. Whether one is moving from childhood to adolescence, from single life to marriage, from employment to unemployment or vice versa, each of these movements involves disengaging from the values, norms, social supports, and ways of thinking that are associated with the group one is leaving. Whether disengagement is desirable or undesirable, good or bad, is a totally different matter, dependent on one's ideological perspective and biases. Throughout this book I use the term disengagement to refer to the process of disassociating and disidentifying with the values, ideas, expectations, and social relationships of a particular social role which a person performed for a given period in his or her life. The term, as I use it, is descriptive and nonperjorative.

While use of the term disengagement usually focuses on the social and psychological withdrawal of the person from society or from previously meaningful roles or social groups, I think it is helpful to return to Cumming and Henry's original conception of a "mutual withdrawal" which involves both the individual's decreased association with a group and, simultaneously, the group's decreased demands on and involvement with the individual. As a group expects less from an individual, the rewards of belonging also decrease, such that withdrawal from the group becomes an increasingly viable option.

In this book I view disengagement as one aspect of the larger social process I call role exit. Rather than assuming the universal inevitability of disengagement, I test the frequency, extent, and nature of disengagement among the people who left roles that they considered significant in their lives. There are cases in which mutual disengagement is minimal, in which the individual fails to withdraw psychologically from the expectations and involvements of the previous role or, conversely, in which society or specific social groups continue to hold expectations of the individual. Disengagement, in the sense of mutual withdrawal from involvement with others in one's role set, is therefore viewed as a variable which can vary from total withdrawal to active involvement with role partners. One purpose of this study is to specify the conditions under which role disengagement occurs.

In addition, throughout the interviews I focused on issues of meaning in order to determine what role exiting meant to the people disassociating from a previous role. Departing from much existing research on disengagement, I was more interested in what the process means to people than in counting the role losses. One major contribution this book offers to the literature on disengagement is an understanding of subjective meanings for the individuals experiencing the process.

While disengagement is an essential part of the role-exit process, it describes only the process of becoming disassociated from a role. What happens after disengagement, in terms of creating an identity that takes into account a previous role, is also an integral part of role exit. I hope, in this book, to suggest some hypotheses and propositions that describe under what conditions disengagement tends to occur and what consequences result when the process of disengagement takes different forms.

Previous Studies

While the concept of role exit has not been elaborated in the general social science literature, some of the subdisciplines in sociology and psychology have generated empirical data on specific types of exits. Family sociologists, for example, have long been interested in divorce and the consequences of divorce, both for the individuals involved and for the society as a whole. Waller's (1930) early work on divorce was one of the first attempts to shift focus from divorce as a social problem to divorce as an event in an individual's life history which implies change, crisis, disorganization, and reorganization for both partners involved. Almost twenty-six years later, as divorce rates began to rise sharply after World War II, Goode (1956) studied the adjustment of divorced women in Detroit. Since then there have been numerous studies of the process of becoming divorced and the readjustment period (see Jacobsen 1983 for a review of these works). Duch's (1982) edited volume on dissolving personal relationships and Diana Vaughn's recent book, *Uncoupling: Turning Points in Intimate Relationships* (1986), present vivid descriptions of the process couples experience when they part ways.

The issues of cult defections, deprogramming, and personal adjustments by ex-cult members have recently caught the attention of sociologists of religion. Zablocki's analysis of American communes (1980) compares "stayers" and "leavers" in a number of areas such as degree of commitment to the group, feelings of trust, and sense of disillusionment with the group's leaders and ideology as well as general demographic differences. Case studies, such as Beckford's (1985) description of the defection process among ex-Moonies, analyze not only why people leave the group but how they negotiate the periods just before and after leaving. Both scholarly journals and popular magazines in the past several years have been featuring articles on the deconversion of people once caught up in new religious groups, especially religious cults (see Wright 1984; Jacobs 1984; Richardson 1978; Richardson et al. 1986; Barker 1984).

Occupational sociologists have traditionally been interested in turnover (see Mobley et al. 1979; Price 1975, for a review of this literature), career changes, commitment and the lack of it

(Becker 1960; Alutto, Hrebiniak, and Alonso 1973; Stevens, Beyer, and Trice 1978; Kanter 1968), and the process of decision making in role enactment or role leaving (Janis and Mann 1977). Much of the occupational literature, however, focuses on the consequences of role exit for the organization rather than for the leavers.

There are also a number of studies in the deviant careers—literature on career patterns, including exits, of drug dealers (Adler 1985; Ray 1964), burglars (Shover 1985), and ex-convicts (Wheeler 1961; Stanley 1976; Erickson et al. 1973). In addition, Goffman's book, *Stigma,* discusses the consequences of societal labeling for ex-convicts as well as for the numerous categories of people in society who find themselves in stigmatized roles.

The numerous case studies of immigrants migrating from a homeland to a new country also exemplify a type of role exit and one in which self-identities are usually drastically altered (e.g., Thomas and Znaniecki 1927; Fitzpatrick 1971; Moore 1970; Rodriguez 1987). This is especially the case when immigrants are confronted with a foreign language as well as strange cultural institutions. The concept of "marginal man," which originated in case studies of immigrants, portrays the immigrant as an individual caught between two cultural worlds as he or she struggles to leave behind the old world and adapt to the new one (Park 1928; Stonequist 1937; Gist and Dworkin 1972).

While there exists a plethora of case studies on unique types of role exits, little scholarly attention has focused on role exit as a generic social process, even though a perusal of the literature from these diverse subdisciplines makes it clear that there are many similarities in the process of role leaving and the reestablishment of identity after a major role change. The two major exceptions in the literature are Blau's seminal paper (1972; reprinted in Blau 1973) in which she introduces the term "role exit" and suggests a framework for viewing it, and Allen and Vliert's (1984) edited volume which presents a series of case studies on role transitions. Blau describes role exit as a process that occurs "whenever any stable pattern of interaction and shared activities between two or more persons ceases" (Blau 1972, 2). While the empirical data in the paper is derived from her work on the elderly, she attempts to develop a theory of role exit that is generalizable beyond the elderly to all types of role exits. While the paper proposes a theoretical framework for analysis, there was no follow-up by Blau or others that tested the ideas with comparative data.

Allen and Vliert's book (1984) goes beyond presenting a model of the role-transition process by presenting a series of case studies of role transitions (e.g., immigration, relocation, adulthood, prison, leadership, work-related and life-cycle transitions). While the book is very informative in terms of a theoretical model and suggestive of intervention strategies, the difficulty with it is that the data chapters are the outcome of a N.A.T.O. symposium on role transitions which included international and interdisciplinary perspectives. The papers were written before the model was developed and therefore constitute an ex post facto test of the model. While much comparative data is presented, there is no consistent perspective or methodology that ties the papers together.

One of the reasons for the lack of general theory in this area may well lie in the nature of our academic subspecializations. The social sciences, like the natural sciences and professions, have become so specialized into subdisciplines and, even more so, into very focused topics within subdisciplines, that we have lost sight of general theories, even theories of the middle range. Most of us focus so narrowly on one limited aspect of the social world that we have lost sight of more general processes that describe human behavior regardless of the specific circumstances in which it is found. Simmel's (1950, 1955) classic analyses of forms of sociation (i.e., processes of conflict, coalitions, and identities and disclosures) are prime examples of the types of "generic social processes" that Prus (1987) is arguing for in the social sciences. We have "developed" and "matured" beyond our founders whose goals were to study and explicate the nuts and bolts of social life. However, in the process of academic specialization, we may be overlooking some very basic and fundamental realities that cut across disciplines and subspecialities. It is my contention that role exit is such a reality, a generic social process (see Prus 1987) that is as fundamental to social life as socialization, social interaction, and social conflict.

Given the fact that there is not a wealth of literature on role exit as a basic social process and the tendency among role theorists to emphasize socialization, this book represents an attempt to explore and suggest basic issues involved in conceptualizing a theory of role exit. I do not pretend to develop a full-blown theory of role exit but rather to take a few first steps by suggesting issues and variables involved in conceptualizing the sociological meaning of an ex-role as well as the process of becoming an ex. Much more research, especially utilizing types of control variables, is needed before we can comfortably claim a "theory" of role exit. However, we must begin somewhere. I hope that the data in this book and the insights drawn from the data are suggestive of the phenomenon I call "role exit" and will provide a starting point toward a general theory.

Role Analysis

Throughout this book, the general perspective that guides research questions and the interpretation of data is that of role analysis. Sociologists and social psychologists have been studying roles and role behavior since the inception of their discipline. In fact, the notion of a social role was developed and used long before the social sciences came into existence. Novelists, dramatists, and other observers of the human scene have long noticed that behavior is often determined less by one's attributes than by the part one is assigned to play in society. Shakespeare's famous line, "All the world's a stage, and all the men and women merely players," is an analogy made by many observers of the human scene.

The term "role" developed as an analogy between the theatrical performances of actors and the many "parts" we play at any given time in life. Just as players have clearly defined parts to play, so actors in society occupy specific positions; just as players follow a written script, so actors must follow normative scripts provided by their culture; just as players react to each other on stage, so individuals in society respond to one another and adjust their behavior to reactions of others; just as players interpret a part, so people with various roles in society have their own individualized interpretations, within limited bounds, of how rules are to be actualized.

According to role theory, social behavior is not random and meaningless; rather it tends to be "patterned"—predictable, meaningful, and consequential for the participants. However, role theorists do not imply a static or rigid view of social behavior but rather view social roles in a dynamic perspective in which broad general norms are specified which allow a considerable range of variability among individuals enacting the same roles.

An important characteristic of role behavior is role attachment or the degree of intensity of involvement in a given social role (Sarbin 1954; Sarbin and Allen 1968). At the low-intensity end of this continuum, role behavior occurs with a minimal degree of effort and with little engagement of self in the role (e.g., behavior toward a clerk in a store, a passerby on the street). At the high-intensity end of the spectrum, a high degree of effort is expended in the role with a high degree of integration between self and role (mother, wife, religious fanatic). As will be described shortly, data in this book are based on a sample of people who exited roles in which their intensity of involvement in the role was high.

While role attachment refers to the degree of emotional intensity that an individual associates with a specific role, role commitment is the probability that the individual will remain in the role. Attachment is only one of a number of factors that an individual takes into account in deciding, consciously or unconsciously, to continue role performance. Another important factor is the side bets an individual accrues while in a role.

As Becker (1960) first pointed out, in the process of performing a role, an individual "stakes something of value to him, something originally unrelated to his present line of activity." These side bets could be friendships that have been established, emotional attachment to the job, retirement benefits, security, or status. Such side bets can enhance role commitment and make it less likely that a person will exit the role.

Individuals have numerous roles at any given time in their lives, a fact that results in both the richness and challenge of life. For example, Jane Smith may function as female, wife, mother, granddaughter, college professor, friend, volunteer, neighbor, and president of the civic club. When behaving as a college professor, the role behavior associated with most of her other roles is latent (Linton 1936). The basic role expectations associated with her behavior in the university are in her relationships to students, colleagues, and the university community. The latent role relationships are expected to become active sooner or later, and many times these latent relationships can color her present behavior. If two or more positions are simultaneously activated, the individual may find it difficult, if not impossible, to conform simultaneously to the two distinct sets of role expectations. That is, inter-role conflict may emerge. Social systems provide structural mechanisms for dealing with such conflicts. Giving priority to certain social roles, isolating roles spatially by providing offices or conference rooms, and even explicit or implicit norms of appropriate dress for given social roles are examples of ways in which social systems deal with role conflict.

In addition, an individual in any social role is related to numerous other individuals, each of whom has expectations of him or her in that given role. For example, a university professor relates to students, colleagues, department chair, dean, president of the university, employees, and staff. The totality of relationships with role senders in complementary positions is called a role set (Merton 1957*b*). Each role partner communicates role expectations to the individual. The person behaves somewhat differently when interacting with each member of the role set as a result of variation in expectations. Frequently, there is conflict within the role set in terms of contradictory role expectations from different members—that is, intrarole conflict arises (Gross, Mason, and McEachern 1958; Kahn et al. 1964). Role conflict, in terms both of competing roles which an individual occupies and of intrarole conflict within one's role set, often triggers discontent in a role and influences the role incumbent to begin to consider exiting the role in favor of a role alternative. In addition, the reactions of others in one's role set to a possible exit is an important factor which influences whether or not the exit occurs. The concepts of role set and role conflict, therefore, are helpful in understanding the dynamics of the role-exit process.

There are two basic approaches to role theory in the sociological literature—the structuralist's perspective and that of the social interactionists. Structuralists (e.g., Linton 1936; Merton 1957*a*; Parsons 1961; Banton 1965; Bromley and Shupe 1979; Stryker 1980) view social roles as sets of behavioral expectations associated with given positions in the social structure. Role socialization involves a process of internalizing the behavioral expectations associated with a given social role as well as learning the existing patterned resolutions that minimize and manage unavoidable role conflict within one's role set. The conflicting demands and expectations generated by various role set members make role conflict and role strain pervasive characteristics of a complex social system (Goode 1960; Merton 1957*b*). To the structuralists, individuals are involved in the process of "role taking," which connotes the fact that expectations exist in the normative system and that an individual takes on and internalizes those expectations.

Social interactionalists (e.g., Mead 1934; Turner 1976, 1978, 1985; Cicourel 1970; Meltzer, Petras, and Reynolds 1975) focus on the way individuals negotiate emergent meanings in order to discover and enact new roles. Based on their subjective perceptions, evaluations, and decisions, they coordinate their actions with the anticipated courses and expectations of others. This "role-making" process involves constant creative modifications as situations change. Role socialization, therefore, consists of individuals forging partial sets of established meanings and behavioral patterns or adaptations within which they can interact. "Role making" is a constant, ongoing process of thinking, feeling, perceiving, evaluating, and decision making. Although individuals are constrained by structural conditions generated largely by others, roles are created and redefined as individuals interpret and assume them. The basic criticism of symbolic interactionism over the years has been its astructural and antiorganizational bias (Denzin 1969; Meltzer, Petras, and Reynolds 1975; Reynolds and Reynolds 1973). In recent years, however, symbolic interactionists, partly in response to the criticism, have given greater consideration to structural and organizational conditions as restraining factors in the role-making process (Handel 1979; Heiss 1981; also see Turner 1985 for a critique of Handel and Heiss).

It is my contention throughout this book that an adequate understanding of a process such as role exiting can occur only in the context of both a role-taking and a role-making perspective. There is no denying the fact that behavioral expectations are associated with given social roles. These expectations are culturally prescribed and exist apart from any single individual in the society. They are, therefore, part of the social structure, and to become socialized implies the assumption and the internalization of those behavioral expectations. On the other hand, however, within broad boundaries individuals do engage in role making, that is, in creatively interpreting and adapting role expectations to given situations. Individuals exiting given roles are highly cognizant of the expectations others have for them, both as exes from previous roles and as neophytes in new ones. There is a range of viable patterned role prescriptions within which individuals make their choices and adapt behavior and self-identity.

There are some ex-roles in society that are more highly

institutionalized than others in their specific role expectations. Such, for example, is the case of the divorced person or the widow. On the other hand, however, there are ex-roles which are relatively new or rare in society and for which there exist fewer specific expectations. Examples are the situations of ex-nuns in the early 1970s and, currently, of mothers without custody of their children. Such ex-roles involve greater "role making" since individuals moving into these roles are faced with an ambiguous situation in which there are few existing behavioral expectations. As such roles become more common, they tend to become more highly institutionalized and better defined by society. The degree of institutionalization with regard to role expectations is a central variable throughout this study.

Role and Self-identity

From one perspective, roles explain the basic social order in society. People act and react in patterned, predictable ways because most people most of the time abide by the normative expectations associated with their social roles. Roles, however, explain more than social order; the self-identity of the individuals performing these roles is closely connected to the roles they perform. Personal identity is not merely the sum of roles played but arises from images of the self formed in the course of role behavior. While the primary and underlying self-concept of a person is formed during childhood, it is continually changing in response to other social contexts in which the person is involved.

While it is inappropriate to equate self and role, given the fact that there are aspects of the self that are formed outside of a social context, research has shown that a person's social roles are a major determinant of the conception of self and self-identity. When individuals are asked the question "Who are you?" the most frequent response is in terms of roles such as male/female, husband/wife, U.S. citizen, lawyer, doctor, Republican, daughter, etc. (Kuhn 1954; Spitzer, Couch, and Stratton 1970).

It follows, then, that transition from one role to another will influence one's self-identity.

Not all roles in a person's role repertoire are equally important to self-identity, nor are they all operative at any one time. Stryker (1980) uses the term "identity salience" to refer to the degree to which a particular role is involved in different situations. The higher the identity in the role hierarchy, the more likely that the identity will be invoked in many different situations (see also McCall and Simmons 1978; Heiss 1968). Likewise, Turner (1978) argues that person (self) and role are said to be merged when there is a systematic pattern involving failure of role compartmentalization, resistance to abandoning a role in the face of advantageous alternative roles, and the acquisition of role-appropriate attitudes. In addition, one's self-concept also helps determine the importance of a role.

Theorists of the self agree that early in life an individual begins to form an idea of self as an object, that is, begins to conceptualize self as an entity that exists and is unique from anyone or anything else. In addition, there is an underlying sameness and continuity of the self that remains despite changes in role. Allport (1961) expressed the sense of identity as follows:

> Today I remember some of my thoughts of yesterday, tomorrow I shall remember some of my thoughts of both yesterday and today; and I am certain that they are thoughts of the same person—of myself. Even an oldster of 80 is sure that he is the same individual as at the age of three, although everything about him, including the cells of his body and his environment, has changed many times over. The sense of self identity is a striking phenomenon, since change is otherwise the invincible rule of growth. . . . yet the self identity continues, even though we know that the rest of our personality has changed. (114–15)

As Blau (1973) points out, with each significant role change the integrity of the self is jeopardized to some degree. When the individual enters new roles and exits from old roles that have been incorporated into the structure of the self, the sense of enduring identity is disturbed. Self-identity is built up gradually over the years by internalizing the meanings and expectations of the roles we play. In Erikson's sense, ego identity is the "accrued confidence that one's ability to maintain inner sameness and continuity is matched by the sameness and continuity of one's meaning for others" (Erikson, 1959, 89). This, in essence, is a congruence in self-image that develops between our evaluations of ourselves as role players and the evaluations of our role performance by others in our role set. Erikson suggests (1959, 1968) that psychologically healthy people have a firm self-identity which he calls "ego identity." They have perceptions of themselves as continuing over time, see their ideas about themselves as being basically unified, and believe that their own self-concepts are essentially shared by other people they know.

Role exits, as well as role entrances, are closely related to self-identity since the roles an individual plays in society become part of one's self-definition. Personal identity is formed by the internalization of role expectations and the reactions of others to one's positions in the social structure. Each time an individual enters or exits a role, self-identity is threatened. Elements of the new or previous role have to be negotiated and reintegrated into one's self concept before stability and security can be reestablished. In some instances, the process of reestablishing identity occurs quickly; in others, the process may extend over many years. Zurcher (1977) has suggested that the rapid social changes in our society and the increasing number of role changes experienced by individuals in the course of their lifetimes is generating a new type of self-concept, one which he calls the "mutable self." The mutable self represents a significant shift, for the individual, from orientation toward the *stability* of self (self as object) to orientation toward *change* of self (self as process). The mutable self develops as a response to the centrality and frequency of role change in the course of an individual's lifetime.

Process Model

Let us review the definition of role exit that was presented earlier. Role exit is the process of disengagement from a role that is central to one's self-identity and the reestablishment of an identity in a new role that takes into account one's ex-role. Role exit is a social process that occurs over time. Very rarely does it happen as a result of one sudden decision. Rather, role exiting usually takes place over a time period, frequently originating before the individual is fully aware of what is happening or where events and decisions are leading him or her. In time, sometimes after years and often after only days or weeks, the individual becomes aware of what is happening and begins to act more self-consciously and deliberately. He or she becomes cognizant of cues being emitted and begins to interpret these cues. At that point, a shift in the role-exit process occurs in terms of decision making, seeking and weighing alternatives, anticipatory role playing, and alterations in significant reference groups.

While the types of roles being exited vary greatly in the sample described in this book, the process itself is identifiable and generalizable across roles. There are identifiable sequences of events which occur regardless of the role being exited.

I use the idea of "stages" or sequence of events very cautiously, fully aware of the criticism that the concept has engendered in the past few years (Brim 1976; Skolnick 1975; Riley 1978; Rossi 1980; Dannefer 1984). There are a number of inherent suppositions usually associated with stage theory, especially as it is used to describe developmental, age-related processes such as the life course, adult development, midlife crises, aging, etc. Dannefer (1984) identifies the basic supposition as "ontogenesis," that is, the assumption that there is a organismically rooted, normal pattern of development. Variation is defined as "deviation from the norm" rather than as patterned variations that can be explained by factors that produced them. Ontogenesis also leads to the supposition that a given sequence of events is inevitable and that one event *must* happen before another can occur, or at least occur normally.

Stage theories also frequently neglect the impact of cohort effects, that is, the influence of historical and social factors associated with the age cohort into which an individual was born. For example, being part of the baby-boom generation (as well as the baby-bust one), has great implications for such life events as educational and job opportunities, housing, recreational patterns, and adapting to old age (Jones 1980). Frequently, stage theories focus on individual development apart from the social factors that influence it. There is also a tendency among theorists using stage theory to assume a harmonious balance between social environmental factors and development rather than testing the effects of environment as an independent variable (Skolnick 1975; Lawrence 1980; Dannefer 1984).

In discussing the process of role exit, I am not assuming, in any way, an organismically based process. The very fact that the frequency of role exit varies by historical period, cultural group, and even for individuals within the same society is evidence enough that there is nothing biologically based or "normal" about role exit. Rather, we are talking about a social process that is determined and shaped by various sociohistorical factors. The fact that the process takes shape and is patterned by a more or less predictable sequence of events does not assume that this sequence is either inevitable or necessary. When events happen and how long each lasts is an empirical question. In fact, occurrence of the event as well as timing and duration of the process are characteristics of the role-exit process that vary and need explanation.

The decision to organize this book into "stages" or sequential events was made in the process of analyzing data when it became obvious that a definite pattern existed with regard to the process individuals experienced in leaving roles. The organization of the book grew naturally as I began to trace what an exiter went through in making a decision, disengaging from an old role, and beginning to acquire a new role identity. There was a natural sequence of events that emerged as the general pattern. In most cases, I was also able to explain those "deviant" cases that didn't fit the general pattern. A major finding of the study, therefore, is the fact that a general process is operative, one which progresses through a series of predictable stages.

Sample and Methodology

Data in this book are derived from four samples: (1) fifty-seven ex-nuns interviewed in 1971; (2) a follow-up of twelve ex-nuns interviewed in 1985; (3) 106 exes interviewed in 1984; (4) ten transsexuals interviewed in 1985. The face-to-face, intensive interviews lasted approximately two hours. With few exceptions, all 185 interviews were tape-recorded so that data could be transcribed and subjected to repeated analyses.

EX-NUNS

The fifty-seven ex-nuns interviewed in the summer of 1971 had exited from three Catholic orders, each at a different stage of change. One order was very liberal and among the first to initiate far-reaching structural and ideological changes; the second order was very conservative and was resisting the Vatican's mandate regarding religious life-styles; the third order was in between the first two in terms of change and was effecting moderate changes at a very deliberate and well-thought-out pace. I selected nineteen women who had left each of the three orders within a five-year time span. I asked the chief administrator of each order (called the "superior general") for a list of members who had left and obtained such a list from the liberal and moderate-change orders, but I received a refusal from the conservative order. For the first two orders, therefore, I was able to draw a somewhat systematic random sample, making sure to include a range of ages and differences in time since exit, length of time in the order, marital status, and educational experiences.

While the conservative order refused officially to cooperate, I made contact with a member of the central administration who was herself planning to exit within the next month. She was frustrated and discouraged with lack of change in the order and felt it was important to find out why others had left and whether the lack of change influenced their decisions. She, therefore, provided me with the names of five nuns who had left recently. I began with these names and easily snowballed a sample because of the close informal network that existed among ex-nuns from that particular order. In fact, these informal ties were so strong that there existed a structure akin to a countergroup, held together primarily by strong negative reactions to the parent group.

I interviewed all fifty-seven ex-nuns for approximately two hours each, using the focused interview as a prototype. There were a number of specific issues I wanted to explore with each interviewee; however, the sequence in which I introduced them was unstructured and determined by the flow of the interview. In addition to asking predetermined questions, I followed up and explored any areas that seemed pertinent and meaningful to the person being interviewed. If one individual brought up an issue that seemed especially important with regard either to the role-exit process in general or to the specific order from which she had exited, I introduced that issue in subsequent interviews in order to obtain additional information. In this sense, I used a grounded theory approach (Glaser and Strauss 1967).

The response of the fifty-seven interviewees was overwhelming. Rather than feeling imposed on, the vast majority were eager to talk and flattered that someone was interested in their story. In fact, the major problem in the interview situation was to keep issues focused so that the interview could be terminated in a reasonable period. No one objected to a tape recorder, so a transcription of each interview was made.

Variation exists in the basic demographics of the sample (see appendix A). The distributions of characteristics reflect the population of women who left religious convents in the early 1970s. Leavers tended to be in their late twenties and their thirties, having left in the late 1960s or early 1970s after being nuns for at least five years, and having completed at least a college degree and frequently also a master's degree. Most ex-nuns were still single, something due at least in part to their having been out of the convent and back in the world only a relatively short time. The sample I interviewed, therefore, is quite representative of the growing population of ex-nuns that existed in American society in the 1970s.

In the fall of 1985, I interviewed an additional twelve ex-nuns who had left religious orders within the past three years. The purpose of these interviews was to ascertain if the exiting process is different for ex-nuns who are leaving today from orders that have undergone significant changes since the implementation of Vatican II. In 1971, changes were just beginning; by 1985 orders had been radically restructured and represented more open systems than was the case previously. Again, I used a grounded theory approach in the interviews, focusing on the issues of role exit that had emerged in the earlier study and that had been refined in the intervening years. In the process of interviewing these later leavers, I used the grounded theory technique of "theoretical sampling," that is, sampling aimed toward the development of an emerging theory (Glaser and Strauss 1967; Charmaz 1983). Rather than drawing a systematic sample beforehand based on a specific sampling design, the sample of ex-nuns was part of the progressive stages of analysis. I realized as my analysis progressed that my previous data on ex-nuns was insufficient to answer the questions that were arising, especially in regard to the organizational contexts of role exiters. Very clear-cut patterns emerged from the earlier sample of ex-nuns, relating the process of leaving to changes in the orders. I wanted to verify this finding over time by seeing if the pattern continued for more recent leavers. Therefore, I sampled ex-nuns who had recently left until I was assured that my questions were answered.

Other Exes

The sample of 106 other exes my students and I interviewed in the summer of 1983 consisted of people who had left a variety of roles which they defined as central in their lives. As we began the project, we had two options: (1) to select three or four major types of role exits and compare people who had left each type, or (2) to study a wide array of types of exits in order to see whether patterns exist across them. Since my major research goal was to try to understand whether there exists a process which I can call "role exit" and under what conditions it operates in predictable ways, I chose the second option and decided to use a snowball technique to locate people who had exited a major role which society defines as centrally important and which the individual perceives as central in his or her self-identity.

Our research team, consisting of myself and five graduate students, knew offhand, through personal acquaintance or via friends, approximately twenty individuals whom we knew had recently exited major roles. We began with these names and our sample grew rapidly, as interviewees knew of other people who had undergone major role changes. We decided not to interview friends and acquaintances but to pass these names to other members of the team.

We determined beforehand that we would try to include exits from major areas of life, including familial roles (e.g., divorce, widowhood, relinquishing custody of children), occupational roles, ideological groups (religious and political), and stigmatized roles (e.g., prison inmates, alcoholics). Appendix A shows the breakdown of types of exits in the sample as well as demographic characteristics.

While we included several people who had experienced role

exit many years ago in order to have some idea of how time span affects recall of the process, the majority of individuals we interviewed had left less than five years previously. Most also had been in their previous role at least five years, long enough to become identified with it. Income was determined in terms of total family earnings; that explains the large percentage of the sample (49%) who made $40,000 or more a year. Our sample, however, is somewhat overrepresented by educated middle-class wage earners, since 61% of our interviewees have at least a college degree. In later analyses, we compared the college-educated with those less formally educated to see to what degree level of education affects the leaving experience.

Each interview lasted approximately two hours and all but two of the 106 interviews were tape-recorded. Each interviewer transcribed the tape onto interview schedules as soon after the interview as possible.

Many interviewees had also experienced multiple exits, such as an occupational exit and widowhood. In these instances, we tried to get data on both exits, with focus on the issue of how multiple exits influence each other.

As in my ex-nun study, the interviewees were, on the whole, eager to talk about their exit experience. For many of them, the interview was therapeutic, either because insights were raised by the types of questions that were asked or because the interview provided an "objective" setting in which they could relive some of the emotions and feelings associated with the usually painful experience. (See appendix B for discussion of the therapeutic aspects of the interviewing process.)

In the fall of 1984, at the suggestion of several editors, I added a subsample of ten transsexuals, eight of whom had undergone sex-change surgery from male to female and two from female to male. Four of them had had their surgeries five or more years earlier and the remaining six had undergone sex changes in the past five years. Their ages ranged from twenty-six to sixty-two, with a median age of thirty-six. Again, in selecting this sample, I used a theoretical sampling approach in which I continued to sample until I felt I had adequate data to understand the process I was studying.

Grounded Theory Approach

As my research on ex-roles progressed, it was greatly influenced by my growing interest in qualitative methods, especially the grounded theory approach (Glaser and Strauss 1967; Glaser 1978; Charmaz 1983). In 1971, my training was predominantly quantitative, with emphasis on the focused interview as a data-gathering technique. This fact is obvious as you read the analysis of the interview data in *Out of the Cloister* (Ebaugh 1977). Luckily, I had the original interviews on tape, and, as my qualitative interests and training grew, I was able to transcribe those interviews and reanalyze the data from a new perspective and with a new set of theoretical categories.

The remaining samples of exes reflect a more qualitative methodological approach. Rather than determining the samples a priori and deductively, I adopted more of a grounded theory approach in which samples are determined in the light of the development of an emerging theory (Glaser 1978). As I analyzed materials and began to develop theoretical categories, especially with regard to the general process of role exiting, I discovered the need to sample more cases to elaborate a category and make comparisons across groups. Theoretical sampling is part of the progressive stages of analysis, and samples are drawn when present data do not answer the questions the existing data raise (Glaser and Strauss 1967; Charmaz 1983; Douglas 1985). Subsequently, samples are chosen that will provide the relevant materials. Comparison groups are selected for their theoretical relevance. Both the latter sample of ex-nuns as well as the transsexual sample were included because of questions that arose in the analysis.

Grounded theory is especially powerful in illuminating social processes since the focus is on the individual's statements and actions regarding patterns, inconsistencies, intended and unintended consequences of action, meaning systems, assumptions that people hold, and social systems and interactions that are part of behavior. To understand a process such as role exit, grounded theory offers a way of understanding both the implicit and explicit dynamics from the perspective of the participants in the process. As my research progressed, because my central interest was in understanding what was involved in the process of role exit and whether a generalizable process did exist, the grounded theory approach emerged as the most viable way to answer the basic questions.

Life History as a Methodology

Along with a grounded theory approach, I was influenced by techniques of the life-history method. In the 1930s and 1940s, sociologists trained at the University of Chicago such as Robert E. Park and Ernest Burgess used the life history method extensively (Park 1952, 1955; Hughes 1928; Anderson 1923; Cressey 1932; Sutherland 1937; Shaw 1931). The technique has since been used by a number of qualitative researchers to describe such experiences as suicide (Jacobs 1967), violence (Prus 1978), professional thievery (Chambliss 1975), recruitment into religious cults (Lofland 1966), and the experiences that mothers of retarded children have with the medical profession (Jacobs 1969). The life-history approach presents the experiences and definitions held by one person, one group, or one organization as this person, group, or organization interprets these experiences (Denzin 1978). The basic assumption behind the life-history method is that every person defines the world differently. In order to explain these definitions and relate them to social behavior, sociologists must understand what events mean to the people experiencing them. The subject's definition of the situation takes precedence over the objective situation since, as Thomas and Znaniecki (1927) have argued, "If men define situations as real, they are real in their consequences." This means, in essence, that the way an individual perceives an event or situation impacts his or her behavior. In order to understand behavior, therefore, it is necessary to take such subjective definitions into account.

Life histories seek to establish the process whereby personal circumstances are interpreted by the person giving the account so as to produce the actions related in the account. Particular attention is given to the temporal sequences of events, the social context in which they occurred, their interpretations by the individual, and how all this led him or her to believe and behave as he or she did (Schwartz and Jacobs 1979).

The life-history approach emphasizes process as an organizing theme. Emphasis is on studying perspectives, negotiations, and relationships in process terms rather than on analysis of the impact of static structures on human behavior. Prus (1987) argues that the life-history approach is sensitive to issues such as the existence of multiple world-views whereby people organize their lives, people's abilities to influence one another's viewpoints and experiences, and the emergent, ongoing nature of group life.

While the life-history or ethnographic approach to gathering data has provided rich data on a variety of social settings, the current challenge is to delineate those processes that describe behavior that is generalizable across contexts and situations, in other words to specify "generic social processes" (Prus 1987). Prus defines these generic processes as transsituational elements of interaction, that is, "parallel sequences of activity across diverse contexts." Such processes highlight the emergent, interpretive features of association and focus on the basic activities involved in group life. The purpose of this book is to delineate and describe one such generic social process, namely, that of role exiting.

By interviewing a number of people in like situations and focusing on their perceptions and behavior, it is possible to discover to what degree patterns exist. One of the basic questions in my study was whether sufficient patterns would emerge among a wide variety of types of role exiters to enable me to specify a unique process called role exit. After years of research on the topic, I am convinced that role exit is a basic social process that operates in many different contexts.

Unlike the complete life history, the present study is a topical life history (Denzin 1978) since only one phase of the subject's life is considered, namely the process of role exiting. Interview questions focused specifically on events, attitudes, and behavior associated with the decision to disengage in one role and take on a new one. The interview guide, or "life history guide" as Denzin (1978) calls it, served to help order the interviewer's thoughts and convey them to the interviewee. It also insured that topics considered important for the research questions being posed were not overlooked. However, interviewers were trained not to overstructure the interview session but rather to guide the interviewee to talk about what he or she considered important in the exiting process.

The life histories presented in this book, like most life histories, are retrospective accounts which interviewees have constructed of what happened to them during some event in their lives. All of the pitfalls and limitations of retrospective reporting must therefore be taken into account (see Snow and Phillips 1980). Not only may the person's memory have faded, but life experiences in one's current position may well influence and taint the perspective with which one recalls past experiences. However, as Denzin (1978) points out, for many events the account is not only the best we have but often the only evidence available. Also, to recall again Thomas's statement that defining a situation as real makes it real in its consequences, the objectivity of a recalled event is less important than its subjective meaning for the person recalling it. Therefore close attention is paid throughout the study to the interpretations placed on events by those experiencing them.

Sequence of Events in the Role-exit Process

One of the major findings in the study is the fact that a pattern exists among exiters with regard to the sequence of events during the exiting process. While some variation did exist in the timing of experiences, the similarities exiters described were suprising. Because of the strong pattern that emerged regarding the sequencing of events in the process, I decided to organize this book in a natural history fashion, delineating chapters according to the major events that emerged as significant in the course of the exit process.

Four major "moments" or stages in the process emerged as characteristic of most exiters' experience. The first stage was that of first doubts, in which individuals began to question the role commitment they had previously taken for granted. While there were a variety of conditions under which such doubting began, cuing behavior and the reactions of significant other people became critical factors once doubts were entertained in determining whether and how the process would continue. This doubting stage is the subject of chapter 2. Chapter 3 focuses on the next stage of the process, the seeking and weighing of role alternatives. The functions of conscious cuing, anticipatory socialization, role rehearsal, and shifting reference groups become important variables at this stage. Turning points and their functions in the role-exit process are the subject of chapter 4. This chapter also includes discussion of how exiters feel after they have left a meaningful role and of the vacuum experience that characterizes many role exits. Chapter 5 describes what happens after the exit in terms of establishing an ex-role identity. The chapter focuses on areas that are important in the postexit adjustment period.

Inspired by the natural history model of research, I found the four stages in the role-exit process emerging in the course of data collection. These corresponded to the accounts of those who had experienced the process. Throughout the book, I will describe the few deviant cases and attempt some explanation of the conditions under which exiters did not fit the general pattern.

Properties of the Role-exit Process

In the course of data analysis, eleven properties of the role-exit process emerged as central variables that influenced the nature and consequences of the process. These variables became major categories that helped differentiate and explain what was occurring throughout the process. Many of these variables are similar to those noted by Glaser and Strauss in their discussion of status passages (1971).

The first two variables, voluntariness and centrality of the role being exited to self-identity, constituted the parameters on which I selected the sample. Each role exiter was selected on the basis of having made a voluntary exit from a role that he or she considered central to his or her identity. However, among our interviewees, there were some differences in degree of voluntariness in making the exit and in how central and all-encompassing the previous role had been. While I selected individuals high on each dimension, there was some variability among the interviewees on each dimension. It is important, therefore, to discuss these two variables before proceeding to the remaining ones.

Voluntariness. This property concerns the degree of choice an individual has in making an exit. In some instances, such as sex change and becoming an ex-nun, the individual is free to make the exit or not make the exit; in instances such as mandatory retirement or being fired from a job, the exiter has little or no control in making the exit. However, the variable is not dichotomous but rather must be conceptualized on a continuum because most exits have elements of both dimensions. Divorce, for example, is usually an interactive process in which the individual chooses to terminate a marriage which is impossible to maintain. Many divorcees will say, "I really had no choice." They did have a choice; however, the alternative of remaining married under adverse circumstances was not a viable option. Likewise, in the case of the air traffic controllers in the sample, there were elements of both voluntariness and involuntariness in their decisions, since the decision to go on strike was a voluntary one but the decision to stay on strike was affected by President Reagan's order that those remaining on strike were fired.

Centrality of the role. At any point in time each of us plays numerous roles in society, including central roles such as sex identity, marital roles, parental roles, career commitments, as well as less important roles such as membership in a society, peripheral roles in organizations, and temporal roles on mailing lists. Some of these roles are more important to us than others and constitute role identities which direct and organize who we think we are in society. Each of us has one or several "master statuses" around which we organize our self-identities and by which we are primarily known in society (Hughes 1958; Merton 1957*a*; McCall and Simmons 1978). For most people, master statuses involve sex roles, familial roles, and primary occupational roles. Master roles help to prioritize and integrate our other roles and are a way of preventing overload and role conflict (Merton 1968).

Roles differ in their degree of centrality to self-identity. Certain role identities are extremely important to the individual and are imbued with strong affect (Stryker 1968; Sarbin and Schiebe 1980). Loss of such roles can have devastating consequences for the individual. The centrality of the role of mother for some women is so important that to give up custody of children creates a sense of utter loss and annihilation. By contrast, other roles are more peripheral to self and can be abandoned with little personal trauma or sense of loss. Goffman (1961) uses the term "role distance" to denote activities that an actor performs with little self-involvement or emotional affect.

In the first stages of this project, I was confronted with a number of decisions regarding the sample I would study. Among those decisions was whether to include both voluntary and involuntary exits. For the sake of focus and simplicity, given the lack of research in the area of role exiting, I decided to include only exits that were primarily voluntary. Likewise, I had the option to include any of a wide array of exits ranging from those highly salient to self-identity to those that were more peripheral. In order to focus more sharply on the decision-making process involved in exiting and the effect of an exit decision on self-identity, I chose to include only exits that were at the core of self-definition. However, a list of role-exit properties must include both degree of voluntariness and centrality of the role to self-identity. Future studies will, I hope, expand the present analyses to include variations in each of the two variables.

Reversibility. In some instances of role exit individuals can reverse their decisions and return to a previous role. This is the case, for example, in most career changes or changes in terms of ideological groups, whereas sex changes are irreversible decisions. In some instances, such as leaving religious orders, there are institutional constraints on readmittance. In other cases, such as divorce and giving up custody of children, these exits are irreversible in most instances although they don't necessarily have to be so.

Duration. The role-exit process may be compressed into a very short time period, sometimes consisting of only days or weeks, or it may extend over many years. Each stage of the process has temporal aspects that are influenced by various factors. The duration of some exits, such as training programs, leaves of absences, and periods of marital separation before divorce, are institutionally scheduled, while others are determined by individual and social factors.

Degree of control. In most instances of role exit, the exiter does not operate in isolation but is dependent on institutions and on other people to facilitate or retard the process. Transsexuals, for example, are dependent on psychiatrists and medical doctors both to recommend and execute the sex-change surgery. Divorced people and mothers without custody are dependent on spouses in the decision-making process. Ex-convicts are dependent on criminal justice institutions to facilitate their period of parole. Ex-nuns are dependent on the Institute for Religious in Rome to approve an official dispensation from vows, but they may also simply walk out of the convent without such official approval. Occupational exiters also have relatively high control over the decision to exit, even though they have to deal with organizational and interpersonal factors.

Individual versus group exit. Some exits are executed individually as the person makes an individual decision and leaves relatively independently of other people, whereas in other instances exiters leave either in age cohorts or as part of an aggregate of individuals. In the latter instance, exiters may be personally acquainted, or they may be part of an aggregate whose members do not know each other personally or interact. In the 1960s nuns left religious orders as members of an aggregate while those leaving today almost always leave as lone individuals since the exodus rate has declined significantly. In contrast, the few individuals who obtained divorces fifty years ago had little company while divorced people today are part of a large cohort.

Single versus multiple exits. Generally people go through more than one role exit at a time. For example, the woman exiting a marriage in many instances also experiences an occupational change. So too the nun leaving a religious order usually changes occupations in the process. Mothers who give up custody of children usually do so at the time a divorce is finalized. While some exits may be relatively independent of each other, others may compete for time and energy, often causing considerable personal strain. Multiple exits often involve problems of priority as a person tries to determine which of the various exits is most important.

Social desirability. Some exits, such as those of the ex-convict, the ex-alcoholic, and the ex-prostitute, carry social approval, whereas other exits, such as those of the ex-physician, divorcé, mother without custody, transsexual, and ex-nun, are frequently socially undesirable and carry social stigma. The process of establishing an ex-identity is highly influenced by the desirability or undersirability of the exit as viewed by society.

Degree of institutionalization. Some exits are institutionalized in society since there are social expectations and rites of passage or ceremonies associated with them. Such is the case with physicians who complete medical school and pass medical board examinations or retirees who are honored with banquets and gold watches. Other exits, however, are less clearly defined by society, and in these cases the exiters create their new identities as they proceed in the process. Such emergent passages characterize the role of the ex-nun, the mother without custody, and the transsexual in society. One indication of the degree of institutionalization of an ex-status is the nomenclature developed by society to indicate these passages. Society has coined terms for the alumnus, divorcé, and retiree; however, less institutionalized role exits are simply known as exes, such as ex-nun, ex-minister, ex-physician, or ex-alcoholic.

Degree of awareness. In some instances, role exiters make a very deliberate and calculated decision to exit whereas in other instances individuals seem to "split" or "glide" through the process with much less deliberation and awareness.

Sequentiality. Some exits are sequential in nature. Examples include age-graded, life-cycle progressions, movement from one grade in school to another, participation in professional and vocational training programs (medical student to intern to physician), and movement out of probationary statuses (engaged to married, novice to nun, rookie to athlete, army recruit to officer). Once individuals begin the sequence, they usually move from one role to the next. In the present study, life-cycle events that occur without individual choice such as the transition between childhood and adolescence, adolescence and adulthood, and middle years into old age are types of involuntary sequential events that are excluded. However, voluntary sequential events, as in the case of the nun with temporary vows facing the lifelong commitment of final vows or the physician opting for retirement, are included.

Each of the above characteristics of the role-exit process influences and determines the process. In each of the following chapters it will become evident how these characteristics of role exit impact on the process. Some characteristics are more salient than others in each particular stage of the process; however, these characteristics crisscross each other and become mutually interdependent in terms of outcomes of the process.

Two major factors underlie the organization of the book: stages or sequential events of the process and properties descriptive of role exit. The next four chapters are divided according to what emerged as the four major stages in the role-exit process. Within each chapter, the importance and impact of the role-exit properties outlined in this chapter are described. In chapter 6, I summarize the role-exit process and the findings regarding each property. In a short epilogue, I apply the role-exit model in several therapeutic and organizational settings and address the issue of the ways in which knowledge about role exit as a major social process might assist in intervention to ameliorate the process.

2
First Doubts

The first definable stage of the role-exit process occurs when role incumbents begin to question and experience doubts about their role commitment. The doubting stage is essentially one of reinterpreting and redefining a situation that was previously taken for granted. Events and expectations that had been defined as acceptable begin to take on new meanings. First doubts involve a reinterpretation of reality, a realization that things are not what they had seemed. Even though the individual may have been dissatisfied previously in his or her role, when doubts become conscious, the person begins to reinterpret meanings and normative expectations associated with the role. The process of doubting, reconsidering role commitments, and admitting role alternatives is basically a process of reinterpreting role requirements and value judgments concerning the costs and rewards of meeting those role demands.

The doubting process is usually gradual in that the individual first experiences overall dissatisfaction in a generalized way and only eventually is able to specify and articulate what he or she finds lacking in the situation. In some instances, this first stage of the exit process is arrested and never proceeds to further stages. In other cases, it is prolonged over many years, while in still other instances it occurs quite rapidly and results in exit within the span of a few months. In this chapter, I explore some of the conditions which led to initial doubts on the part of our interviewees and then specify conditions which both encourage and discourage the process of moving from initial doubts to the consideration of alternative roles. Essential in this process is the function of cuing behavior on the part of role exiters, the positive and negative impact of others' reactions to first doubts, and the interpretation of subsequent events once the individual begins to question and reevaluate role commitment. As a way of summarizing this descriptive data, a flow chart depicting the initial stage of the exiting process is presented as a conclusion to the chapter.

Circumstances that Give Rise to First Doubts

There are a variety of conditions that influenced the interviewees in our study to begin doubting their role commitment and reinterpreting the costs and rewards associated with continuance in the role. These conditions varied for the different groups we studied but can be categorized as follows: organizational changes, job burnout, disappointments and drastic changes in relationships, and specific events.

Organizational Change

Some of our interviewees first began to question their role commitment when the organization with which they were affiliated underwent significant change. While organizations are constantly changing, there are two types of situations in which organizational change creates doubt and disillusionment for its members and results in membership turnover. The first occurs under conditions of rapid change which some members are ill-prepared or unwilling to accommodate. In some of these instances, members lose their original commitment because their goals and interests are no longer parallel with those of the organization. A second situation occurs when change is gradual over time but eventuates in structures which no longer accommodate the needs or interests of some members.

Organizational change was the reason many ex-nuns in my sample began doubting their commitment to religious life; however, a number of professional and occupational exiters also traced their initial doubts to organizational changes. The fact that leaving religious convents was practially nonexistent prior to the Second Vatican Council in the Catholic church (1962–65) is one indication that the process of leaving was related to changes occurring within the orders since Vatican II. In 1950, 381 nuns left their orders. The number rose to 765 by 1960. However, by 1970, one decade later, the number increased to 4,337 (Neal 1984). It is not coincidental that the rise in rates of leaving occurred during the decade of rapid change within religious orders. It is impossible to understand the process of exiting religious life without understanding the context of the changes occurring within these institutions.

The entire social organization of the traditional convent was built on the goal of death to self and rebirth to God. The three vows of poverty, chastity, and obedience were designed to eradicate selfish desires and encourage nuns to be instruments of God's will. To assure total concentration and commitment to these ends, since the twelfth century nuns were isolated within the cloister. Convent walls and clanging doors kept outsiders out and nuns secure behind closed doors. Physical isolation was buttressed by an even more powerful social and psychological isolation manifested in various rules and customs which preserved strict boundary maintenance between life inside the cloister and "the world."

A series of historical events occurred within the larger church structure that not only permitted but mandated critical reevaluation of the system. Pope Pius XII's mandate to religious superiors in 1952 to upgrade the professional preparation of nuns to place them on a par with lay colleagues and the *Decree on Religious Life* (Abbot 1966) promulgated by the Second Vatican Council about ten years later disrupted the isolation and totalistic way of thinking that was characteristic of orders for centuries. As a result of educational experiences and the intensive self-scrutiny and renewal demanded of orders by Vatican II, religious orders emerged in the late 1960s and early 1970s as radically transformed institutions. While the three vows remained, they were interpreted to place less emphasis on self-denial and greater focus on the human and community dimensions of the vows. The hierarchial notion of superior and inferior was replaced by that of dialogue among groups and individuals. The stress on cloister and isolation from the world gave way to emphasis on availability and witness in the world. The medieval black habit was discarded for contemporary dress and nuns were allowed greater choice in types and places of work as well as in where they lived. In short, the religious order changed from a total institution par excellence to a contemporary form of voluntary organization committed to providing resources to members (Ebaugh 1977).

Central to changes in structure and life-style within religious orders was redefinition of what it meant to be a nun. The well-defined image of the pre-Vatican II nun was gone and the image of the nun in the modern world was still emerging.

When the Vatican Council mandated that religious orders reevaluate their life-style and structure, every nun was asked to become involved in the renewal process. As a result, religious orders set up numerous self-study groups and committees, whereby every nun was encouraged to be part of the reevaluation process. Whereas superiors had previously told nuns what was expected of them and what was to be done, an environment was now created for democratic processes of discussion, reevaluation, and creation of a new life-style and image. Approximately one-half of the ex-nuns interviewed indicated that in the course of these group discussions, they first began to question the value of religious life for themselves. In these discussions not only was attention given to daily routines of religious life but, perhaps more important, discussion centered around the value of religious life, the meaning of religious life in the contemporary world, and the new theology behind the three vows of poverty, chastity, and obedience. In addition, nuns were now allowed to watch television, read newspapers, and participate in group processes outside the order, such as social movements, political groups, and discussion clubs, activities which were prohibited in traditional orders. Therefore, changing cultural mores were brought to bear on the discussions within religious life. These ideas included the reevaluation of traditional forms of the family, women's rights, and increased emphasis on self-fulfillment and self-understanding.

The Second Vatican Council itself was a response to intellectuals within the church, and laity as well, who were questioning the traditional authority and outdated structures of the Roman Catholic church. As Sarason (1977, 72) points out, "The Vatican Council, like the Constitutional Convention of 1787, did not occur because someone thought it was a good idea. It was a consequence of an approaching crisis within the Church." And the heart of that crisis revolved around concepts of authority. Not only were infallibility and theological authoritarianism publicly debated by the bishops at the Council, but issues which were normally not discussed, especially with laymen, were broadcast openly by the press. As Goldner, Ritti, and Ference (1977) argue, this open communication led to production of "cynical knowledge" on the part of various ranks in the church, including clergy and laity alike—that is, the knowledge that presumably altruistic actions or procedures of the organization actually serve the purpose of maintaining the legitimacy of existing authority or preserving the institutional structure. Goldner, Ritti, and Ference (1977) present data on the development of cynical knowledge on the part of priests in the church, but a similar process occurred for Catholic nuns.

The atmosphere that permeated group discussions within religious orders was one that emphasized the processes of reevaluation, discovery, and creation of new forms rather than the acceptance of forms that had been traditionally accepted both in the culture and in the church. For many nuns, these group discussions within their orders provided a first opportunity to begin questioning the religious life that they had taken for granted until this point. While for some nuns these discussions simply provided an outlet for preexisting doubts, for many they raised new issues and doubts never before entertained, especially in regard to the legitimacy and altruism of religious life and obedience to authority within religious convents. As one ex-nun described, "All of the theology on which I'd kind of pinned my life, Vatican II was questioning. Just because you're a priest or nun doesn't automatically make you one whit better than anybody else. And I learned that there are all kinds of alternative ways to be a good person and serve God. All of this was news to me and, at first, very unsettling."

As nuns began to consider the fact that religious life itself was changing, they were also challenged to consider whether they, themselves, wanted to maintain their commitment to religious life. In addition, throughout this process nuns became more and more aware of and in touch with their own personal feelings and needs. As one ex-nun said, "I never should have entered. It took me twenty years to be able to admit that and be true to myself."

Strangely enough, as convent life became freer and in many ways less demanding, more and more nuns found it difficult or impossible to maintain their commitment. Kanter (1972) found a similar relationship between sacrifice and commitment in her study of nineteenth-century utopias. Those groups that made intense demands on members tended to outlive the more lenient groups. One possible explanation offered by Kanter is that sacrifice tends to go along with clearly defined goals and role expectations. In other words, if a cause is clearly seen as worthwhile, members are willing to make extreme sacrifices to bring it about. When goals and expectations become more nebulous, members reevaluate the benefits of self-sacrifice.

In addition to the discussion groups and renewal efforts within religious orders themselves, another major influence that led nuns to doubt their commitment was exposure to advanced education. Going away to study was normally the first time a nun found herself outside the cloistered environment. While before things had been secure and well-defined for her, all of a sudden she found herself negotiating in a world where her role was not so clearly specified. Among fellow students, she was often an anomaly. She sat in classes where the existence of God was not necessarily assumed. The world was seen not as a result of a magnificent anthropomorphic creator but rather as operating according to its own natural laws.

For many nuns the initial questioning of religious life occurred, strangely enough, when they began studying contemporary theology. Many of them realized that theological notions regarding God, the church, the secular world, and religious vocation were changing. For example, as one ex-nun expressed it, "I entered because I felt it was God's will for me. In a contemporary theology course, I learned that God is a loving Father and cares about our happiness. Vocation, we were taught, was a decision from within, a free response to live full human lives and be faithful to our inner selves. When my notion of God's will changed, I began to question my being in religious life when I felt basically unhappy." Another ex-nun described a similar experience: "I always wanted to leave, but was brainwashed in the idea that God wants me here. What I wanted was not important. Then I went away to study and heard a priest in a class tell the story of a young sister who didn't want religious life, but thought God wanted it for her. The priest told her she should leave because God as Father wants what she wants. It hit me like a thunderbolt to think what I wanted might be important as part of God's will for me." Another nun was exposed to modern liturgical changes and began to realize that traditional forms of liturgy were not necessarily the best and that liturgy, essentially, was man's response to God and therefore had to be adapted throughout the ages. Such a sense of relativity and changeableness led her to question the rigidity with which religious life had been lived for centuries.

In addition to the intellectual challenges presented to nuns away studying, nuns were also exposed to all types of new associations and social contacts. For the first time in years, many of them were interacting with lay persons, colleagues, and fellow students. In addition to formal class associations, nuns socialized with male and female fellow students. For the first time, a life-style other than that of "celebate religious women" became prevalent on a day-to-day basis. Nuns learned that laywomen with families were living very happy, meaningful lives. Many ex-nuns commented that during those days they began to realize the high cost involved in being a celibate religious. Likewise, for the first time in years many of them became aware of and admitted sexual as well as friendship needs that were not being met in their lives in the convent. Frequently, male students and male professors reacted to them not just as members of religious orders but as women. For many nuns it had been years since they were in a dating situation and had personal relationships with men. For many of them such male attention evoked dormant sexual and emotional needs and raised doubts in their minds about a future life of celibacy.

Both of these major influences that led nuns to question a total way of life—discussions within orders themselves and educational opportunities—came from the church itself as part of the renewal and adaptation movement formalized by Pope John XXIII in calling the Second Vatican Council. By "opening the windows and allowing the breath of the Spirit to enter," Pope John led the way to what became a major dilemma for convents and the nuns in them. The process of questioning disrupted the totalistic system and the underlying symbolic meanings that sustained orders. This eventuated in the exodus of large numbers of nuns from their convents. In some instances nuns left because they felt the radical changes meant that religious life no longer afforded opportunities and rewards not available in lay life. Others left because they opposed the rapidity and nature of the changes; still others left more conservative orders because they felt changes were not rapid or substantive enough (Ebaugh 1977). Religious orders were in a no-win situation. Once the underlying structure of an isolated, totalistic institution gave way to evaluation and questioning, it was impossible to maintain the same kind of membership commitment that was based on rigid socialization and strict adherence to authority and discipline.

Beginning in the late 1960s and continuing throughout the 1970s, large numbers of nuns left almost every convent in the United States. Even the national media publicized the trend and raised issues regarding the future of religious orders. Nuns could no longer take their commitment for granted but were challenged to reconsider whether they wanted to be part of a dwindling institution.

In a similar manner, an ex-navy man also first began to question his commitment when he saw that the U. S. Navy was beginning to move in a more liberal and less restrictive direction. In Goffman's scheme of total institutions (Goffman 1961), the traditional Navy and pre-Vatican II religious convents shared many similar characteristics, such as physical and social isolation, rigid rules of discipline, social distance between staff and inmates, and well-defined socialization mechanisms whose purpose was to create an institutional identity and loyalty. As a result of societal pressures, the U. S. Navy, along with other branches of the service, experienced far-reaching organizational changes at about the same time as Catholic religious orders. Interestingly, the navy also moved in the same general direction of less social isolation and strict discipline, placing more emphasis on individual freedom and adaptation to twentieth-century society. While the effect of such change was to increase commitment on the part of some navy men and to encourage new recruits, there were others who found it difficult to adapt to such organizational change. One ex-navy man in our sample described his first doubts as follows:

> After I had about ten years in the navy, I realized at that time that the navy was going through a very significant change. A lot of the old values and principles seemed to be suddenly considered outdated and so I started looking

> at myself as being a little bit slow to change or started questioning even if I wanted to change, what should be my response to the changes. So I started deciding maybe I'm just being overly critical. I realized I don't control the whole navy. Well, it tended to mount. It just tended to have cumulative effects, and by the time I had about sixteen years in I saw the navy was changing faster than I was changing with it. I realized I've simply got to go. It was a rather straightforward choice for me to make because when you seriously see yourself as being a square peg in a round hole then there's not too much of a choice to be made. It's pretty well logical what you need to do. And I could see that I was doing myself and the Navy no good by staying longer.

Likewise, increases in the bureaucratization of the medical profession created organizational conditions which influenced doctors in our sample to question their professional commitment to medicine. Sarason (1977), in his study of physicians, also found that many of them became disillusioned and frustrated by a sense that they were becoming mere cogs in the wheels of bureaucracy rather than personal healers. Most noteworthy and frequently mentioned among our sample of doctors is the increased threat of malpractice suits that significantly raised malpractice insurance premiums and gave rise to the increased practice of "defensive medicine." As one ex-doctor put it, "Every patient I saw was a potential malpractice suit. It used to not be like that. I could relate to patients as people and treat them for what they needed. Nowadays, you have to cover yourself on all fronts and be sure you run enough tests to protect yourself in court if necessary. The whole profession of medicine has changed so drastically that doctors and patients are often in an adversary position rather than in a caring, cooperative, human relationship. I reached the point where I didn't want any part of it anymore." Another ex-doctor got frustrated with the amount of time he had to spend with insurance companies and occasionally lawyers who were threatening malpractice suits on the part of patients. He said, "My main surprise in beginning practice was having to deal with third parties and insurance companies and other things that are more in the business side of medicine and the time it takes out of your medical practice to take care of business things. It used to not be like that and we were not prepared in medical school to deal with these things. Medicine is becoming too big-business to be effective."

We also interviewed a top-level hospital administrator who had very recently resigned his position to take up commercial real estate. After ten years as executive director, he was happy to resign his job, in part because of the changes occurring in hospital administration. As he said,

> Over the years my hopes and aspirations for the institution were achieved beyond my expectations. My typical days were really devoted with top executives to developing and expanding new opportunities for patients and doctors. However, in the past several years medicine is moving more and more into the business areas such as determining the affordability of programs for patients rather than developing good people programs. Medicine is becoming more customized and coordinated in terms of millions of test exams, many of which are not really necessary. The major decisions of hospital administrators are more and more big-business decisions in terms of market shares and all of this new corporate financing and management. The size and scope of the whole organization has become so enormous and health care has become so competitive that it is not the same situation I entered.

Organizational change, therefore, was the condition that encouraged a number of our interviewees to begin questioning whether they wanted to remain in an institution that was significantly different from the one they first entered.

Burnout

Many of the professionals and semiprofessionals in our study became frustrated, lost enthusiasm, felt exhausted, lost their original ideals, and gradually realized that they were taking out their dissatisfaction on the clients and patients they were supposedly in the business to serve. Usually, these professionals identified their feelings and behavior as "just being plain burned out with my work." Burnout is not a sudden phenomenon but happens over a period of time, sometimes several months but more usually several years. While the loss of idealism and commitment can and does occur at any point in a professional's career, Cherniss's work (1980) shows that the early years immediately following professional training and the beginning of professional practice often comprise the period when burnout is most likely to occur. This is due to the disjuncture between the idealism instilled in aspiring professionals during their training and the jolts of reality experienced during the first few years of practice.

The idealism inherent in professional training programs has often been noted by researchers (Becker, Geer, Hughes, and Strauss 1961; Sarason 1977; Cherniss 1980; Dworkin 1986). In fact, in order to motivate students to undergo rigorous studies in a situation with few immediate rewards, idealism and a sense of the future value of their contributions keep students committed to assimilating as much knowledge and as many skills as possible in order to be productive professionals in the future. Built into the very nature of the helping professions is commitment to the welfare of others. These ideals are ingrained as part of professional training. While such idealism is functional during the training period, these ideals are seldom realized fully in a real-life work context as the professional has to deal with bureaucratic structures, ungrateful clients, boredom, incompetent and sometimes selfish peers, etc. The clash between ideals and reality provides the opportunity for burnout to set in. The cynical knowledge that Goldner, Ritti, and

Ference (1977) discuss on the part of Catholic priests who realize that seemingly altruistic actions really serve the legitimacy of the existing institutional structure occurs with many types of professionals once they leave the haven of professional schools and face the realities of bureaucratic structures.

Freudenberger (1974) coined the term "burnout" to describe people in the helping professions who experience fatigue or frustration brought about by the lack of the satisfaction they were led to expect during their training. In 1976 Maslach described the process of burnout in an article in *Human Behavior* (Maslach 1976). The overwhelming public response to the article, both on the part of individuals who identified with burnout as well as organizations who recognized the potential costs of burnout, indicated that this is a major concern for many people.

Despite variations in descriptions and definitions of burnout, there are some similarities and core ideas in the literature that differentiate it from other related concepts such as stress, turnover, and job dissatisfaction. First of all, burnout is a negative response on the part of individuals to role-related stress. This negative response is manifested in three basic ways. (1) Exhaustion, described as wearing out, loss of energy, fatigue, loss of feeling and concern, loss of interest, and loss of spirit. Exhaustion is manifested physically by bodily symptoms such as loss of appetite, insomnia, headaches, and frequent illness. Emotional exhaustion results in lack of energy to do one's job with enthusiasm and lack of interest in job requirements. Mental exhaustion is associated with feelings of lack of self-worth, incompetency, inadequacy. (2) A negative shift in responses to others is indicated by depersonalized relationships, especially toward clients and patients, loss of idealism, and irritability. (3) A negative response toward oneself and one's accomplishments is manifested by depression, low morale, withdrawal, diminished productivity, and a general inability to cope with job demands and social relationships (Maslach 1982*b*).

Several of the ex-doctors in our sample first became

conscious that they were burned out when they began to have excessive weight gains or losses, always felt tired, and began smoking three to four packs per day, had heart problems, or simply "felt lousy." One doctor checked himself into the hospital and was told by his internist that all of his physical symptoms were psychosomatic and that he had better figure out where the stress was coming from and do something about it. During his hospital stay he realized how much he hated his work and how pleasant it was to be away from it. While in the hospital he decided that he would give up medical practice within one year and begin to do something he enjoyed. Another ex-doctor said, "I was overweight, smoking three packs a day, drinking too much. However, I think the thing that got me after a while was that I saw no way out. It was the same thing over and over every day with no variations, no options, no choices, and I kind of wanted to break out of that and sort of take control of my own life. But I couldn't see a way out at the time."

While the concepts of job stress, job dissatisfaction, and job frustration may refer to transitory and specific aspects of one's job or role, burnout indicates a more global, nonspecific, all-encompassing negative attitude manifested in behavior responses. Dworkin (1986) defines burnout as an extreme form of role-specific alienation characterized by a sense that one's work is meaningless and that one is powerless to make it more meaningful. A sense of normlessness or normative conflict and feelings of social isolation also characterize burned-out people. Besides lethargy and general disinterest in one's job, the predominant manifestation of burnout is withdrawal and anger toward clients or patients. One burned-out ex-physician described how he felt toward patients:

> It was a tremendous amount of responsibility, a tremendous amount of worry, long, tiring hours. Always the question: Will this be the patient who sues me for malpractice? Or would this patient pull out a gun and shoot me because in her mind I have not done everything

> I could for her? I went out of my way to do as much as I could for my patients. I am afraid the image of the TV doctor was burned into my mind. You can spend an entire career trying to help the health and mental health of one patient, but the realities of practice are that you have hundreds of patients and I would make an appointment with someone for twenty minutes for a problem that should have taken five minutes and an hour later I would be sitting there listening to her complaints.

Cherniss (1980) found that burned-out lawyers, public health nurses, mental health workers, and teachers in public high schools lost their idealism regarding what they could do for clients, were less trusting and sympathetic toward clients and patients, and began to treat them in a detailed, mechanical fashion. Maslach (1978) reports that clients and patients of burned-out public professionals complain of being pushed around, ignored, mistreated, and/or deceived. While she admits that clients have many legitimate reasons to protest the quality of the treatment they are receiving from frustrated, dissatisfied professionals, she also argues that the structure of staff-client relationships in public bureaucracies contributes to burnout of professional staff.

The fact that clients and patients are people with problems means that it is this negative side of them which professionals see and with which they deal all day long. Further, there are rules structuring the interaction between professionals and clients that can introduce sources of emotional stress such as a requirement that the professional ask a series of questions about the client's financial ability to pay, or rules that limit the amount of time a staff member may devote to a client. Other potential sources of stress are lack of agreement and understanding of the expectations between the client and professional, and a broader cultural norm that views the professional as an authority figure and socializes clients to behave in a passive and dependent way.

An ex-physician in our sample first began to doubt his

profession when he realized how angry he was at the lack of appreciation shown by patients:

> I partially believed in the television image of the physician—that the physician would be shown some personal attention by his patients, that they would develop a personal relationship. That there would be gratitude, not hand-kissing gratitude, but at least the gratitude to send a Christmas card, a bottle of scotch. Call him up and see how he is doing now and then. And there would be periods when I would be deadly tired or discouraged and could have used a card or a telephone call. I found that in five years of practicing medicine I got one Christmas card and one invitation to dinner. You patch somebody up and send them out from the office or from the hospital, they were gone and you were not anymore part of their lives. When they got through with you as a doctor, they were gone and you were not anymore part of their lives. I also found in medicine, in general, it is more or less of a racket since Medicare came in.

Another ex-doctor said, "I think most doctors go into medicine for humanitarian reasons. When the patients start biting back at you and threatening malpractice, that's very distressing." For another ex-physician the hostility of some patients was difficult to accept: "I think what really disappointed me were those people who became hostile if you didn't care for them. This is particularly true when you are sending a bill and they don't get well and they say 'the mechanic in the garage guarantees the work on the car, why can't you?' Also disappointments come from a few negative comments from patients and very few positive ones."

Among the ex-doctors we studied, there was a lot of professional burnout, due largely to the idealized image of the physician which is part of medical socialization, as well as to a general societal image of a physician as one who deals continually with life and death issues and places the good of the patient before all other personal concerns. The ex-physicians had internalized the Marcus Welby image of the good doctor and found that idealized role expectations did not always match the day-to-day reality of medical practice. The majority of them first realized their discontent when they lost interest in caring for patients and began dreading interaction with them.

Among the ex-physicians we interviewed was an ex-thoracic surgeon who had spent thirteen years preparing for his medical speciality and had been well-known and nationally respected for seventeen years. Despite his many years in practice, he never really enjoyed it or found satisfaction in what he was doing. As he expressed it, "I never identified with the content of the work. This is the age-old lesson that I learned. It's not in the achieving of the goal that gives one happiness but it's in the process of doing it. Unless you enjoy that, once you get there, it's an empty victory. I was so goal-oriented that I thought I was going to be happy when I achieved the goal. When I got there and had the fortune to achieve my goal at an early age, it was empty."

Another group that were prone to job burnout were the ex-police officers we studied. In this case, also, the idealized image of the police officer as the "good guy" who protects innocent people against dangerous criminals often did not materialize in everyday police work, which led officers to become disillusioned. As one ex-officer expressed it:

> It took me about three years to come to the realization that my idea of what I was going to do in law enforcement was wrong. At that time in my life it was difficult for me to accept things as they were. I was trying to make them the way I thought they should be. I suppose idealistic is good, but I thought that I was going to catch bad guys and help good guys, and really do something for the community. I thought that. I really had that in my heart. And it took me about three years to figure out that the system—the administration of justice system in general—doesn't allow for that. And the

department doesn't have room for that. It's sad, but that's the way it is.

Another ex-officer described the stages police go through when they join the force:

> We're all about the same and they all go through basically the same kind of stages. When they first come in and they're young bucks and man, they got that gun, and they got that badge and they are smoking them Camels and boy, it's great. Some guys are more mature and more quick on the uptake and they can make that transition real fast. And then they get into the eight-hours a day routine and "Hey, I do *my* job." If somebody's getting stabbed over there and this spot's my beat, call the other car. I'm not taking that report. This is where my job stops. Or I'm on my way home, I'm not going to stop.

Like the physicians in our sample, several of the ex-police officers were disappointed and surprised by the apathetic and often negative responses of the people they were supposedly serving. As one policeman said,

> I didn't expect that the general opinion of the public would be so against you. I thought that the crooks would be against you but I thought that Joe-average-citizen out here living in a housing tract with two cars and a wife and 2.5 kids and the red wagon and the mortgage and the house, why I thought that he would be for you but he's not. No, he's not. He doesn't like you. He doesn't like to see you behind him when he's out on a Saturday drive because right away his palms start getting sweaty and he checks the speedometer and he thinks to himself "what's this guy going to stop me for?"

Idealized images of professionals that are presented in television, movies, magazines, and novels had been internalized by many of the ex-professionals in our sample. In the process of being socialized into their professions, they accepted and "bought into" the media image of the ideal physician, lawyer, police officer, or teacher. Once in real practice, life was much more complicated and unexciting than the media portrayed it. Routine and even drudgery were more common than the periodic thrills and unusual challenges of the media doctor or police officer.

Thornton and Nardi (1975) in their research with professionals found that though the anticipatory stage of socialization is generally considered functional for subsequent adjustment to acquired roles, adjustment is in fact dependent on the degree of accuracy of what is conveyed and perceived. Studies by Thompson (1958), Johnson and Hutchins (1966), Wright (1967), and Olesen and Whittaker (1968) also indicate that anticipation helps adjustment only to the extent that it is accurate. If it is not accurate, it may actually impede adjustment in that performing the acquired role will necessitate unlearning as well as learning.

Likewise, individuals who exit one role and enter a new one are prone to eventual burnout to the degree that they lack realistic knowledge of the new role and have built up idealistic expectations. Louis (1980) describes individuals making career transitions as experiencing discrepancies between anticipation and experience which indicate an error in the individual's "mapping of the situation." The development of anticipations about a new setting is a natural part of any transition and serves much like beliefs in guiding choices. When predictions or ideals are not borne out, transitioners may feel a sense of failure, frustration, denial, and regret. In order to resolve tension and deal with the new situation, individuals engage in a "sense-making" process whereby they revise their expectations and attempt to understand and interpret events in the new setting. If the discrepancy between anticipated ideals and reality is too great, over time these individuals experience burnout and begin to seek a way out of the situation.

Several ex-nurses and ex-teachers that we interviewed also experienced burnout. In the professionalization literature (Etzioni 1969), these groups are usually classified as semiprofessional since they share some characteristics of professional groups such as formal training, service orientation, and a code of ethics but lack other essential characteristics such as role autonomy and peer review. Among the semi-professionals in our study, burnout was frequently the condition that initiated the process of doubting role commitment.

An ex-nurse first began doubting her commitment to nursing when she realized that the ideal of service and caring for patients that she had been taught in nursing school was impossible to achieve because of bureaucratic rules and time demands of the hospital. As she expressed it, "I like people and the satisfaction of helping people is a strong thrust with me. I am a service-oriented person. I never felt that I could give total care to the person. There was a lot of pressure to do so much by a certain time. You could not address your care to the emotional needs of the sick person." An ex-teacher expressed similar feelings regarding his teaching role: "The simple things that you never thought about is what irked me about teaching. The checking roll, locking [doors], check all the equipment, and check all this and all that. When you're a kid you don't see that coach or that teacher doing that stuff, or coming up there on in-service days or those extra hours at night. You don't see that. You just think they are here eight hours and they are through. But it's not like that. The kids don't see that. And they don't tell you this in college, either."

While burnout sometimes leads to exiting a job or a profession, burnout and role exit are not synonymous. There are many people who leave roles who have not experienced burnout and, conversely, many burned-out people continue in their work roles. Role entrapment, as Dworkin (1986) points out, is common among teachers in public schools, many of whom remain in disliked jobs for entire careers. The same is true in practically all careers where individuals are entrapped because of the lack of job options or because they have built up such substantial side bets in terms of investment of time, benefits, skills, or personal obligations that make exiting too costly (Becker 1960). A projected next step in our role-exit research is to compare those individuals who burnout yet remain in roles with those who have actually exited. This next step is essential in order to specify more exactly under what conditions burnout leads to exit. At this point, we know that burnout is a sufficient, though not necessary, condition for reevaluating role commitment.

While the concept of burnout has been used to describe stress, alienation, and frustrations in all kinds of roles, including marriage, parenthood, sports, and school, it applies most directly to professional and semiprofessional occupations in which there exists professional-client relationships. In their work on burnout, Maslach and Cherniss have reserved the term to describe negative reactions and fatigue experienced by professionals who deal with clients on a continuous basis. Burnout results as a disjuncture or contradiction between what a professional is taught to expect by his or her agency of training and what actually occurs in the course of practice. To restrict the term in this way is to maintain a more precise and meaningful description of burnout. To expand the term to all types of roles and situations is to make its meaning less precise and specific. Empirically, in our role-exit data, the kinds of job-specific frustration, disappointments, and feelings of alienation that characterize the professional and semiprofessional exiters are different in character from those experienced by people in other roles, such as divorced people, mothers without custody, parolees, alcoholics, ex-nuns, or transsexuals. While in these cases there is also loss of idealism and disappointment in outcomes, the sources of idealism are usually parental or media socialization and are frequently harder to identify. It makes sense, therefore, to restrict burnout to professional and semiprofessional exiters.

Disappointments and Changes in Relationships

Among the divorced people and mothers without custody, a major factor which led to initial doubts revolved around disappointment that relationships did not turn out as one was socialized to expect. As was the case in professional burnout, many of the individuals who exited marital and parental roles were disillusioned when an idealized image of the role did not materialize in reality. In American society, we place strong cultural values on the institutions of marriage and parenthood and socialize children and adolescents to place sometimes unrealistic expectations on what it will be like to be married and begin a family. As one divorcée explained, "My mother engraved in me, and my sister too, that in order to be happy you will grow up, get married, have babies. But she never really got too far into the discussion on what you look for to make you happy in the marriage. So, when I went off to college and met my husband, he was the first man that asked me to marry him and so I said yes because I never thought anybody else would ever ask me."

The failure of a relationship frequently leads to self-doubt. As one divorcée explained, "And I just had all these romantic, immature ideas of what marriage was. I truly believed in the vine-covered cottage, picket fence, walking off into the sunset and everything was going to be wonderful and I was going to be in control. Well, I wasn't. I went from one mess into another. Once we were married it was different. It wasn't the same. He was no longer courting me and his life-style was just totally different from what I had been used to." Another woman had similar feelings: "I was expecting it to be like a bed of roses. I was expecting a more traditional marriage. I expected him to take care of me, kind of shelter me. I was really expecting a traditional marriage but it just didn't turn out like that."

Among the mothers who gave up custody of children during divorce proceedings, disappointment in what it was like to be responsible for children played a big part in first entertaining the idea of relinquishing custody and day-to-day care for children. One mother without custody expressed her disappointment: "It was so disappointing to have to stay home with her and just so unchallenging to be with a small child all the time. I just felt like I was going to lose my mind if I'd stay there; if I stayed home and played tinker toys one more day I felt like I was really going to lose it. It was just so intolerable and I began to realize I wanted out." Another mother without custody said she came to realize that she wanted to finish college more than anything in the world and she began to see her small daughter as an obstacle to going back to school. She began to see her child as more trouble than enjoyment and felt very guilty because that was not how she had imagined motherhood. She felt relieved to realize that her husband wanted custody and saw his having custody as a way out of a bad situation.

One characteristic predominated among the ten mothers without custody and was integrally related to finally relinquishing custody of children: low self-esteem. This was usually associated with having strong, domineering husbands. While we have no way of measuring self-esteem before their divorces, respondents repeatedly reported that they felt very inadequate and thought little of themselves while in their marriages. Eight of the ten were full-time homemakers and had their identities totally wrapped up in being spouses and mothers. While the majority felt they were good mothers, they felt they were failures as spouses and could do little other than change diapers, buy groceries, and maintain a home.

Concomitantly, all ten women had husbands whom they described as aggressive, ego-centered, domineering men who wanted control of the house, wife, and children. The husbands reportedly tended to downplay, derogate, and humiliate their wives by telling them how weak, incompetent, and/or dependent they were. In two instances, the women were physically abused by husbands, and for years they accepted it silently as something they deserved. The women, on the whole, tended to accept their husband's evaluations, which simply reinforced their low self-regard.

In all of the ten cases, in varying intensitites, the women wanted more personal freedom and control over at least simple household decisions such as check writing, freedom to buy things without their husbands' permission, and freedom to go to school or pursue a career. Low self-esteem and the desire for more freedom were crucial factors in giving up custody of children for seven of the ten women. These seven women felt they couldn't care adequately for the children alone and that their husbands were better equipped financially and/or psychologically to care for their children. These women had either no jobs or very low-paying jobs and had little confidence in being able to build a career. In a number of cases, the husbands threatened to pay no child support and these women feared not being able to support their children.

Feelings of inadequacy and low self-esteem, as well as disappointment in marriage and motherhood, therefore, caused these women to begin to give serious consideration to giving up custody of children to the father. As one woman said, "My self-esteem during those years of marriage just got worse and worse and worse and worse because of all the rejection I felt from him because he chose to be away from the house so much. I took it all personally, as a personal rejection, and I felt I was no good. I was no good as a wife, a mother, you name it, I felt no good at it. I had no sense of worth at all."

In their study of battered women, Johnson and Ferraro (1984) found that one catalyst that stimulates battered women to begin questioning their victimization is a drastic change in their relationships with their husbands. In the early stages of physical abuse by husbands, violent incidents are usually followed by periods of remorse and solicitude. Such phases are often very romantic and bind a wife even more closely to her husband. However, as the battering increases, this romantic phase tends to shorten or disappear altogether, eliminating the basis for maintaining a positive view of the marriage. Extended periods devoid of any kindness or expression of love may alter the woman's feelings about her marriage and lead to doubts about wanting to stay in the marriage. We found a similar pattern among a number of our divorcées, especially two instances in which women were physically abused by husbands. The abuse usually occurred two to three years after marriage and stunned the women, who had never anticipated such treatment. Their initial reactions were shock and severe disappointment that their spouses would engage in abusive behavior. The intermittent periods of remorse and solicitude led the women to define the abuse as "loss of temper"; they thought, "I must have deserved it," or "he was probably just drunk." When the abuse became more frequent, the women found it harder to excuse, and eventually they realized it was becoming a way of life.

In three other instances, significant changes in behavior on the part of spouses influenced partners to begin questioning their relationships. In six cases, spouses were having extramarital affairs and began acting differently. In another case, a woman became bored with her marriage and "just didn't feel anything toward him anymore." These shifts in relationships suggested problems in the marriage and eventually led to divorce.

In the cases of both burned-out professionals and individuals who exited familial roles, a central theme that emerged throughout the interviews was the discrepancy between an idealized image of the role and what it was like in reality. Once individuals recognized and admitted the discrepancies, disappointment and disillusionment usually followed and provided the impetus for beginning to doubt commitment to the daily demands of the role.

Events

In some instances, events trigger initial doubts about one's role commitment. While the individual may have vague, ill-defined, usually unconscious feelings of dissatisfaction, some event will focus these feelings and make them conscious to the individual. Among the divorced people in our sample, six first realized their unhappiness when they discovered that their spouses were having affairs. In two instances, this realization led to immediate divorce proceedings. In the remaining cases, the affair was simply the beginning of prolonged attempts to make the marriage work. As one woman explained, "I began to doubt my marriage six months after my marriage when my first daughter was born. That's when I questioned his being faithful and caught him having an affair. But at the time I was not prepared to deal with the problem so I let it go away." In two additional cases it was not marital infidelity that raised initial doubts but discovering that husbands were alcoholic and had hidden the fact until after marriage. In both cases the women had strong religious feelings about alcohol and both were upset about the deception as well as their husbands' hidden drinking problems. As one woman said,

> I probably first realized that I had made a very serious mistake about six months after we were married. I discovered that my husband had lied to me on a number of very important things. I had a very close friend commit suicide while drunk—over alcoholism. And, I had a very strong feeling about drinking, and my husband told me he did not drink. But six months after we got married, I discovered that he himself was almost an alcoholic. And I was very angry about that. I was already pregnant with my first child at that time and I really didn't feel like I had a whole lot of alternatives. And he led me to believe he would get help with this problem. I discovered he had lied on several other things—his first divorce—the reason for it. So I began to lose respect. So, as I discovered those things, I thought, "Oh, my heavens, what have I done here?"

In two instances the deaths of children instigated doubts about continuing in current roles. An ex-navy man began to question his long absence from home after his eighteen-year-old daughter died from cardiac arrest after being in a coma for three months. He said, "At that time of my life I was pretty cocky, self-sufficient, and it really made me wake up. I didn't have my 'house' in order properly and I thought I was the controlling factor in everything. And then I ran up against something that I didn't have control of. I resented the fact that I had a daughter eighteen years of age that had passed away and approximately nine years of my life that I spent away from her. That's when I began to question whether I should be in the service."

A physician also began reevaluating his professional commitment when his eighteen-year-old son died while pole vaulting in a high school track meet. He decided, then, that there was a lot of life his son didn't get to live and he was going to live it for him and not get so caught up in his medical profession that he didn't have time to enjoy life. When he began to have chest pains several years later, he decided to retire completely from medicine and enjoy some of the things in life his son had missed out on.

Among the twelve recovered alcoholics we interviewed, first doubts usually took the form of realizing that a drinking problem existed. This was usually the beginning of a long process of denial and trying to cover up the problem with family, friends, and business associates. Frequently, some event such as a car accident, a spouse's departure, a frightening medical report, failing grades in school, or a blackout caused the alcoholic to confront the fact that he or she had a serious drinking problem.

Some roles in society are sequential in nature such that one role leads into another. Medical students, for example, become residents and then licensed physicians. Novices in religious orders become full-fledged nuns at some specified point in time. As the next step in the sequential process nears, role incumbents frequently reexamine whether they really want to make a further, more intensive commitment to the role. One of the institutionalized purposes of training programs is to give recruits an opportunity to experience and learn future role requirements in advance so that they can decide whether or not they want such commitments. It is quite common for some trainees to opt out before they move into the specified role. Five of the ex-nuns interviewed left the convent shortly before they were expected to pronounce their final vows, that is, to make a lifetime commitment. The event of having to make a final decision raised doubts in their minds and triggered the exiting process.

The transsexuals in our study demonstrate a unique pattern with regard to first doubts. When asked at what point they first began to question their gender identity, without exception the interviewees said they knew by age three or four that they "were in the wrong body." While all of them had to postpone sex-change surgery until adulthood, most felt certain by a very early age that their physical apparatus and gender identities simply didn't match.

As one male-to-female transsexual expressed it, "I knew at three to four years old I was not really what people saw. I was raised in a Baptist home and I prayed that when I woke up I would be a little girl. I never wanted to be a boy. I felt out of place in the boy's locker room. I knew the body I was in was not really my body. As a child, aged four to five, I dressed as a girl when nobody was around. I had a little red skirt I wore every day I could when nobody would find me." Another male-to-female transsexual said, "Since age two or three I knew I was in the wrong body. I head a pretty red dress I hid and wore whenever nobody was around. I was very jealous of my sister who was seven years younger because she was a girl. I stole my mother's panties and wore them whenever I could. I was just never attracted to girls but to boys."

Most of the interviewees in our transsexual sample had married at some point; however, marriage was simply a response to social pressure rather than attraction to the opposite sex—these transsexuals were usually attracted to people of the same sex and identified emotionally and psychologically with the sex of their spouses. Interestingly enough, they did not define their sexual preference as homosexual, since they identified as the opposite sex from that indicated by their physical appearance. For example, the transsexual males who identified as female tended to be attracted to natural-born males. Even in situations in which they had sexual relationships with males prior to their sex change surgeries, they tended not to label these sexual encounters as homosexuual affairs. A male-to-female transsexual told of her early marriage and later gay life: "At eighteen I married a girl. I felt it would cure my problem. Five months before we had sex and she got pregnant. We split when the baby came. I snuck into gay bars because I knew I couldn't live a heterosexual life. However, I also knew I was not really gay."

Transsexuals, therefore, indicated few doubts about their sexual gender identities prior to surgery. Any doubts they expressed revolved around apprehension that they would ever be able to bring their physical appearance in line with their psychological and emotional life as a person of the opposite sex.

As demonstrated in the previous pages, first doubts might be triggered by a number of circumstances ranging from changes in the organization to which one belongs to unique events that occur in one's life. Regardless of the varied factors that initiate or first suggest doubts to the role incumbent, once doubts exist and are entertained by the individual, the process of exiting takes on a character of its own, and exiters share many of the same experiences such as cuing behavior and reinterpretation of role-related events. Even though transsexuals report that they never really doubted their gender identity, once they realize they have the option to change their sex organs and physical appearance to match their identities, their role-exit process is similar to that of individuals who exited other roles.

Cuing Behavior

In the course of the first phase of the role-exit process, as they entertain initial doubts about role commitment, individuals frequently emit cues that indicate role dissatisfaction and the desire for alternative courses of action. Cuing can be defined as those signs, conscious or unconscious, that an individual is dissatisfied in his or her current role and is seeking role alternatives. These symbolic behaviors may be early warning signs of erosion in commitment. As the role-exit process continues, unconscious cues become conscious and are taken into consideration when judging the amount of commitment one has to a given role.

Cues are often used in retrospect as justification for a role change. When interviewees are asked to recall the process of deciding to exit a role, it is impossible to distinguish the interpretation of cues at the time they occurred from retrospective justification for behavior. It was common for interviewees to point out early cues as a way of demonstrating that they were unhappy in their roles long before they made a conscious choice to leave. For example, an ex-prostitute who allowed herself to get pregnant and have a son commented that for years she was very careful in using contraceptives. She interpreted her carelessness as a cue that she was becoming dissatisfied with her work and was looking for an excuse to get out of it and do something more socially acceptable. She ultimately left prostitution because she feared that her son would someday find out about her profession and suffer social stigma because of it. She admitted, however, that getting pregnant was probably a cue that she was beginning to consider other options.

One of the latent consequences of cuing behavior is that cues are noticed by other people, especially those with whom the person interacts frequently and/or who are significant in one's life. These cues serve as early indicators that the individual is unhappy or discontented in his or her present role.

While Goffman (1959*a*) does not explicitly use the term "cue" in his analysis of the dramaturgical analogies of social life, he indicates that actors engage in numerous expressions, both verbal and nonverbal, which present an image to others of one's identity. Individuals, therefore, constantly engage in behaviors that define the situation and present an acceptable self to others engaged in the interaction. Life, for Goffman, is analogous to a stage on which actors play out their parts in terms of managing impressions for an audience. Through words, gestures, and action, players communicate who they are and what is happening in their lives. Likewise, in real social life, actors are enacting roles and emitting cues to others which suggest who they are and what is going to happen. In addition to mannerisms, expressions, and behaviors that are consciously learned in training for a theatrical part, actors and actresses emit all kinds of unconscious cues regarding the person they are portraying. That is why seasoned players who are enacting parts of people who really lived frequently get to know as much as possible about them. Goffman suggests that in real life, individuals likewise give off unconscious cues concerning self-identity and courses of action.

The manner in which significant others react to cues can provide critical feedback and can serve as either positive or negative reinforcement for the further consideration of exiting a role. Positive response, in the form of empathy, support, understanding, and even encouragement to leave, often reinforces initial doubts and confirms a person's feelings of dissatisfaction. This, in turn, may encourage the dissatisfied person to interpret further events negatively and to begin looking at alternatives. On the other hand, if significant others react negatively to cues that one is dissatisfied, such negative reinforcement of initial doubts may cause the person to reinterpret his or her early signs of dissatisfaction and reevaluate the positive aspects of the current role. This reevaluation may end the doubting process, or at least prolong it until other events or conditions arise that again elicit doubts.

While we did not explicitly ask interviewees whether they were aware of cues they had given off in the early stages of considering a role exit, many of them mentioned behaviors which they later realized were early signs of discontent. Given the difficulty with retrospective reporting, it is also possible that they made a decision to redefine them as cues and as a way of justifying their exit. In some instances other people reminded them of earlier actions which were indicative of later decisions. A young man who worked for a mental health agency commented that a year and a half before he quit his job his Cadillac kept breaking down, and that when he finally decided to get a new vehicle he chose a truck. When questioned about his choice by surprised friends as well as by his spouse, he said it was for camping and hauling dogs around, although at the time he neither camped nor owned dogs. However, his father was in construction work and he had always thought that construction work was something he might like to do. He ultimately left the agency and became a construction superintendent. He commented that, in retrospect, he realized he had probably bought a truck just in case he ever left the mental health field and engaged in construction work. In fact, owning the truck became symbolic of what he really wanted to do with his life and of his early dissatisfaction with mental health work.

An ex-police officer commented that significant changes in his behavior about a year before he quit were early indications of his desire to get out of police work. Even though he didn't relate his behavior at that time to a desire to change careers, he realized later what his behavior was saying:

> I've always been, not a health nut, but I've always eaten good, and, I think, taken care of myself except for that last year. I was living on doughnuts and tacos, drinking more. Honest to God, living on doughnuts in the morning after I was working and, at night, eating Jack-in-the-Box tacos and drinking after work. I'd get off work at 2 a.m. and go down and drink until sunrise at the beach. I have an old pick-up truck and I always had beer bottles and beer cans in the back of it. I had one headlight that worked, the taillights didn't work and I didn't register it.

Finally, his wife and several close friends confronted him with his bizarre behavior and suggested that maybe he was trying to get the message across that he was miserable in police work. When confronted by them, he broke down and admitted that he was "living in hell" and hated being a policeman. They encouraged him to get out and find something he could enjoy, which he eventually did through a medical discharge.

Three different ex-police officers whom we interviewed left the force on medical discharges with lifetime medical pensions. All three of them were unhappy in their work and suffered job-related injuries. Each of them was relieved when doctors testified that the injuries made them unable to function any longer as police officers. In two instances, injuries while on the job led the men to face their basic discontent with their jobs. In both cases, the ex-policemen commented that they seemed more accident-prone at times when they were fed up with their jobs, and they wondered if they were really looking for a way out of police work without losing the pay benefits they had accrued.

Among the sample of ex-nuns, cuing behavior in the early stages of doubt was widespread. In the traditional convent structure, there were so many rigid rules regarding appropriate dress, mannerisms, and behavior, all intricately bound up with and interpreted by an overriding religious ideology, that deviance from the rules was symbolic of questioning the total system. For example, nuns wore their hair short and in a nonstylish fashion underneath their headdresses and veils. Even after religious orders abandoned their traditional habits, nuns were expected to wear modest and simple hairstyles. Frequently, those nuns who allowed their hair to grow long or engaged in more modern hairstyles were those who ultimately left the convent. The development of close social ties with "outsiders," that is, with lay friends, was also an early cue that they were beginning to seek options. Many of the nuns we interviewed said that they look back on such behaviors as early warning signs of discontent with their lives and that gradually they began to realize what these signs were saying in terms of commitment.

Another group in which cuing behavior was very evident was the alcoholics. About a third of our sample recalled instances of early events which they later interpreted as cues that they were having problems and wanted help. One alcoholic said he probably subconsciously chose his spouse because she came from a nondrinking background: "I think that I was, even in choosing her as a mate at that time, looking for help. Subconsciously, I think it was an attempt to somehow not continue this life-style that part of me saw as being detrimental to me, a kind of a way of life I abhorred but just didn't know how to get out of." It was his nondrinking spouse who ultimately forced him to get help by threatening divorce if he didn't get sober.

In three other cases, alcoholics kept names and telephone numbers of people who offered help. In one instance, an alcoholic met an old high school friend who had also had a drinking problem but had sobered up through Alcoholics Anonymous. He was angry at the friend's suggestion that he was alcoholic and needed help. However, he accepted his friends's card and kept it in his wallet "just in case I ever needed it." Two years later, when he realized he was killing himself by excessive drinking, he called his friend in desperation.

Another alcoholic woman went to see her doctor and was interviewed by an intake receptionist who asked if she was perhaps having a drinking problem. Even though the patient denied it, the receptionist gave her a card with AA's telephone number on it. Several years later, the woman found the card in her purse at a point where she realized she had to have help. In a drunken stupor, she was admitted to an AA rehabilitation center.

Several alcoholics went to see psychiatrists for what they thought were not drinking-related problems and were confronted with their alcoholism. In retrospect, they realized they were reaching out for help.

Role of Significant Others in the Exit Process

The entire process of role exiting is influenced by interactions of the individual experiencing exit with significant others in his or her life. While the decision to exit is a very personal one, it is inevitably made in a social context and is highly influenced by the reactions of other people. At the stage at which the exiter is first questioning role satisfaction, other people serve a number of functions in the process including reality testing, enhancing the rewards of staying, and suggesting alternatives.

One of the most frequent functions of sharing doubts with others is reality testing. Persons experiencing doubts often wonder whether they have a one-sided, biased view of the situation. Either significant others can reinforce the reality of the problem by being sympathetic, or they can downplay the reality of the problem and challenge the individual to reconsider aspects of the situation. In the first case, the potential exiter is likely to have his or her doubts reinforced and to be encouraged to seek alternatives, while in the latter case the person is likely to reevaluate the reality and seriousness of the situation and to be less encouraged to admit a problem.

An ex-policeman was greatly relieved when his wife confronted him with his apparent fears of retribution from angry citizens whom he had arrested or sent to jail. She assured him that she also feared for his safety and that he was justified in wanting to get out. In fact, she wondered how he had survived the pressures and dangers as long as he did. Her reassurance encouraged him to begin considering what other type of work he might do. An ex-teacher was also relieved when his wife pointed out how depressed he had been lately and encouraged him to quit. He had always assumed she was proud of him as a teacher and coach and would object to his changing careers.

On the other hand, an ex-physician's wife was very discouraging and negative when she realized her surgeon husband was unhappy at his work. She valued both the prestige and financial rewards of his medical practice and tried to encourage him to realize how talented he was and how much patients benefited from his skills. In part as a result of her negative reactions to his initial doubts, he procrastinated for years in making the decision to exit. He stated that if his wife had been more supportive of his discontent, he would probably have left medicine years before he did.

In the case of another ex-physician, his father and grandfather had been physicians and a medical career was highly valued in his family. When he expressed doubts about his desire to spend a lifetime practicing medicine, his parents were shocked and assured him that the doubts were temporary and that "every doctor loses confidence and gets bored at times in his career." Each time the doctor considered a career change, he feared disappointing his parents who were proud of the medical heritage in their family.

In traditional Catholic families, having a daughter-nun or a son-priest was considered being "blessed by God" and conferred status on the parents. It was common for Catholic parents to encourage their children to consider a "religious vocation" as a nun or priest. On the other hand, defection from the convent or priesthood, besides being a rare phenomenon, was seen as humiliating for Catholic parents and perceived as scandal in the local Catholic community. The fear of disappointing parents was one factor that made many discontented nuns in our study hesitant to entertain doubts regarding their commitment. In many instances, parents picked up early cues that their daughter was unhappy. The reactions of parents was significant in whether the nun pursued her questioning and evaluation of alternatives. In those five cases in which parents reacted negatively to early cues, the nuns procrastinated in their decisions to leave and tried to be happy in their religious orders. Only one nun whose parents were very displeased with her early thoughts of leaving actually proceeded without hesitation to leave the order. In the cases in which parents were supportive of early signs of unhappiness, the nuns were further encouraged to reevaluate their commitment.

Another role of others in the early stages of the doubting process is to attempt to dissuade the individual from exiting by enhancing the rewards of staying. The most dramatic example occurred in the case of the thoracic surgeon who was well known and well respected by colleagues. He had been in practice seventeen years but had never been completely happy. When he finally faced his discontent and began thinking about options, he approached the head of his surgical team and expressed his doubts. His "boss" was very discouraging and told him he was crazy to leave a very lucrative and prestigious practice. As the ex-physician expressed it,

> My boss, a nationally renowned thoracic surgeon, had a philosophy which could be described as "slopping at the trough," a philosophy of management. What that means is if you've got a bunch of pigs that you're feeding and one of them wants to start wandering away you yell "souie" and you pour a little more slop in the trough to sweeten the pot again and the pigs come running back. Every time I kept wanting to move away and, in fact, even before I left, I went and asked him if I could have a sabbatical. He always sort of joked about how I could have a sabbatical. I wanted to do something for a year. He said, "Well, you don't really want to do that. I need you here and you'd be making a mistake leaving this career. You're one of the top surgeons in the country. I really need you and wish you'd stay. The sky is the limit." He was very persuasive. He's a leader and a dynamic person.

In addition to providing financial incentives, the boss sent him to national and international meetings in order to enhance his prestige. He was also given coauthorship on major research reports. As he said, "Those little things keep you going and you're willing to stay on." While his boss continuously discouraged his exiting, in time the costs of staying outweighed the advantages, and, after many years of doubting, the physician finally left the practice of medicine.

A third function of others in the doubting stage of the process is to suggest alternatives. In many instances, individuals who first realize unhappiness or problems in a role feel caught or trapped in that they see no alternatives. Other people who are sympathetic can point out alternatives and suggest the noninevitability of one's current role. In several cases, lay friends challenged discontented nuns to consider the option of leaving the convent and establishing a life as a single person with future possibilities of marriage and a family. In the case of a mother who was unhappy with both her marriage and role as mother and felt trapped, her sister continuously challenged her to get out of the marriage and let her engineer husband raise the children. The presentation of options can give a sense of emotional relief by helping a person to realize that he or she is not necessarily trapped in a role but can consider viable alternatives.

Finally, the very act of making a private problem public can have important consequences for the exiter, especially in the early doubting stages of the exit process. Literature on battered women shows that significant changes in the situation often occur when there is a change in visibility and other people become aware of the problem (Johnson and Ferraro 1984). Most cases of physical abuse in marriage are kept private, sometimes for many years. Abused women create a web of rationalizations in order to overlook or ignore violence. This is enhanced when the violence is private and no outsiders are present to question the validity of these rationalizations. However, if the violence occurs in the presence of others or other people become aware of it, a reinterpretation process can be triggered. An objective observer will apply a definition to the event inconsistent with the victim's prior rationalizations, thereby challenging the victim to reconsider her interpretations. Likewise, Vaughn (1986) found that "going public" had a profound effect on the uncoupling process of those involved in intimate personal relationships. As significant others learn of the separation, their responses confirm the reality of the situation for the couple involved, thus reinforcing the separation and creating obstacles to reconciliation.

A similar situation occurs when others become aware of a drinking problem of a family member or friend. The alcoholic may be able to rationalize his or her drinking as long as it occurs in private. However, when other people become aware of the problem and begin challenging prior rationalizations, the alcoholic either has to work harder to cover up and strengthen his or her rationalizations or is challenged to reconsider prior excuses. In each of the dozen interviews we conducted with recovered alcoholics, a shift either in drinking patterns or in rationalizations occurred because of challenges from other people. In each case, ultimate rehabilitation was triggered in some way by the reactions of significant others to the drinking problem. Ray (1964) found the same pattern among the drug addicts he studied. Significant others, especially parents, spouses, and best friends, had great influence in triggering doubts in the addicts.

A significant variable throughout the role-exit process is the reaction of significant others to the exit of the individual. At this point in the process, negative reactions of others can halt the process altogether or at least prolong it. In other instances, doubters who experience negative reactions from one group may seek out other individuals who are supportive of a role change and use this new group as a focal reference group. In contrast, positive feedback from others frequently encourages the process by providing reality testing, encouragement, and suggestions of viable alternative roles.

Interpretation of Subsequent Events

Once an individual admits doubts about his or her role commitment, and especially under conditions in which significant others further support and reinforce those doubts, it is often the case that subsequent events are interpreted in ways that support initial doubts. Events that may have had little significance earlier suddenly take on meaning in the light of making role decisions. For example, a wife saw her husband's sudden attention to her birthday with flowers and a gift as a way of "making peace and averting problems" after she had discovered his extramarital affair. Rather than being flattered with such attention, the wife was offended and angry that he would try to please her.

A group of Catholic nuns in our sample were very active in bringing about changes in their order as a response to Vatican II in an attempt to make religious life more appealing to modern young women. However, once these nuns began questioning their basic commitment to religious life, they interpreted the accomplishment of structural changes negatively because religious life no longer held the challenge and uniqueness to compensate for the costs of celibate commitment.

Physicians who realized they were no longer content with practicing medicine began to interpret emergencies and unusually challenging patients as evidence of how annoying and stressful medical practice is. Whereas they had earlier seen such events as the challenges of medicine and what kept practice from being boring, in situations of role ambivalence and doubt they often interpreted these events as justifications for role change.

Unconscious cues of role dissatisfaction are usually picked up by people who interact with the individual. Reactions to these cues either support the person in the doubting process or influence the person to abandon their doubting and recommit him- or herself to role obligations. If doubting is further reinforced and the individual continues to experience role dissatisfaction, current events come to be interpreted as further evidence of how bad things are. Likewise, past events are frequently reinterpreted as evidence that one cannot continue in the present situation.

Duration of the Doubting Process

How long this initial stage of the process lasts varies significantly among interviewees, ranging from two weeks for one divorcé to forty-three years for one of the transsexuals. Among the factors that determine how long the initial doubting phase lasts are degree of awareness, degree of control over the exit, institutionalization of doubts, and whether the individual is a lone doubter or part of a group of people who are beginning to question their role commitment.

In some role situations, such as that of the nun in the cloistered convent or that of the transsexual, roles are part of a totalistic, given system that goes unquestioned. Individuals buy into the ideology of the system, thereby accepting the norms, values, and role prescriptions that flow from the all-encompassing ideology. Therefore, role expectations, as well as one's acceptance of role prescriptions and commitment to role behavior, are taken for granted and may go unquestioned and unexamined for many years. Individuals may assume, as nuns did for years, that they had no control over staying or leaving. Once they assumed the role, they were told repeatedly that doubts were unacceptable and a temptation from the devil, and that if they really didn't belong in the convent, their superiors, as representatives of God, would let them know. Awareness of the limitations of the sacred elements of the system can cause individuals to begin to look at the previously unexamined life and can lead to doubts about role requirements in themselves and/or personal commitment to a given role. As individuals begin to see institutions as manmade, imperfect social structures, capable of change and error, they begin to realize that they have a choice to accept the role or abandon it. Degree of awareness, therefore, is influenced by the nature of the institution in which a given role is imbedded. Institutional change, especially from totalistic, closed systems to more open, democratic ones can lead to greater awareness of role options on the part of members. The nature and timing of organizational changes encouraging greater individual awareness impact when the exit process is begun and how long it lasts.

The amount of control the individual has over an exit also determines the nature and duration of the doubting process. Until the early 1960s, sex-change surgery was only a dream because medical technology had not yet been developed to effect such surgical and hormonal changes. People "born in the wrong body" had no way out of it, regardless of their doubts and misery. Even though nuns who had taken final vows could physically walk out of the cloister doors prior to 1960, the social stigma and formal denunciation by the Catholic church made the prospect of being an ex-nun so dismal that most nuns saw such a possibility as outside of their control. Even though role incumbents were dissatisfied, it was years before they were able to exit, because of either social norms or undeveloped medical technology.

Some roles in society are sequentially organized in such a fashion that individuals are challenged to reconsider their commitment at given points in time. For example, time frames (Merton 1984) are built into the social structures of entering and exiting certain roles. Many states require a three-day waiting period between obtaining a marriage license and being legally married. One function of this waiting period is to encourage couples to be sure marriage is really what they want. Similarly, separation periods before divorce serve the same purpose. Transsexuals are required to cross-dress for a specified period of time in order to challenge their initial doubts. Nuns are required to make temporary vows of religious commitment for three to six years before they are allowed to make final vows for life. It is quite common for a nun to begin doubting as the time for a permanent commitment draws near. The very institutionalization of the process timewise encourages doubts among the aspirants to full-time status.

In some instances, role incumbents begin to entertain doubts as lone individuals, whereas in other instances they are part of a group of individuals who are questioning role commitment. Our data clearly show that the initial process of doubting is more prolonged for lone doubters than for individuals who are moving through the process with others. This is the case whether or not the doubters are aware of each other and communicate in the process. While communication with others allows both sharing ideas and mutual support, just knowing that others are also questioning role commitment seems to provide social support for the doubter. This was true for the divorced people and mothers without custody who did not formally associate with anyone who had gone through the process, but who were aware that others had done so. As one divorcée said, "I didn't know anyone personally who had gotten a divorce, but I realized that many other people were going through the same thing and it helped me a lot."

The ex-nuns who left in the early waves of the 1960s and 1970s were part of cohorts of nuns who were exiting. Whether they knew and shared personally with others who had left or were leaving or were simply part of the large numbers of nuns exiting, the doubting process was shorter-lived for them than for the later sample of ex-nuns who left as lone individuals, neither with friends nor as part of the numerical wave that characterized an earlier period.

There are a number of factors, therefore, that influence how long the doubting process goes on before the individual takes the next step of actively seeking role alternatives and making a decision to exit. The factors include the degree to which individuals are aware of their dissatisfaction, the degree to which they feel they have control over the exit, and whether they are part of a group or cohort making the exit. The greater the awareness of dissatisfaction, the shorter the doubting stage seems to be. Likewise, the more control individuals perceive they have in the choice, the shorter the doubting stage. Individuals who experience the exit process along with others, either people they know personally or a cohort, tend to go through a shorter process than individuals who are lone doubters.

Summary

The following flow chart depicts graphically what typically occurs in the first stage of the role exit process, from the point of first doubts to the onset of considering alternative role options.

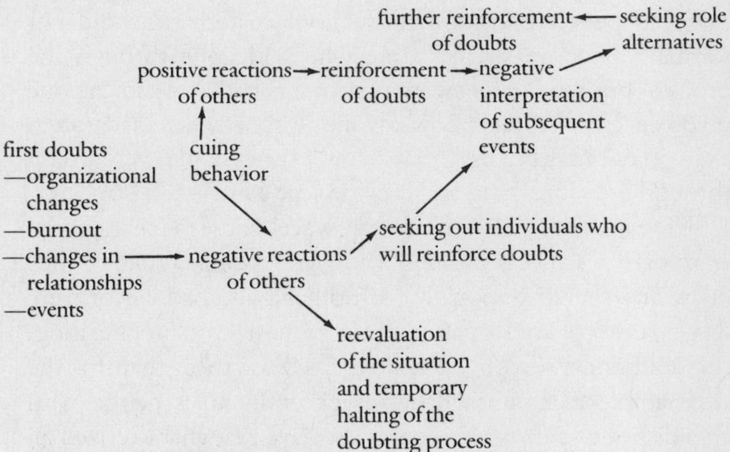

First doubts, that is, the initial reinterpretation of a social role previously taken for granted, are influenced by a variety of conditions such as organizational stresses and changes, occupational burnout, role disappointments, and specific, idiosyncratic events. Once individuals begin to question their role commitment and consciously admit doubts and reservations regarding a desire to continue in the role, they frequently emit cues that indicate both to themselves and to others discontent with their current social role. At some point, individuals realize these cues and use them either as further reinforcement of discontent or, later, as evidence of early dissatisfaction in their role. They are also picked up by others, especially people who are significant in one's life, and serve as initial indicators and clues that the individual is dissatisfied and is questioning role commitment.

When significant others react negatively to the cues indicating discontent or a questioning of role commitment, the individual tends to retrench and reevaluate the costs and benefits of role performance. Negative reactions challenge the individual's perception of the demands and rewards of his or her specific role, with regard to both the current role and the feasibility of alternative roles. At this point, either the doubting process is disrupted altogether and the individual reinterprets the situation, highlighting the positive aspects of the role, or the process is temporarily halted until some future situation or event again raises doubts and the process is repeated.

When the reactions of significant others to these cues of discontent are positive and supportive, initial doubts are reinforced and strengthened by a kind of reality testing. Some other person or persons are now aware of one's dissatisfaction and the reasons for it and by their positive response give reassurance that there is a basis in reality for doubts and reevaluation of a current role commitment. Frequently, the positive reactions of other people also take the form of suggesting role alternatives, thereby providing relief from feelings of being trapped in a role and opening up alternative possibilities.

Positive reactions of others usually reinforce initial doubts and expand the range of areas and issues that come under scrutiny and reevaluation. Once the individual becomes aware of the specific issues and conflicts that are causing the dissatisfaction, he or she tends to scrutinize and examine an ever-wider array of areas. In addition, subsequent events are now interpreted in light not of role commitment and a taken-for-granted role performance but of the reevaluation and conscious examination of every aspect of role demands. As a result of a changed outlook on role demands and role commitment, subsequent events are frequently interpreted negatively as a way of bolstering or justifying initial doubts about role continuance.

The utilization of events to reinforce and justify earlier reinterpretations of role demands and role commitment solidifies and gives substance to doubts that at first may have been vague and nonspecific. Now the individual has further concrete evidence of how stressful or unpleasant role demands are and of the misfit between these role expectations and his or her ability or desire to meet them. The more aware individuals are of their role dissatisfaction and the more control they feel they have in making a role choice, the shorter the doubting stage of the exit process tends to be. Likewise, individuals who are part of a group of others who are doubting experience a shorter exit process than individuals who struggle alone with their doubts. At the point at which individuals become aware that they no longer desire to meet the expectations of their roles, they enter the second major stage of the role-exit process, the search for viable alternatives.

3
Seeking Alternatives

The initial stage of experiencing doubts about a current role situation, especially under conditions of positive social support, is followed by a period during which the individual seeks out and evaluates alternative roles. In some cases the individual is aware of alternatives during the doubting process, and the existence of alternatives either provokes or encourages the doubts themselves. However, in most instances the availability of viable alternatives is a vague or general awareness. At some point, however, usually after the person admits dissatisfaction in a current role, alternative seeking becomes a conscious step in the exiting process.

Alternative seeking behavior is essentially a comparative process in which alternative roles are evaluated in comparison with the costs and rewards of one's current role. While role incumbents are familiar with the costs and rewards of their present roles, most alternative roles are less familiar. At the point at which individuals face the fact that they are dissatisfied with their present situations, they begin more deliberate exploration of the costs and rewards of alternatives.

While the exploration and evaluation of role alternatives is in fact a deliberative and rational process, there are also many spontaneous, nonrational, emotional elements involved. For many interviewees, circumstances, unexpected events, feelings, and intuitions were as important in shaping the process as deliberate calculations. However, in many instances in our sample, respondents did proceed in a very deliberate and rational fashion, often making lists of possible alternatives and itemizing the costs and rewards of each alternative role. A physician, for example, showed us the list he made of the occupational alternatives he considered if he chose to leave medical practice. These included the oil business, hospital management, independent investments, establishing a computerized EKG company, hospital consulting, graduate school, and even "doing nothing." He carefully evaluated each alternative in terms of his skills and training, demands of the job, the life-style each would afford, physical and emotional demands, monetary and emotional rewards, and, most important to him at the time, the degree of personal control over his life that each would afford in comparison to his lack of control in his current occupational role.

In other instances, the evaluation process that respondents went through was less systematic and deliberate. However, the majority of respondents considered alternatives before making a final decision to exit a current role. In fact, only twelve of the 185 people we interviewed indicated that they left an established role without considering other alternatives. Three individuals left jobs which were intolerable without considering what they would subsequently do. All three of them commented that they felt anything would be preferable to their current jobs and that their only consideration was getting out of a situation they hated. Four people, three women and one man, went through a divorce without much thought of what single life would entail. In each case, their exclusive attention was on getting out of a painful relationship. Only after the divorce was finalized did they consider what being divorced entailed. For two of them, adaptation to the single life was traumatic and for several years they regretted their decisions.

The group least likely to consider alternatives were the mothers who gave up custody of children. Five of the ten said they never seriously weighed the consequences of relinquishing custody but were so miserable in their marriages that their only thought was getting out of the marriage at any cost, even if it meant giving up custody of their children. In four of the five situations, their ex-husbands demanded custody before signing divorce papers. Typically, the presence of children aggravated the marital relationship and these women were tired of emotional struggles and couldn't imagine supporting children as well as themselves. Since a woman without custody of her children is a relatively uncommon figure in society, most of these women knew no one in that role situation and therefore had no notion of role expectations. In desperation they gave up legal custody, often with verbal assurances that they could have free access to the children. As soon as the papers were signed, verbal promises were forgotten and the mothers found themselves cut off from their children.

With the exception of these twelve respondents, the remaining 173 individuals experienced a process of seeking and weighing alternatives before making a final decision to exit. With minor variation, the process was strikingly similar among those we interviewed. The process included seeking and weighing role alternatives, responding to social support or the lack of it from significant others, realizing one's freedom to choose an alternative role, shifting reference group orientations, and engaging in role rehearsal.

Weighing Alternatives

Essential to understanding the seeking and evaluation of alternatives is the exchange perspective—the evaluation of costs and rewards of one's present situation as compared to alternatives that are available and potentially viable for the role incumbent. Thibaut and Kelley (1959) present a framework for analyzing the way in which individuals evaluate outcomes of interaction in terms of the degree of satisfaction and reward a particular interaction has for them. While they apply their framework specifically to interaction among individuals, their basic analysis is helpful in understanding broader role considerations. The consequences or outcomes of interaction in their scheme are described in terms of rewards and costs. Reward refers to those aspects which the individual finds pleasurable, enjoyable, gratifying, or otherwise satisfying. In their words, "the provision of a means whereby a drive is reduced or a need fulfilled constitutes a reward" (1959, 12). Costs refer to anything that inhibits the performance of a behavior or action. Therefore, the greater the inhibition that a person must overcome to perform a given action, the more costly the enactment of that action.

Outcomes are evaluated by comparison with two internal standards which Thibaut and Kelley call the comparison level (CL) and the comparison level for alternatives (CL_{alt}). The CL is a subjective standard that is developed as a consequence of the interpersonal relationships and situations an individual has experienced during his or her lifetime. In general, the CL will be an average of the range of experiences the individual has had, ordered by the goodness or satisfaction of outcomes. Once the CL has been established, the individual will evaluate positively any situation that he or she judges to fall above the CL in terms of outcomes and negatively any situation that falls below the CL. If a given situation yields outcomes which fall above the CL, it should be relatively attractive and satisfying to the person; if the outcomes fall below the CL, it should be relatively unattractive and dissatisfactory. The CL, therefore, is a measure of degree of satisfaction based on the subjective comparison of one's present situation with situations previously experienced.

For interviewees who experienced job burnout, their CL was expectations established during professional and job training and included idealized images of the profession provided by the mass media. Disillusionment and frustration occurred when demands did not correspond to what they were led to expect. Ex-physicians, teachers, and police officers were particularly prone to professional burnout due to the lack of correspondence between idealized images and real-life experiences.

For those interviewees who began doubting their role commitment because of changes in the system, the CL was usually the degree of satisfaction they had experienced at an earlier point in time before the organizational changes. Several of the ex-physicians recalled how happy they were in their early years of practice before Medicare, insurance companies, and "defensive medicine" required extensive record keeping and red tape. The trend toward highly specialized medical practice also meant that several no longer felt as qualified to treat patients as in the earlier days of the general practitioner. These organizational changes led to feelings of inadequacy and loss of personal satisfaction in the day-to-day practice of medicine.

A number of people who exited occupations realized their unhappiness when they compared their current jobs to ones they had previously held. Several commented that their dissatisfaction was caused in part by comparison of present employment with former jobs that offered more challenge and satisfaction. As one man put it, "I knew how miserable I was and how much I hated my work because I had been in a job before this one that was much more fun."

Individuals who began doubting as a result of unhappy personal relationships tended to use previous relationships or idealized images of the "perfect" relationship as a CL. Divorced people in our sample tended to compare their unhappy situations with courting days or early years of marriage. Many of them said they knew something was wrong because things weren't like they used to be. As one explained, "If we hadn't had a good relationship during our first five years together I wouldn't have known how miserable things had gotten. But we used to like each other and enjoyed being together. Now it's nothing between us but fights and bitterness."

Several of the mothers who gave up custody of children said they remembered how free they were before having children and how tied down and trapped they felt subsequently by constant responsibilities and demands. As one mother said, "I longed for those days when I could go when I wanted and where

I wanted without feeling guilty. Or just to be able to read a novel, even for an hour, with no interruptions."

Strangely enough, the ex-nuns were least likely of all the interviewees to compare convent life with preconvent days. Perhaps this was due to the fact that most nuns entered the convent at a very young age and realized the life-cycle changes that were involved. In addition, most nuns grew up in conservative Catholic families prior to the changes created by the Vatican Council. Very few of them looked back nostalgically to those days as a point of comparison. Rather, the ex-nuns focused on current alternatives to their celibate, cloistered way of life.

While the comparison level (CL) is a basis for determining costs and rewards of a current role, Thibaut and Kelley (1959) propose that the comparison level for alternatives (CL_{alt}) is the standard an individual uses to decide whether to remain in a situation or to leave it. The CL_{alt} is the lowest outcome that a person will accept in view of alternative possibilities. Theoretically, an individual might choose to enter into or to maintain a present situation which is unattractive (below his CL) if it is the most attractive one available at the time and if it is above his CL_{alt}.

The process of seeking and evaluating alternatives is an interesting and complex one. As long as individuals are content in given roles, they are aware of numerous alternatives in a vague and general way. They have family, friends, and acquaintances engaged in all kinds of alternative roles. Through the media and casual conversation, these alternatives are known and perhaps even vicariously experienced. However, under conditions of personal dissatisfaction with an existing role, vague alternatives take on a new perspective and focus.

In most instances, the vast array of role alternatives is limited by the degree of translatability of skills, personal interest, and experience that the individual perceives between his or her present role and an alternative one under consideration. In his study of commitment and burnout among urban public school teachers, Dworkin (1986) found that the degree of translatability of skills on the part of teachers was a major factor in determining who stayed in teaching and who quit. Teachers in the natural sciences, mathematics, business, industrial arts, and bilingual programs were considered "translatables," since their skills were applicable outside the classroom to the business world and public-sector jobs. These teachers tended to have more viable job options than did the "non-translatables" in elementary education, humanities, and social sciences, who often experienced "role entrapment" due to the lack of viable alternatives.

As interviewees in our sample began to explore role alternatives, translatability of skills and interests was a major factor in determining which alternatives were explored. This was most obvious among the occupational exiters who tended to consider alternative jobs or careers in areas related, at least tangentially, to what they were doing. Several business and computer teachers found jobs as accountants and computer technicians in businesses; a math teacher became a graduate student in engineering; several police officers took up private security work. The ex-physicians, surprisingly, tended to consider and eventually move into areas unrelated to medicine. Two of them entered law school and eventually became lawyers; three others became involved in commercial real estate. There are several reasons for the interest ex-physicians seem to have in real estate. Many doctors invest their personal incomes in real estate and become familiar with the area as a kind of hobby or adjunct to their medical practice. Because obtaining a real estate license requires relatively little training (especially compared to medical training), it is appealing as a second career.

Eight of the thirty divorced people in the sample met another partner while still in their marriages and evaluated the new relationship as a preferable alternative to the existing marital relationship. Having an alternative made the divorce process much easier than for those individuals who had not met someone else before leaving their marriages.

In weighing the rewards and costs of a current role in relation to an alternative one, other factors that enter into the equation are the "side bets" that a person has accrued in his or her current role. Becker (1960) defines commitment as persistence in a "consistent line of activity" that occurs through a process of placing side bets. When an individual has made a side bet, he has "staked something of value to him, something originally unrelated to his present line of activity" (Becker 1960, 35). For example, in the course of a job, an individual accrues status, longevity, retirement benefits, security, friendships, emotional attachment to the job, and the public respect of being employed. Becker contends that, in general, the greater the number of side bets, the greater the commitment of the individual.

Among the interviewees in our sample there were dozens of types of side bets that became costs in deciding to exit a given role. These ranged from monetary considerations such as pension plans, financial security in marriage, good incomes, and inheritance, to emotional issues such as emotional investment in a relationship, feelings of security, status, and public approval. In considering alternatives, these side bets frequently constituted a central factor in weighing costs and rewards.

Three career military men forfeited their twenty-year retirement pension by exiting. In each case, however, these men made very calculated decisions to suffer the costs because of greater rewards they saw in alternative roles. One navy officer left just three years prior to completing his twenty years, at which time he would have been eligible for full retirement benefits. However, he felt three more years of "hell" was too high a price to pay. In addition, he feared his marriage was in jeopardy if he stayed because his wife was tired of his long absences and their irregular home life.

A female executive resigned from her high-status position and returned to her previous lower-status job because she felt inadequate as an executive and constantly pressured by the demands of the job. She gave up a high salary, excellent retirement benefits, and the prestige of being the only woman executive in the company.

Several young teachers were advised by principals and older teachers to get out of teaching within five years or to plan to stay for their entire careers because after that time retirement benefits begin to accrue, which would make it difficult to leave. In addition, it becomes more difficult to retrain for another career as one gets older. A major side bet for teachers, like other professionals, is the investment of time and energy involved in preparing for a teaching career. Several teachers in our sample hesitated to leave teaching because of these side bets. It was only when other alternatives arose that promised to outbalance these costs that they made the decision to exit. Likewise, an ex-sheriff said, "If you are going to leave you got to do it the first couple of years. You don't have too much invested. You're still young. You can go out and start doing something else. You haven't accumulated all the creature comforts like cars and houses and all that stuff that keeps you tied down."

A side bet that played an important part in a number of exits was the fact that the individual always wanted a given role and was socialized to identify with the role from early childhood. This was the case for two police officers who wanted to be policemen as long as they could remember, three doctors whose fathers and/or grandfathers were physicians and who never considered any other career, a minister who had always dreamed of being a minister, and a large number of nuns who wanted to be nuns from the first or second grade. Several mothers who gave up custody also experienced guilt because they had always thought they wanted to be full-time mothers. In all these cases, prolonged identification with a specific role became a side bet over time and resulted in a sense of loss when the individual considered giving up this long-standing aspect of self-identity.

In most instances, the process of comparing a current role with role options took place in a vague and off-and-on way over a period of years until pressures mounted or events occurred which significantly altered the perceived advantages and disadvantages of either the current or the alternative role. At this point, the CL_{alt} tended to shift and challenge the role incumbent to a new evaluation of his or her situation.

Conscious Cuing

At the point at which individuals began actively to search out viable alternatives, their cuing behavior tended to become more conscious. They began to realize and focus on behaviors that were indicative of dissatisfaction. This had the effect of reinforcing their initial doubts and served as justification for the deliberate pursuit of alternatives. In addition, as cues became more conscious and public, other significant individuals noticed changed behaviors and responded, either positively or negatively, to the realization that the person was unhappy in his or her present role and was looking around for possible alternatives. This social response became an important variable in determining whether alternatives continued to be explored or whether the searching process was either aborted or delayed.

An ex-astronaut in our sample was approaching the age of fifty and began to feel age "closing in on him." He viewed being an astronaut as an "age-related business," much like that of an athlete who goes through rigorous training, reaches the peak of his career early in life, and then "tries to stay in the sport too long and sort of goes ungracefully downhill as a faded hero." About ten years earlier, he had begun investing in real estate, a venture which mushroomed over the years to the point that he realized he was spending more time and effort as an investor than in his career. Right before his fiftieth birthday, he faced the fact that he had been laying groundwork, somewhat unconsciously, and that he was now more an investor than an astronaut. That admission led quickly to his resignation from NASA.

Another ex-navy officer who had been unhappy for several years with changes in the navy realized that his gradual interest in tennis and physical exercise was an attempt to be in top physical shape to compete for a job outside the navy. For four to five months he had intensified the time and effort he devoted to exercise and suddenly realized that it was not because he enjoyed the routine but rather because he was unconsciously preparing for a shift in jobs.

The female executive who returned to her previous lower-status job admitted that for six months she would cry uncontrollably because of her insecurity in the job. She rationalized her outbursts as due to the new demands and stress of the job; however, after several weeks of wishing she were back at her old job she admitted that her outbursts were an indication of how miserable she was. This realization focused the problem for her and gave her courage to do something about it. The crying was also a cue to her husband indicating she was unhappy and with his support she gave up the position and returned to her former job in the company.

By comparing one's present situation with both past experiences (CL) and possible alternatives (CL_{alt}), the individual makes judgments about the costs and rewards of each role. In addition, the person weighing alternatives takes into account both the translatability of skills involved in making a role change and the side bets that have accrued in a particular role. The balance of the costs and rewards of a current role as compared with an alternative one is also greatly influenced by the evaluations significant others place on each role and the influence other people exert on the exiter attempting to weigh alternatives.

Role of Social Support

As cues become more conscious and deliberate, other people notice them, make interpretations, and respond to the cues. In about one-fifth of our interviews, someone significant to the individual responded negatively. This negative response, in most instances, interrupted the exiting process and caused the individual to reevaluate his or her role situation. In five instances, negative responses on the part of spouses or close friends retarded the process for five or more years. For example, in the case of two ex-physicians, negative responses from wives regarding loss of income and prestige caused the physicians to hesitate and rethink exiting medicine in favor of some other field. In one case it took the physician ten years to overcome his wife's objections. He finally left despite her intense disapproval.

Eight of the ex-nuns we interviewed procrastined in leaving their convents because of intense disapproval from parents. Three of them were threatened with disinheritance should they leave. All eight admitted that parental disapproval caused them to reconsider earlier decisions to exit and resulted in their postponing their decisions, sometimes for many years. San Giovanni (1978) found a similar pattern among the ex-nuns she studied.

Among the divorced people there were also six who said that negative reactions from significant others, usually parents or friends, made them reevaluate how really bad their marriages were as compared with the loneliness, social stigma, and financial problems involved in being divorced. As the mother of one divorcée warned, "You better look twice at what you've got now because single life is no bed of roses. It is not the heaven you are imagining. Bob makes good money and doesn't beat you and provides a roof over your head. You're crazy to give that up for pipe dreams."

In addition to negative reactions from significant others, role exit from some social roles carries negative societal sanctions and casues individuals leaving these roles to face widespread stigma. In our sample we deliberately included some ex-roles that involve social stigma. An obviously stigmatized role is that of mothers who give up custody of their children. In general, pervasive social norms regard motherhood and maternal care of children as a permanent commitment. To give up this responsibility carries with it social stigma. For the majority of the mothers without custody we interviewed, facing the stigma and prejudice of peoples' reactions was a major cost in making their decisions. The women reported that "people feel there is something wrong with you," "you're considered a weirdo and totally irresponsible to give up your children," "people stigmatize you," "people express shock and disbelief when they find out." Most women internalize the norm of the responsible mother and feel guilty when they give up custody, even when they feel it is best for their children. As one woman expressed it, "You feel incredibly guilty about doing that because there are very few things that make you feel like you're OK when you do that." Guilt along with the stigma placed by society on the role are costs that mothers about to give up custody considered in their decision.

Catholic nuns who left their orders also faced social stigma, at least from many Catholics who are socialized to consider a "religious vocation" as a permanent commitment. In fact, exiting convents was a rare occurrence prior to the mid-1960s. While some candidates in their two- to three-year training period left voluntarily and others were denied admission to full membership in the religious order, it was very unusual for nuns with vows to opt to leave. When a group of nuns from a midwestern college left in the early 1960s, the media picked up the event as "a most extraordinary happening."

Most of the ex-nuns interviewed in our study left their orders during the late 1960s and early 1970s. While the phenomonon of exiting nuns was becoming more widespread in American society, many of those interviewed experienced negative or at least shocked reactions on leaving. The fear of negative criticism and stigma was a deterrent for some of our interviewees and was viewed as a high cost of leaving. As one ex-nun said, "I knew people would be shocked and consider me a sinner. However, things in the order got bad enough for me that I finally didn't care what people thought." At that point, the costs of staying were higher than the costs of facing the social stigma she feared if she left.

Since we have no data on individuals who are dissatisfied in their roles but have not exited, it is impossible to describe what happens to people who respond to negative reactions by retreating from their consideration of alternatives and accepting their current roles as the best they can do. Other studies, however (Dworkin 1986; Ebaugh 1977), suggest that role entrapment is a common occurrence.

Positive social support in the serious consideration of role alternatives frequently accelerates the process of evaluating alternatives and ultimately of exiting itself. Many of the people we interviewed expressed relief when someone they valued sympathized with their current role situation and encouraged them to seek alternatives. In fact, six of the interviewees described feelings of reassurance that they really weren't "crazy" when someone else thought they were doing the right thing by considering alternatives. One divorced woman said she "felt grounded again and no longer so anxious when her mother said she should have reached this point years ago." She felt perhaps she was overreacting to her marital problems until her mother assured her she had a choice and that life could be much better for her outside of marriage.

A divorced woman who had also given up custody of her children was constantly challenged by her sister to stand up to her unfaithful husband and confront him with his behavior. She admitted, "My sister, I swear to God, I owe her everything, literally. She's the one, I'd say, 'but my kids,' and she'd say, 'Oh, bullshit!' We were just at each other's throats. But she made me snap out of my old fears. She'd say, 'You're weak, you're weak, you're just a shadow of yourself. I can't believe what you've become.' And when she'd say these hateful things to me, I'd just hate her. But, when I was alone, I retrenched and thought about it and I decided to get out of my misery at all costs."

A divorced man went into therapy to try to get some advice regarding his marriage. After interviewing both him and his wife, the therapist said she was a bitch and that he ought to leave her to preserve his own sanity. The therapist's evaluation confirmed the man's own feelings that the costs of staying married were too high and gave him the support he needed to file for divorce. Likewise, a woman interviewee said her friends called her husband a "schmuck" for the frequent affairs he had while married and encouraged her to wake up and get out of a crazy situation. These comments forced her to face reality, stand up to her husband, and begin seeking viable alternatives.

A mother without custody was encouraged to dissolve her marriage, even though she knew she would have to relinquish custody, when she met a woman at the local Planned Parenthood Association who had given up custody and was very happy and content with life. After a few weeks of knowing her, realizing that someone else had been through it and not only survived but was quite happy, she gained the confidence to agree to a divorce and give her spouse what he insisted on, namely, the three children. The costs associated with divorce were outweighed by the desire to be free of the situation.

Social support, both positive and negative, is an important variable throughout the role-exit process. At this stage of seeking and weighing alternatives, the support of significant others can help clarify the costs of one's present situation and the rewards of other possible role options.

Realization of Freedom to Choose

The process of considering role alternatives was essentially an intellectual, rational one for most people we interviewed. In fact, many of them proceeded in a very systematic fashion to explore viable options, often making lists and noting the pros and cons of each alternative. For a number of people, especially those in roles considered permanent such as nun, mother, and sexual identity, the stage of alternative seeking is followed by a stage of emotional euphoria in which individuals experience feelings of freedom in actually perceiving a choice of roles, described as "freeing," "having a tremendous weight lifted off my life," feeling "so relieved to know I had a choice."

The most striking cases of emotional euphoria occurred among nuns at the point they realized that religious vows, even final vows, were revocable. Nuns redefined the meaning of final vows in various ways. Some came to realize that the life to which they committed themselves had changed drastically and the nature of their earlier commitment was no longer the same. An even greater number came to redefine the meaning of final vows. Whereas previously final vows meant a commitment to live poorly, celibately, and obediently for life, now, in the new system of religious orders with the emphasis on personal needs and a changing institution, nuns began to feel that such a lifelong commitment was simply impossible and that they couldn't possibly have such a "forever" commitment.

The interview data show that many nuns were aware that Rome was quite routinely granting dispensations from final vows, a fact that further indicated that what one might have promised years ago might no longer be binding. The process of requesting freedom from vows from Rome was well known among these nuns, and the fact that it had become quite routine suggested to them that they now had a choice to stay or not to stay.

In the stage of considering alternatives, the nun in the process of leaving disengaged herself intellectually from the meanings associated with the traditional role of nun and became convinced that she did have the moral right to sever her vows and consider options as a single lay woman. For many of the ex-nuns the discovery of their freedom to leave resulted at some point in an emotional disengagement from previously internalized meanings of role commitment. This realization was accompanied by feelings of freedom and elation.

In the traditional system of religious orders, nuns were forbidden to eat in public places. One ex-nun reported the exhilaration she felt while studying in New York City. She decided to break the rules and have a candy bar along Amsterdam Avenue. She reported her great desire just to be "normal" and a "plain ordinary person." She was tired of living up to people's stereotypes and expectations of the nun and began to realize how much she wanted to break free of that role. The feelings of freedom associated with breaking the rule of not eating in public became an issue in her decision to leave.

The mothers who relinquished child custody experienced similar reactions when they realized, often very suddenly, that they had the option of allowing their husbands to have custody of their children. Most of the mothers commented that they never even considered the possibility until their husbands requested or demanded custody, or until they met some other woman who was without custody of her children. In four of the ten cases I studied, this sudden realization opened up new possibilities for the women and gave them an option they never seriously entertained before. Several of them said they knew intellectually that they could give their husband custody; however, they never really considered the option seriously until some remark or event caught their attention, usually at a time when they were desperate and feeling trapped in their situation. As one mother without custody said,

> I really felt like I couldn't get divorced because I couldn't provide for my daughter. It never occurred to me that I might not have to have her with me. For most of the time I was married, I assumed that the child should always go with the mother. But, I think it was desperation, you know. He said if we separated I wouldn't get to take the baby and that he wanted custody. And I thought, bing, that is a great idea. I think it was in the back of my mind but I never really admitted it even to myself. When he brought it up, it seemed the perfect solution. I felt so free again—like life could go on.

Several of the transsexuals I interviewed had similar experiences when they became aware that sex-change hormones and surgery were a realistic possibility for them. While they had heard and read about sex changes and knew vaguely that such an alternative did exist, most of those I interviewed spent years thinking about that alternative and collecting what information they could before finally contacting a doctor or medical program that did sex-change operations. Such contact, however, was a first step in a long, involved process of therapy sessions with a psychiatrist to determine whether the person was a viable candidate, a minimum of six months of cross-dressing and living as a person of the opposite sex, medical evaluation of possible response to hormone treatment, and efforts to raise the finances necessary for lengthy hormone treatments and surgery. After months, usually years, of such evaluation, the individual arrived at a point of realizing that sex change was a viable option. All of those interviewed expressed tremendous emotional relief and feelings of hopefulness that they were no longer doomed to living "in the wrong body," but could now "be physically who they were emotionally and psychologically." The experience of going through an emotional stage of feeling free again and not being condemned for life was uniform among all the transsexuals I interviewed.

Some of the divorced people also experienced a period of emotional relief and feelings of freedom at a point at which they admitted they could get out of their marriages. Especially for individuals from traditional, conservative, often religious backgrounds, the thought of divorce was simply not a viable alternative to a bad marriage until some event or person convinced them that divorce was an acceptable solution. It frequently took many months or years for them to accept this reality, but once they did, they felt free again with the realization of options. The most dramatic case was a traditional Catholic woman whose parish priest "gave her permission" to divorce her husband. She said she drove away from his office ecstatic that it was OK to leave her husband, who had been beating her for years.

In instances of group exits, that is, where exiters left along with other people, there was more awareness of having the freedom to choose. The awareness that others are choosing to leave the role was a major factor in creating a sense of control and choice among interviewees. Several divorced people commented that knowing that divorce rates were increasing and many other people were in the same situation helped them realize they had an option. Mothers who relinquished custody also had an easier choice if they knew at least one other woman who had done the same.

Feelings of being free to consider role alternatives were usually a bridge between the vague awareness of options and a period of very deliberate attention to specific options.

Weighing Pros and Cons

By this point in the role-exit process, most people had narrowed their role alternatives to one or at least a very limited number of options and began to compare very concrete alternatives with the rewards and costs of their present situations. When asked how they went about making a decision, approximately two-thirds of the people we interviewed described a deliberate process of weighing pros and cons of the existing role with one or several alternatives which seemed viable to them at the time. Interestingly enough, many of the interviewees could readily recall the list of pros and cons they had considered in their final decision to exit. For example, an ex-police officer said, "I sat down and did an old sales technique where they list on a piece of paper the goods and the bads. The pros of my job were about ten lines and the cons about forty lines. And I went, 'That's it!' "

The ex-physicians were among the interviewees who could most easily recall the pros and cons that entered into their decisions, a fact that was indicative that for all of them the decision to leave medicine was very calculated. One ex-physician wanted to retire in order to hunt, sail, enjoy his bay home, and work on his ranch. However, he felt very guilty about retiring at the age of fifty-seven and felt he would become "a leech on society." He also worried about missing medical practice and feeling less useful to society. After several years of weighing these pros and cons, he had a major heart operation and used his medical condition as justification to no longer work. Another doctor wanted to do something over which he would have more control and carefully weighed three viable alternatives before deciding to leave medical practice in order to engage in independent investments. He was willing to sacrifice a good income and prestige in order to enhance control over his own life.

An ex-coach and teacher listed the six advantages he saw in staying in teaching, including camraderie of colleagues, contact with kids, and use of his teaching degree, and then described the eight advantages of exiting teaching in order to work for an oil company: more money, being with buddies who had joined the oil company, better retirement benefits, more time with family, more money for the child he and his wife anticipated, freedom from the hassles of parents, kids, and administration at school. After two years of considering the pros and cons, the advantages of leaving began to outweigh the disadvantages and he finally handed in his resignation.

Many of the divorced people listed loss of children, financial setback, and loss of social friends as major disadvantages of divorce, and freedom from an unhappy situation, a more independent life, and a better emotional life as advantages to being divorced and single again.

Regardless of the numerous and varied advantages and disadvantages each interviewee considered, the majority went through a deliberate process of narrowing down alternatives and finally considering very systematically the specific pros and cons of each alternative, including the choice to remain in the present role. While the deliberation process was quite calm and rational for some interviewees, in other cases the decision making was marked by tremendous emotional tensions and confusion. This type of emotional agony characterized the experience of more of the divorced people and mothers without custody than any of the other types of exiters, probably because of the personal relationships involved in the decision to exit. Such exits involve negotiations and mutual disengagements with another person who is not necessarily at the same stage in the exit process (Vaughn 1986). Particularly for the mothers facing the option of giving up custody of children, the decision was frequently tumultous. As one woman put it, "It was like I was pulling my brains out, like I was being pulled at both ends. My conscience was telling me, 'Well, you dirty rat—you're a rotten mother.' While, on the other hand, there was a little voice in my head saying, 'Well, just think of it this way. You won't have anything to worry about but yourself.' I was being torn at both ends and I couldn't think straight. I was confused and felt torn apart." Another divorcée said, "I was miserable, there was no emotion, no feeling. Either the marriage had to die or I would have died, physically."

At this point, individuals were very close to making a final decision regarding their role exits. One indication that they had already made a decision on an unconscious level was the fact that they began identifying with new reference groups.

Shifting Reference Groups

Once alternatives are narrowed down and the individual is close to making a definite choice, there tends to be increased focus on the alternative role that seems most viable and desirable. In fact, there is a pattern among people seriously considering a role change to begin identifying with values, norms, attitudes, and expectations held by people who are already enacting the role being considered. There is a shift in focus from the role expectations of the current role to those associated with the anticipated role. Individuals begin evaluating themselves in terms of standards and goals that are part of the desired role, a process sociologists call anticipatory socialization.

Sociologists refer to groups with which an individual identifies as reference groups. Interestingly enough, a person need not be a member of a group or role in order to use its standards as a basis for judging his or her own actions. A major part of "anticipatory socialization" is the process whereby people take on the values and norms of the role to which they aspire.

Reference groups, whether membership or nonmembership groups, serve three major functions for the individual oriented toward them: comparative functions, normative functions (Kelley 1952; Merton and Kitt 1950; Stouffer et al. 1949), and gate-keeping functions (Shibutani 1955). In the first case, reference groups provide a framework of comparison relative to which the individual evaluates him- or herself and others. The reference group becomes a context in which an individual makes judgments about him- or herself and others. Secondly, reference groups set and maintain standards that are assimilated by those oriented to them. Individuals internalize and make part of themselves the values set by these groups. It is possible for these two functions to be served by different groups, a fact which has led sociologists to distinguish analytically between normative and comparative reference groups. In other instances, the same group may serve both functions, as is usually the case when an individual begins identifying with a group to which he or she aspires. The third function, gate keeping, refers to groups or individuals to whom a person looks for approval or support of actions or decision. A shift to a new gate-keeping reference group can facilitate an exit by making it legitimate while the failure to make such a shift might retard the process by, for example, reinforcing continued role performance. A therapist or parish priest can give an individual "permission" to divorce, give up custody of children, or leave a convent. Likewise, an individual's family can be important in either facilitating or discouraging role change.

Anticipatory socialization has consequences both for the aspiring individual and for the group he or she eventually enters. For the individual, prior identification with group norms and values aids his or her rise into that group by increasing the probability that such a shift in role will actually occur and also by easing the person's adjustment once he or she becomes part of it. Prior identification with a group to which one aspires helps the person internalize values, norms, and attitudes of the new group and serves as a kind of bridge to membership in the group. The person, in a sense, psychologically becomes part of the group before he or she actually becomes a member. This identification makes one a stranger in one's own current membership group and makes it difficult ever to retrench and be satisfied with an old role. Anticipatory socialization is in fact a first real step away from an existing role and toward a new role identification. It is the bridge between the old and the new. Simultaneously, identification with a role one anticipates eases adaptation to the new role once one is a member and mitigates the shock of internalizing a new set of role expectations (Burr 1972).

While anticipatory socialization serves these functions for the individual, there are simultaneous consequences for the group one is leaving that also make continued membership problematic and less a viable option. As Merton points out (1957*a*, 324–25), what the individual experiences as estrangement from a group of which he or she is a member is experienced by associates as repudiation of the group. As social relations between the individual and group deteriorate, the norms of the group become less binding for him or her, and, simultaneously, he or she is less likely to experience rewards for adherence to group norms. As a person identifies with other groups and social roles and takes their norms and values as a point of reference, he or she tends to be less oriented toward and involved with current group members. In turn, people in the exiting role set sense this alienation and emotional distancing and, in turn, reduce both their expectations and rewards for the individual. This process, therefore, further reduces the advantages the individual sees in remaining a group member.

The prevalence of shifting reference groups at some point in the role-exit process is evident among the vast majority of our interviewees. Furthermore, the shift tends to occur at the point where an individual has begun to focus on one or a very limited number of role options and is seriously weighing the pros and cons of a specific role alternative as compared with an existing role. The process of identifying with a new reference group either comparatively or normatively is usually a factor that accelerates the exit process insofar as it helps in disengaging from a current role and in becoming socialized into an anticipated one.

Among the ex-nuns in our sample, shifting reference-group behavior frequently took the form of changes in dress and mannerisms. As mentioned earlier, hairstyle, physical appearance, and apparel tended to be of great concern to nuns who were considering leaving the convent to return to single lay life. Rather than comparing themselves to other nuns, many of the nuns about to exit admitted that they began to read fashion magazines, consult hairstylists, browse in department stores, and become more aware of what lay women were wearing. In fact, probably because of the distinctive garb and "other-worldly" appearance of traditional nuns and their desire not to be labeled an ex-nun on leaving, many nuns made a deliberate and very conscious shift in reference group prior to leaving. Along with taking a new interest in appearance, many of them also began comparing themselves to single women involved in the dating game and social scene. Many of them commented that they deliberately began to nurture relationships with both lay men and women and used these contacts to evaluate how they might adjust to outside life.

For the physicians who were contemplating an exit from medicine, comparisons with friends and acquaintances who had more leisure time and fewer job pressures became an important factor in making the exit. As one physician stated, "During the two years I was seriously thinking about leaving medicine, I found myself envying my friends in other jobs who worked eight to five, five days a week and had a lot more free time than I did. In fact, I became very reflective about how I would spend leisure time if I had it and I even found myself cultivating old hobbies I once enjoyed, like golf and fishing. As I look back now, I was probably anticipating my move and beginning to build bridges so I wouldn't feel lost once I left my hectic involvement with patients." Another ex-physician said he found himself beginning to associate more with his nonmedical friends than with the doctors he had known and worked with for years. He said at that point in his life he wanted a life-style very different from the one he had had for fifteen years.

Two of the mothers who had given up custody of children said they found themselves focusing on other women who had finished college and had careers, and they began to compare their lives with those of women who seemed to be doing more exciting and fulfilling things. As one mother said, "I always wanted college and a career and never was able to manage it with a husband and children always making demands. I wanted to be successful by a lot of other standards." As soon as she filed for divorce, she moved out of the house and into a college dorm. She said she finally "felt at home after years of being unhappy."

The transsexuals in the study identified with members of the opposite sex long before they underwent sex-change surgery. As indicated previously, it was very common for them to cross-dress and take on the mannerisms and self-presentation of a person of the opposite sex long before they underwent sex-change surgery.

As individuals came closer to a final decision to exit a role, and as part of the process of weighing alternatives, they began to engage in anticipatory socialization. Their reference groups shifted from current membership groups to those they were considering as alternatives to their present situation. In addition to shifts in orientation, attitudes, and values, individuals at this point in the process also began rehearsing the roles they were anticipating.

Role Rehearsal

Anticipatory socialization, that is, the process of learning about and identifying with values, norms, and orientations of social roles before one actually assumes them, involves not only studying alternative roles at a distance but also some types of role rehearsals that help prepare for playing the new role. Some rehearsals are institutionalized, such as the requirement that medical students "make rounds" with doctors, engagement periods prior to marriage, student teaching for education majors, and halfway houses for prisoners returning to society. In addition to institutionalized role rehearsals, however, there are numerous informal rehearsals that individuals experience in the process of deciding whether they will "fit" into a new social role.

Role rehearsal can take place in two basic ways: by imaginary role playing and by trying out new roles in reality (see San Giovanni 1978). Transsexuals frequently observe the behavior of the opposite sex and other people's responses to them and imagine what it would be like to be treated similarly. Males role-play by imagining that people see them as women and respond to them accordingly, especially in sexual terms, and the same process applies for females who feel they are males. Many of the transsexuals we interviewed said they would spend hours dreaming of being a person of the opposite sex.

Nuns likewise engaged in a lot of imaginary role playing by observing the behavior of friends and acquaintances who had left religious orders. At the stage of seriously questioning their religious commitment, nuns about to leave routinely intensified their contact with friends who had already left the order. By spending time with such friends, a nun was able to get an idea of what it was like to find an apartment, manage household chores, hold down a job, dress like a lay person, begin dating, get married, and establish a family life. By making such contact and becoming familiar with what other role options involved, she was able to imagine whether such roles were viable options for her. It was like "trying out roles" in one's imagination to determine how they fit.

Teachers and school coaches on a nine-month contract had built-in opportunities to try out alternative roles during the summer months, and many of them in our sample used summer jobs to engage in activities they were considering as options to teaching. One male teacher, for example, worked for an oil company during the summer and enjoyed the better pay, more regular hours, and fewer intellectual demands. The following year he resigned from teaching and accepted a job with the company. A math teacher took a calculus course during the summer and decided to continue in school as an engineering major rather than return to teaching.

In addition to rehearsing roles in their imaginations, many people about to exit a role actually try out aspects of the role in reality before making a final decision. Some real role rehearsals are either dictated by societal norms or required by specific institutions. Transsexuals who apply for sex-change surgery are required to cross-dress for a specified period of time in order to experience what it is like to be regarded as a person of the opposite sex. It is at this point in the process that most transsexuals change jobs and begin to establish a social identity as a member of the opposite sex. The person usually begins hormone treatments at about the same time so that physiological changes are occurring simultaneously with social changes.

Most of the transsexuals had cross-dressed even before they were mandated to do so by the therapist preparing them for sex change surgery. As one woman, who had previously been male, said, "After I married I traveled a lot and kept two suitcases with me at all times, one with men's clothes and one with women's. I had a closet at my work with female clothes. I kept it well locked but wore them when I could." In many states cross-dressing is illegal and proves a difficult stumbling block for transvestites and transsexuals. One interviewee, for example, dressed as a woman to go shopping to prove to herself that she could be a woman in all circumstances. She was picked up in Woolworths. When police officers asked her for her ID, she gave them a driver's license that had on it "sex—male," although she was dressed as a female. Since there was an ordinance against cross-dressing, the officers took her to the men's jail with women's clothes on. She was married at the time and had three children.

She was embarrassed and called a neighbor attorney who had to come down to the jail and bring her men's clothes because they wouldn't let her leave dressed as a woman. After this incident, she determined that she would try to dress and act like a man. She went home and locked up her women's clothes, determined to go straight. She dressed like a man for two days. However, on the second day she looked at herself in the mirror and, as she reported, "My vision changed. I didn't see Charlie. Instead I saw Faye in that mirror. It was almost unbelievable, a figment of my imagination but real to me. I went over and unlocked my closet. I put on my female clothes again and knew I just couldn't go straight."

While transsexuals before surgery are stuck with what they call "excessive baggage," meaning either breasts or penises, there is very little they can do about it until the time of surgery. However, transsexuals do everything they can to hide those body parts which they detest. For example, the same transsexual reported, "When I had my 'excessive baggage' that is, my penis hanging out, I hated it. I even tried to cut it off on several occasions. I did things to me that tried to get rid of it. I put pins in it, I tied weights on it to stretch it so I could use my rectum to have sex with myself. I even took a knife at one point and tried to saw it off, but unsuccessfully. That's characteristic of transsexuals, it's baggage they feel they shouldn't have and don't want."

The purpose of cross-dressing before surgery is not only to become comfortable with a new identity that is emerging but also to become comfortable with society's reaction to that changed identity. Transsexuals have six months or so to experience how society reacts to the opposite sex before actually becoming part of that gender. At the time that transsexuals begin to cross-dress, it is frequently mandatory that they change jobs because most report that employers and fellow employees are not willing to accept cross-dressing. Companies were also afraid of what clients and customers would think if they allowed a transvestite to continue in the present job. In several instances, transsexuals began a new job at the time that they began cross-dressing and underwent sex-change surgery while in their new jobs. In three different instances, transsexuals filed for health insurance to cover their surgeries through their companies, and a secretary or clerk noticed that the surgery involved a sex change. In all three instances, the individual was fired from his or her job when this was discovered by employers.

Identification records were of major concern to the transsexual. Birth certificates, driver's licenses, passports, and other official documents list sex of the individual. The difficult thing to have changed in many states is a driver's license. Highway departments are very reluctant to make sex identification changes without an order from a judge. Therefore, in most instances, transsexuals have to appear before a judge in order to obtain a court mandate that they have changed sexual identity.

Nuns who were considering leaving their convents frequently began to experiment with role options before they made a final decision. Much of this experimentation was an anticipated consequence of changes occurring within the orders themselves. The change in religious dress that was implemented as a way of breaking down barriers between lay people and nuns, for example, had the result of redefining the role of nun both for nuns themselves and for the people they served. As Joseph and Alex (1972) point out, uniforms are a device for identifying group members and ordering the priorities of role obligations for the individual. The traditional habit was a symbol, for the nun and for outsiders, of membership in a celibate, otherworldly group. The habit, which was worn at all times both in the convent and outside, was a constant reminder of the nun's religious role. It also served to channel other people's responses to her. The master status of nun was symbolically confirmed by the habit and ordered all social relationships with that status in mind. The changes in the habit after Vatican II had the intended result of encouraging more open dialogue and accessibility between nuns and those they served. However, that openness and accessibility had numerous unintended and unanticipated results as well. The habit change required that nuns pay more attention to matters of appearance, style, and personal habits. As one ex-nun remarked, "Before you just automatically knew what you would put on in the morning. Your hair never showed and neither did your legs or tummy bulges. All of a sudden, with the modern habit, we had to decide what colors matched, curl our hair, shave our legs, and face the fact that we were out of shape. In fact, all of a sudden we changed from neuter to woman. And that had all kinds of implications. Rome never knew what it let loose when Pope John opened those windows to let the Spirit in."

In addition to impacting the nun's gender-role identification, the modern habit affected the responses of other people to her. By appearing in clothes that were secular in appearance, nuns were able to mingle in public places without being noticed and were treated like "ordinary women." This meant that nuns had the opportunity to learn the skills and routines of secular living and to practice them without being noticed. This role rehearsal provided opportunity for nuns to experience what it was like to be in the secular world.

Because of the liberalization of social as well as physical barriers between nuns and seculars, many nuns in the process of deciding to leave shifted their dealings with men, especially priests with whom they worked and had social contact. While previously there had been strict norms regarding association between nuns and men in general, in the renewed system there were few formal restrictions regarding social relationships. Because of the increased emphasis on professional preparedness, many nuns were pursuing educational degrees in both Catholic and secular universities and were fellow students with men as well as lay women. In addition, the liberalization of work settings meant that nuns were working alongside male colleagues on a regular basis. Romantic and sexual involvements were a consequence of the renewed structures in religious orders. These involvements provided nuns in the transition of exiting the opportunity to try out male-female relationships and were a socializing factor in the exit process. While very few ex-nuns in our sample left because of a specific relationship or to marry someone they had known while a nun, these sexual experiences awakened them to options that they never seriously entertained in the traditional, cloistered system.

The majority of male-female relationships cultivated by nuns prior to leaving were priest-nun relationships. In the traditional orders, dealings with priests were carefully prescribed by strict norms. During the time of renewal in religious orders, friendships with priests were often encouraged as part of the attempt to help religious men and women deal with their own sex-identification roles. Under these conditions, platonic relationships quite often turned to romantic ones. These experiences were a form of role rehearsal that provided the nun a basis for deciding whether to pursue role options.

Once an individual allows him- or herself to engage in role rehearsal, either imaginatively or actually, the process of making a final decision is usually close at hand. It is almost as though once people "see the lights of the city, you can't keep them down on the farm." If the alternative role is indeed a good "fit" and the individual feels comfortable with the anticipated role expectations, the new role takes on an attraction and compelling force which serves to draw the person away from a current role; the "pull" of the new role becomes an added incentive to the "pushes" or dissatisfactions of the old one. At this point, the CL_{alt} shifts in favor of the new alternative. The stage is set. All that remains is a final decision to make the transition.

Duration of Seeking Alternatives

A number of factors determine how long the process of seeking alternatives lasts. These include reversibility of the exit, degree of social support, social desirability of the exit, degree of institutionalization, status as a lone traveler or as part of a group, and, finally, degree of awareness of the process occurring.

Irreversible exits are associated with more intensive deliberations, more careful weighing of alternatives, and more involved anticipatory role rehearsal than are exits that are more easily reversible. The intensive, deliberative process tends to take more time and postpones the readiness to make a final decision. Both ex-nuns and transsexuals made irreversible decisions in abandoning their previous roles, transsexuals because of irreversible physical changes and ex-nuns because of institutional prohibitions against returning to the order. Both groups tended to experience prolonged processes of deciding to make a role change. The same was the case for ex-professionals (ex-physicians, ex-dentists, ex-lawyers), all of whom had gone through lengthy training programs. Even though professional careers are reversible and it is possible to return after an exit, professional norms strongly inculcate a sense of changed identity and lifetime commitment. Individuals who gave up professional careers tended to view their exit as permanent and irreversible. These irreversible exits tended to extend over longer time periods than exits that were seen as reversible, such as divorce, giving up custody of children which most interviewees felt they could regain at a later date, retirement, or nonprofessional occupational exits. In all of the latter cases, interviewees felt that there was the choice of returning to the previous role if circumstances or life events changed. This realization tended to speed up the exit process and was associated with a somewhat shorter time span between first doubts and the decision to exit.

As data in this chapter indicate, positive social support also speeds up the process by encouraging the individual to look at alternatives and seriously weigh the advantages of other role options. Positive social support is one of the most critical variables facilitating the exiting process. Another important factor is the social desirability (or lack of it) associated with ex-roles in society. Role change from alcoholic to recovered alcoholic, prostitute to straight, drug user to former drug user, gay to heterosexual, are seen by society as "the right way to go." Rehabilitation connotes positive role change. However, other ex-roles such as divorcé, mother without custody, ex-nun, transsexual, and ex-physician carry varying degrees of social stigma. The anticipation of entering an ex-role that is stigmatized by society is a factor in the deliberation process of those anticipating such a role change. Such anticipation was a retarding factor in many of the exits.

Institutionalization of the role-exit process can also effect duration since the timing of some exits is specified by society. For example, in most organizations, retirement benefits accrue to a member only after a specified number of years of service. Likewise, one can exit a training period only after completing certain requirements. Many states require a period of marital separation before a divorce is granted. Institutionalized role exits, therefore, dictate the duration of the exit process.

In many cases, interviewees exited multiple roles simultaneously, roles that were usually intertwined in some way. It is frequently the case that when exits are multiple in nature, exiters have control over one exit but little or no control over related exits. Transsexuals who chose to have surgery and become people of the opposite sex usually lost their jobs once their bosses learned of the situation. Transsexuals who had control over their sex role exit, therefore, had little or no control over job-related exits. In like manner, nuns who left the convent frequently jeopardized jobs in church-related schools. Likewise, divorce and custody of children were intricately bound in my study so that each of the mothers who gave up custody saw this as necessary in order to exit a miserable marriage.

The more an exiter was aware of the multiple exits involved in the decision, the longer and more deliberate the process of weighing alternatives was. The individual then had to weigh not only the pros and cons of exiting one role for another but also the costs and rewards associated with related exits.

Finally, the more aware and self-conscious an exiter was with regard to his or her process of exiting, the longer the process tended to take. Twelve of our interviewees indicated that they decided to exit without a lot of forethought and deliberation. In each case, the situation was viewed as unbearable and the predominant motivating force was simply to get out of a bad situation with little or no thought of weighing alternatives. Interestingly enough, the shorter the process of exiting, the more guilt and regret were associated with the adjustment process. Especially in the cases of the mothers who gave up custody of children just to get out of an intolerable role and the divorced people who made rapid decisions to exit a marriage, a short deliberation period was usually associated with a long period after the exit during which they had to deal with guilty or mixed feelings and regret for a hasty decision. On the other hand, the longer and more deliberative the process, the easier was the postexit adjustment.

Summary

The following flow diagram depicts the process through which individuals seek out and weigh role alternatives:

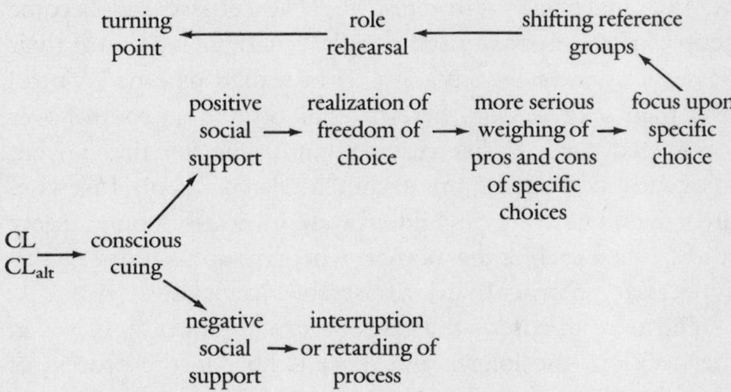

Once a role incumbent begins deliberately to seek out role alternatives, cuing behavior tends to become more conscious and serves the functions of reinforcing initial doubts, providing justification for the pursuit of alternatives, and indicating to significant others the degree of dissatisfaction in a current role. While negative reactions from others interrupt or retard the alternative-seeking process, positive support from significant others and awareness of general social desirability of the change enhance the process of seeking role alternatives. Many individuals at this point in the process also experience the emotional relief associated with the realization that choice is possible. As alternatives are narrowed and focus is centered on one or several viable options, individuals begin to shift reference-group orientations, with regard to both comparison groups and actual behavioral expectations. Imaginary and real role rehearsals begin to occur as the exiter anticipates the norms of a new role. This anticipatory behavior helps individuals imagine their fit in a new role and readies them emotionally for a turning point event which leads to a final decision to exit.

4
The Turning Point

After a period of weighing alternatives, identifying with new reference groups, calculating the costs and rewards of leaving a current role, and rehearsing new roles, there comes a point in the role-exiting process at which the individual makes a firm and definitive decision to exit. This decision usually occurs in connection with some turning point in the individual's life. A turning point is an event that mobilizes and focuses awareness that old lines of action are complete, have failed, have been disrupted, or are no longer personally satisfying and provides individuals with the opportunity to do something different with their lives (Lofland and Stark 1965; Lofland 1966). Old obligations and lines of action are diminished or seen as undesirable and new involvements are seen as possible.

The decision to exit a role is usually accompanied by some type of external expression or indication that a decision has been made. The person either hands in a job resignation, files for divorce, announces to patients that he or she is quitting practice, applies to Rome for a dispensation from religious vows, admits him- or herself to a hospital for treatment, or seeks out a physician who performs sex-change surgery. This public announcement has the function of finalizing the decision. In this chapter, we explore types of turning points, functions of turning points in the exiting process, and feelings which frequently accompany the turning point.

Types of Turning Points

Approximately one-fifth of our interviewees *gradually* evolved to the point of making a decision about a role choice. In these cases individuals went through a long process of being unhappy and discontent with their current role and deliberately exploring role options. At some point, they simply realized they could not continue in the present situation and made the decision to do something about it. Seven of the ten mothers without custody fit this pattern. Giving up custody was simply part of a divorce package, usually brought about by the husband's insistence on custody and the wife's feelings that she could not support her children adequately, either financially or emotionally. The decision to relinquish custody was seen as necessary in order to make the divorce and life as a single person possible.

For some of the occupational exiters, the final decision to resign was a gradual one that occurred over many months or, in some cases, many years. As one ex-school teacher said, "Those little things got to me, a little nick here and a little nick there, and a griping here and somebody eats you out there. And my wife griped at me because I didn't make enough money and we can't get this or that. It all built up and built up. And finally I said, 'Hey, I've had enough of it and I'm tired of it.' I handed in my resignation the next day." Likewise a hospital administrator simply "ran out" of reasons not to leave and knew that if he was really serious about giving up his job he no longer had any good reasons to stay. He felt that if he didn't make the decision soon, he probably never would.

About one-fourth of the ex-nuns also said that they just gradually came to realize that convent life was no longer what they wanted. In some instances the person felt the structure and life-style had changed so dramatically that she no longer felt she wanted to be a part of it. In other instances, the woman herself had changed such that she no longer opted for a celibate religious life. An added factor in almost half the ex-nun interviews was the realization that many friends and fellow nuns had left and that community life was no longer the same as it had been previously. Gradually, these nuns came to the point of deciding that they also wanted out in order to begin a new role in the secular world.

The vast majority of those we interviewed experienced a more abrupt and dramatic turning point in their decision-making process. In some cases these turning points were major events in the individual's life; in many other cases, the event itself was relatively minor and insignificant but took on great symbolic importance because of the time at which it occurred or the fact that it symbolized the culmination of feelings and role ambivalence. There are five major types of specific turning points that emerge from our data: (1) specific events, (2) "the straw that broke the camel's back", (3) time-related factors, (4) excuses, and (5) either/or alternatives.

Specific Events

Specific events are occurrences that crystallize one's ambivalence toward a current role and place the choice to exit in bold relief. These events are sometimes significant in themselves, such as a death in a family or the infidelity of a spouse. In other instances, the events themselves are relatively insignificant but take on symbolic meaning in the context of the decision-making process. For example, in the case of one ex-nun we interviewed, a decision by the order to forbid smoking because of its worldly and immoral connotations became very symbolic of what she defined as the order's infringement upon individual rights. While she herself was a nonsmoker, a close friend whom she had recruited into the order was a chronic smoker and was told she had to quit smoking immediately or leave the order. The ex-nun admitted that the issue itself was much less important than the symbolic value the mandate had in signaling an authoritarian stance on the part of the order. After she protested the mandate and argued that the superiors were placing undue emphasis on minor issues, she was told the decision was irrevocable and that she should reevaluate the independence and worldly attitudes she was recently displaying. Her response was a request to be dispensed from her final vows so she could "return to the world." The interviewee admitted that the confrontation over the smoking issue simply crystallized for her several years of reevaluation and increased her realization of the fact that she no longer held the values and life-style espoused by the order.

Another event that became symbolic occurred when a young woman in the computer business who was bored with her job went on vacation. In Arizona she stopped at a small Ma and Pa grocery store located in a scenic and quiet spot off the main highway. She met the owners, who had left jobs in a nearby city to establish their own business in the country. Their contentment and enthusiasm about working together in a scenic area became symbolic of her desire to quit her hectic job and do something more relaxed and satisfying. As she said, "I was working fifty weeks in order to have two weeks that I enjoyed. I thought this imbalance can't go on. I have to earn a living, but I don't want to do so with the repetition and tedium of my present job." The first day back at work she resigned and returned to Arizona to find a job as a schoolteacher on an Indian reservation.

In the instance of a divorced woman, her husband's refusal to give a daughter a car for high school graduation became the symbolic turning point because he had given a son a $10,000 car the year before when he graduated. The woman protested what she saw as unfairness and the incident ballooned into an argument over many deeper issues which had been bothering her for many years. The argument resulted in her filing for divorce.

In addition to symbolizing conflicts and ambivalence, significant events in themselves became turning points for individuals in some cases. However, in all but a few of these cases, the individuals were already doubting their role commitment. The events, therefore, simply hastened the process. In the case of two physicians, the premature deaths of teenage children challenged the doctors to reevaluate their commitments and what they wanted out of life. One of the doctors who lost a teenage son came face to face with "a realization of no immortality." He said, "My son's death influenced me very, very deeply. I sort of thought, way back in my mind, that some of the things he missed, I'll do for him." This meant finding time to fish, hunt, read, and enjoy people and life while he could.

In ten of the fifteen divorce interviews, the turning point involved either finding one's spouse in bed with another partner or discovering a relationship with another person. In all but one of the ten cases, the interviewees admitted that their marital relationships were already "on the rocks" and that the discovery of an extramarital affair simply brought the marital problems to a head and was the occasion to do something about a bad situation.

Two individuals left their jobs very suddenly when their wives left them and also left children behind. In one instance, an ex-CIA agent who was very devoted to his work and loved what he was doing decided while on vacation to remain in his hometown and change jobs. His wife had left him to marry another man and did not want to have custody of their daughter, and he felt CIA work was not compatible with raising a child. He therefore opted to begin a new career in order to be with his daughter.

A second man, a U.S. marine who was divorced and had a son, was home on leave when he received a telegram terminating his leave and ordering him back on ship. When he protested, he was told to board ship or take an early discharge. He opted for the latter in order to spend more time with his son.

In several cases of occupational exits, coming into an inheritance provided resources for the individual to make a move out of a current role. In all such cases, the individuals left their occupations to oversee family estates; however, all such individuals I interviewed saw the managing of money as temporary involvement until they could find something else to do.

The Last Straw

A second type of specific turning point was an event that followed a gradual build-up of feelings. These events were often described as "straws that broke the camel's back." These events also tended to be insignificant in themselves but were the culmination of a long process of doubting and evaluating alternatives. The specific event came at a point where the individual was ripe to make a decision. A specific event simply became the occasion to take a firm stand and announce an exit.

A Protestant minister had been questioning his role commitment for several years and feeling that he and his family were "living in a glass house" in that his every action was scrutinized by colleagues and parishioners. He also felt he could please no one because of the variable standards of different people. As he said, some people called him a snob for not accepting a cocktail while others were upset if he did. He was also tired of being on call at all times and at the mercy of people who needed him. To refuse to be available on days off when a parishioner had a pressing problem or death in the family created conflicts for them and for him, given his commitment to be of service. While he was on vacation, a woman he had counseled told a colleague of the minister's that he had been "less than professional" with her. Upon his return, the colleague confronted him with the accusation. As the minister said, "That was really the straw that broke the camel's back." He resigned immediately and began looking for another job.

An ex-nun decided to leave the order when her superior sent a representative to negotiate a salary increase with her boss. She felt she was being treated as a child since she had earned a Ph.D., had a national reputation in her field, and had administered several research grants. As she admitted,

> That was the final straw. I had had several run-ins with the administration in the past several years, especially over financial issues. We were required to turn in our paychecks every month and were given a limited budget to live on in return. I objected to the whole system and felt it perpetuated dependence and immaturity. But the real issue was broader than that. I was questioning celibacy and the whole value of religious life. The salary issue just came up at a point where I had pretty much decided to leave at some point anyway. It just focused things for me, like a very ripe pimple.

TIME-RELATED FACTORS

A third type of event that served as a turning point related to time factors. Two of the ex-career people decided to change careers as they approached age forty. An ex-engineer, for example, said, "That approaching benchmark of turning forty was what made me finally do what I wanted to for four or five years and just give up a career I disliked even though I didn't have any other clear cut options at the time. It was now or never in my mind." Likewise, an ex-schoolteacher felt turning forty was a momentous occasion in his life, and it forced him to rethink whether he wanted to teach school forever: "I passed my fortieth birthday. A lot of women say they have trouble at their thirtieth birthday. I had it at the fortieth. It was a traumatic time in my life. Everyone, in my mind, has certain ambitions, certain ideas about what they'd like to do, what they'd like to become. And I thought to myself if you want to be a teacher forever, great, but it you ever want to stick your neck out you'd better do it right now or it's going to be too late. So, I knew a little about real estate and decided to stick my neck out and did so. And left teaching."

Surprisingly, only two of the people we interviewed mentioned the midlife crisis as central in their decision process. I had predicted, based on literature on midlife crises (Levinson

1978), that reaching midlife would be a turning point in the exiting process for many people, especially those who divorced and changed careers. This was not in fact the case. Age-related variables in terms of life-cycle changes were quite insignificant in my data.

The time factors that played a more important part among our interviewees were related to opportunities that the interviewees saw as time-limited, such as alternative jobs that were then available or, alternatively, side bets that would accrue in a job and would eventually make exiting that job all the more difficult. These types of time factors did become turning points for 28 percent of our sample. This finding supports Lawrence's (1980) argument that cohort, environmental, and time factors are frequently confused with life-cycle explanations of a "midlife crisis."

For about 20 percent of the ex-nuns we interviewed, the mandatory time for taking final vows, usually six years after their novitiate year, was the turning point that prompted them to leave. These nuns had been taking temporary vows annually for six years and were now at the point where they were forced either to make a permanent commitment or to leave. These nuns did not want to make a final commitment for a variety of reasons. Some felt ideologically that they could not commit themselves to anything for life, others were unhappy in the order and simply wanted a different life-style, and still others objected to the way the order was changing or not changing. The institutionalized time or "socially expected duration" (Merton 1984) for taking final vows became a turning point for these nuns.

Excuses

A fourth type of turning point was an incident that provided excuses or justifications for the need to leave a given role. In these instances, some event or authority figure made it clear that an exit was necessary for the well-being of the individual. Such advice was used as justification that the exit was necessary, regardless of the individual's supposed degree of role commitment. The ex-thoracic surgeon who was unhappy for years in his medical role used a diagnosis of arthritis in his neck as the excuse that he could no longer practice surgery. He saw his medical problem as the perfect excuse he could give his family and colleagues for his decision to leave medical practice. As he said, "When this came up, it was an opportunity. Like all of a sudden, somebody gave me the key and I made the decision spontaneously and took the key." He admitted that he had been waiting for the right excuse to exit and, even though the arthritis was relatively minor, he saw it as a good opportunity to justify what he wanted to do for years.

Two other ex-physicians made their final decisions to exit after heart surgery. In both cases, the doctors were seriously considering giving up their active practices. Both admitted that they could have continued to practice medicine even after surgery, but they used this medical excuse to do what they wanted to anyway. A fourth physician discovered he had high blood pressure and used his doctor's advice to take it easier as a justification to retire early. Interestingly enough, all four ex-physicians commented that medical problems were accepted by their families and medical colleagues as acceptable reasons to exit medicine and aroused sympathy and concern rather than the stigma associated with giving up a humanitarian profession.

While physicians found a good excuse in medical ailments, three of the ten ex-police officers we interviewed used injuries as excuses for leaving police work. Injury in the course of police duty is a constant threat and viewed as honorable. To have to retire from police work because of on-duty injury is not only acceptable but laudatory in the eyes of fellow officers as well as the general public. In all three cases in which police officers used injuries as the official reason for leaving, they were unhappy in their work and had seriously thought about leaving prior to their injuries. In fact, one ex-officer wondered if discontent made an officer more prone to injury since he had never had even a scratch on duty during the years he enjoyed his work. It was only when he came to hate what he was doing that he sustained injury. He questioned whether "discontent made an officer more careless." He knew five other cases in which disgruntled policemen got hurt and were laid off because of it. An ex-sheriff remarked, "Oh yes. I thought about it (leaving) but I would have never done it because of the type of individual I am. I have known a few guys that did have the guts to get out and I admired them greatly, but I didn't. See, I am very much into security and safety and I didn't want to have to go back out into the real world and start all over as management trainee at Penney's or something. I 'dreamed' a lot, but I would have never done it. I'd still be there right now if I hadn't become injured."

As in the cases of the physicians who left medical practice for health-related reasons and the police officers who left because of injuries sustained in the course of duty, a legitimate excuse for leaving may well be provided by the very group one is leaving. For example, nuns who left the liberal religious order in the early 1970s articulated reasons that were considered legitimate in the order at the time, namely, that religious life had lost its uniqueness, a fact that the order was struggling with in its attempt to renew and adapt to modern conditions. Nuns who left the moderate order, on the other hand, left predominantly for reasons of self-fulfillment and personal growth, issues that were considered legitimate and valuable in the order at the time. Interestingly enough, institutions themselves may provide the rationale and justifications for their members who decide to leave.

Either/Or Alternatives

The final type of turning point is the either/or situation that some interviewees face at some point in their exiting process. This was most common among the alcoholics and divorced people who felt that they had to exit or lose their physical or mental well-being. Most of the alcoholics reached a point where they realized that either they received help or they would die from health problems or drinking-related accidents. The either/or turning point was verbalized by over three-fourths of the recovered alcoholics. The realization usually occurred after some dramatic event, such as a car accident, blackout, or fight with a spouse. In one instance, an alcoholic hit a bridge going seventy miles per hour and went through the windshield. The police gave her a choice: either hospitalization or jail. She decided the time had come for help. Another man had a serious accident and had no recollection of it. He awoke in the emergency room and was "scared shitless" because "I had no idea of what had happened. I knew then that something was drastically wrong and that I either got help with my drinking or would end up in some road ditch." A third alcoholic had a blackout while driving home from school in rush hour traffic and could not recall how she got home. She panicked and called Alcoholics Anonymous but got no answer. However, she put the AA number in her wallet and when her doctor told her she was an alcoholic and needed help she retrieved the number and called AA.

Three alcoholics knew their jobs were being jeopardized by their drinking and that they had to get help or they would lose their jobs. One individual's boss found him drinking and smoking marijuana on the job and gave him one last chance to get help. Another alcoholic was on probation and knew if he lost his job he would go to the penitentiary for eight years. He admitted himself to the hospital for a psychiatric evaluation.

Two recovered alcoholics admitted that their spouses gave them a last chance: if they didn't get help their spouses would leave them. As one man expressed it, "The third time my wife left I really realized that she was not going to go for the shit this time and I was really going to have to do something and that's the reason I tried to quit drinking and went to AA seriously this time. I wanted her more than I wanted a bottle." Another man finally quit when he saw that his wife and son would leave him if he didn't quit drinking.

Several divorced people also reached a point where they felt they had to leave the marriage or "lose my sanity," as one put it. In several cases, they described a "drowning feeling" as if they were being overcome by forces beyond their control. They saw their choice as one between leaving the marriage or losing themselves.

While some exiters go through a gradual, evolutionary process in making a decision to exit a role, the vast majority of individuals experience a more dramatic and identifiable turning point. While in some instances the turning points were significant events in themselves, in many cases the event itself was insignificant but became symbolic of the dissatisfaction and ambivalence individuals were feeling in their roles. As we shall see, turning points serve positive functions in the exiting process.

Functions of Turning Points

Turning points serve three basic functions for the individual in the process of exiting: announcement of the decision to others, the reduction of cognitive dissonance, and the mobilization of the resources needed to exit. Whether the turning point is a significant event in itself or becomes significant because of the emotionally charged symbolism projected onto it by the role exiter, the individual uses the particular turning point event to justify and rationalize the decision to exit, both to him- or herself and to others. It is as though the specific event becomes the reason why the individual cannot now do other than leave his or her present role. To stay in a role in the face of such evidence would make the person appear foolish and weak. Such is the thinking and argument which exiters make not only to others but, equally as important, to themselves.

One function of the turning point event is that it becomes a focal point for announcing one's decision to others. The majority of the people we interviewed announced their decision by word or action or both within a month of the event that finalized their decision. In many cases, such an announcement was made within several days of the event. It is as though the turning point event energized the individual to make a definite decision and then make a commitment to that decision by making it public.

Once other people are aware of the decision, the wheels are in motion and it is very difficult to revoke the decision or turn back. A course is set. Supporters reaffirm the decision and offer assurances that it is the right one; the opposition, or people whose attitude about the decision is negative, make it necessary to justify the choice or at least explain the reasons for it, thereby causing the individual to outline again why the decision was made.

A second function served by a turning point event is the reduction of cognitive dissonance on the part of the exiter. The cognitive consistency theorists in social psychology have long emphasized the need people have to balance and harmonize perceptions of the world. They hold that humans seek orderly and coherent views of their environment, of themselves, and of the important people in their lives. Problems emerge when individuals face contradictions in their perceptions. Cognitive dissonance is a state of tension that occurs when a person holds two incompatible or contradictory perceptions at the same time (Festinger 1957). Dissonance is not so much the objective contradictions in a given situation or incompatible beliefs that may be observed by an outsider; rather, dissonance results from the individual's experience with the absurdity of the contradictions that he or she perceives.

Dissonance may result from two or more incompatible beliefs such as "women should stay home and raise children" and "my wife ought to work because we need the money," or it may result from a conflict between self-attitudes and behavior. For example, the fact that a person smokes cigarettes may be incompatible with the knowledge that cigarette smoking causes cancer. A state of dissonance exists if the person thinks of himself or herself as a sane, reasonable person. Under such circumstances, according to cognitive consistency theory, the individual would seek to work out some resolution to the contradiction. For example, the individual might stop smoking or he or she might regard the linkage between cigarette smoking and cancer as a statistical relationship that does not apply in all individual cases. Or the person may justify continued smoking to him- or herself, as well as to others, on the grounds that an enjoyable life is preferable to a long one. The point is that somehow the individual must reduce the cognitive dissonance and justify his or her actions to put them in balance with attitudes and beliefs. Once an exiter makes a final decision to exit a role and announces that decision publicly, he or she has a need to justify that action. Frequently, the turning point experience becomes central in demonstrating how one's current role is impossible or how that experience is indicative of a broader problem.

The third function of the turning point experience is to mobilize the resources, both emotional and social, needed to carry through the exiting process. The decision has now been made and things have to be done to carry it through, whether this means filing for divorce, signing relinquishment of custody papers, handing in a resignation, checking into a hospital, joining AA, or signing dispensation from vows papers. The majority of interviewees reported increased energy, or at least determination to do what needed to be done. The period of deliberation or evaluation is over and action is now required. In many instances, negative emotions such as anger, resentment, being fed up, or feeling used generated action; in other cases, feelings of relief and freedom mobilized whatever actions were needed.

Feelings after the Final Decision

The kinds of feelings that followed the final decision to exit varied among the interviewees but tended to pattern themselves by the type of role being exited. Among the ex-nuns, the most common experience was euphoria, relief, excitement, a feeling of freedom, and a sense of being released from pressures and expectations. San Giovanni reports a similar experience for most of the twenty ex-nuns she interviewed. These ex-nuns characterized their first days out as "exciting," "crazy," "new," "free," "fun," "peaceful," and "terrific" (San Giovanni 1978, 70).

Feelings of freedom and independence characterized both samples of ex-nuns, the early and the late leavers. For the first couple of weeks, ex-nuns were excited about and enjoyed their new independence. However, simultaneously, they began to realize that that independence provided challenges. Can I live alone? Can I relate to men? Can I support myself financially? What do I do when I get lonely? After years of living in a convent environment with fellow nuns, being alone was a new and challenging experience. This fear of independence seemed to occur only several months after the actual exit. For the first several months, ex-nuns seemed to revel in their newfound independence and freedom. As one ex-nun expressed it, "I was now totally on my own with no institution backing me up. I felt normal again, just an ordinary person with no unusual expectations made of me because of my nun status and it felt terrific." Very few of the ex-nuns expressed any kind of guilt upon leaving. Since all of those who had final vows had received formal dispensations from Rome, this "rite of passage" whereby Rome gives formal approval to the exit seemed to assuage any kind of guilt that they might have experienced in the process.

The common reactions among transsexuals immediately after sex-change surgery was tremendous relief at now being the person they always felt they were. Common reactions were "tremendous relief," feeling "finally at peace with myself", elation "that now my outward appearance matched my inward self", being "glad to be rid of that extra apparatus." Only one of the transsexuals experienced guilt in the process of sex-change surgery. This occurred the day before she was to have surgery. In her words, "I kept thinking how will God view this. Will I be condemned to Hell for this? When the time for surgery came, the night before the surgery I prayed that God would let me die if this is wrong. I woke in my room after the surgery and have never felt any guilt. I felt I had my answer from God."

Among professional occupational exiters, primary feelings after the exit seemed to be twofold. On the one hand, there was relief at having made the decision, but, simultaneously, they experienced feelings of fear and apprehension about the future. As an ex-minister expressed it, "It felt a little scary. I would be a liar if I didn't say I had some fear because there's always apprehension about whether or not you can make this transition into the secular world after you've been in the religious world all your life." The majority of the ex-physicians said they went through a period immediately following their exit of feelings of loss and insecurity along with feelings of relief. As one ex-physician said, "I had a period of feeling lost and useless. I was so used to getting up early to go to work and being called any time of the day or night for emergencies. All of a sudden, I was no longer needed and I felt useless for a time. I felt I was not contributing very much to society, either. One thing about medicine, even if you are paid well when you're practicing medicine, you feel you're performing a service that people need. Sometimes I still feel I'm wasting time when I am managing my money and tending to my own needs." Another ex-physician said the first six months after he left medicine were difficult for him because he was no longer doing what he had been trained for and what he felt comfortable doing. As he said,

> Occasionally, I thought maybe I shouldn't have done it. It's hard to explain. But I felt lost for about six months. It's like you can't go home again. I remember when I graduated from high school. I went back to visit and I was no longer part of that institution. I was an outsider. That's kind of how it felt when I went back to the clinic those first few months or met other doctors I had worked with. They were all very friendly but I was not part of the

> team anymore. There is some pleasure in being a member of the team. So, occasionally, I still think maybe I made a mistake.

Still another ex-doctor said the major change for him was that he used to be inundated with people. All of a sudden, it wasn't like that anymore and he missed it, especially the first few months.

Mothers without custody had two predominant feelings immediately after their exit: first, feelings of numbness and, second, feelings of guilt. Most of the mothers who formally signed away custody of their children expressed feelings of not really being in reality, of a general numbness, of being out of it, of being in shock, of not really knowing what was going on. As one mother put it, "I immediately went into therapy because I thought I was going to die. Not kill myself, just completely disappear. I don't know why. I felt like I was floating somewhere. It wasn't me and I'd say maybe I don't belong here but where did I belong. I didn't belong anywhere. My family was gone, completely." Another mother said, "I thought that giving up custody was best at the time. Well, to be honest with you, I didn't even think. I just did. I was like an automated person. There was someone pushing a button and I just did things and I don't know why I did them. It was like it was, well it was another person. It really wasn't me. It was like I went to sleep for a couple of years and I was watching this person live this crazy screwed-up life, who didn't know what the hell she was doing and yet knowing that's me and she's hurting."

The other predominant feelings among the mothers who gave up custody of their children were feelings of guilt. As one mother expressed it,

> I didn't forgive myself for a long time. I felt like I must be some kind of monster. I felt like I must be what people perceived me to be and I don't even know if they were judging me at all. But I felt that I deserved to be

> punished somehow. I guess I did what I had to do. I'm ashamed of a lot of it, not proud of it at all but it's done. But the entire time that I was running around acting like a single girl, the kids were in the back of my mind and I would think at times, I'm a mother, mothers don't do this sort of thing.

Another mother said, "In looking back on everything that has transpired over the years, it was the worst mistake of my life. Leaving those children with him is something that I will regret till the day I die. It's something that I'll live with every single day. That hurt every day, that it's done and there's not much I can do about it." The guilt that most of the mothers without custody feel is exemplified by the statement of one woman, who said, "You feel incredibly guilty about doing that because there are very few things that make you feel like you're okay when you give up your children."

Because most of the mothers who gave up custody of children had very low feelings of self-esteem at the time of the divorce and the signing of the document, the weeks and months after the exit tended to be traumatic and difficult periods. Most of them had not worked outside the home while they were wives and mothers and therefore faced new jobs at the same time that they were establishing a new family life.

In only one case did a mother without custody express euphoria and relief at the freedom she felt in not being responsible for the children anymore. She said she felt free like a butterfly. She also commented that it was very frightening all of a sudden to have total control over everything and yet to realize she had control over nothing because she didn't know what she had control over. Her children were no longer with her. She had only her own self and her own life to tend to. She found herself totally incapable of making decisions on her own and therefore turned to total strangers for assistance. For most of the mothers without custody the months and frequently years after their divorce were traumatic. In most cases, it took two to three years for them to take hold emotionally after being separated from their children. Added to this was the fact their relations with their ex-husbands tended to deteriorate, making visitation all the more difficult.

There tended to be two patterns of adjustment to being divorced: first, feeling elated at being free again and throwing oneself into the singles dating game, and second, being scared to venture out and proceeding very slowly. Four of the fifteen interviewees became socially and sexually involved immediately after divorce and went out almost every night and with many different people. The excitement of being free again and able to experience self tended to be the predominant feelings for this group. All four of these people had been in marriages that they considered stifling to self-growth. This "wild fling" usually lasted one to two years before they got tired of it. They then felt caught in the "meat machine" and realized that many of the people they were going out with were bums and no-goods. At this point they tended to slow down the dating and reevaluate who they wanted to be and what future they desired.

Eleven of the fifteen divorced people felt very shy about dating again. As one man said, "It was hard to draw on things you learned so long ago." For this group, predominant feelings were those of relief at leaving a bad situation but also shyness and fear about reentering the dating game again. About three-fourths of the divorced people we interviewed said that one of their main problems was dealing with feelings of failure after their divorces. One said, "Divorce is failure no matter how you slice it." Several said they still can't cope with being divorced even after several years. One woman said her greatest desire in life is never to have been married but realizes that that's dead-end thinking.

It was obvious that these respondents considered divorce negatively and in terms of personal failure. They also tended to feel that society stigmatizes them. Several wanted to be called uncoupled or single rather than divorced because of more positive connotations. However, about two-thirds reacted initially to the divorce with feelings of freedom and relief. As one man expressed it, "When I finally signed the final papers, it was like someone pulled a weight off my shoulders. Like I'd been released from a cage. Nothing is 100 percent but it was 99.9 percent relief." For most of the divorcees, mixed with relief were feelings of both excitement and fear of the unknown future. As one divorced man said, "It felt good. It's like being a kid and walking around in a toy store with all the new opportunities that are stimulating. Yet at the same time all these opportunities are still unknowns so it also gets a little freaky."

Feelings experienced after the exit were also affected by the degree of control which the individual felt he or she had over the exit. In the three cases in which a spouse filed for divorce against the wishes of the person we interviewed, reactions tended to be those of anger, disappointment, embarrassment, shock and self-pity. A common pattern for these people was fear of getting too close to anyone again because it makes one too vulnerable. When relationships were becoming too close and personal, they tended to withdraw. As one person said, "I'm never going to let myself in for that again."

Likewise, the air traffic controllers who were fired by President Reagan after they refused to return to work experienced feelings of anger, resentment, and self-pity. Their anger was directed not so much at the president as toward "the system" that refused to negotiate with them. In addition, several of them were furious with former supervisors who encouraged the strike initially and then returned to work when it was obvious that there would be serious repercussions for the strikers. These interviewees felt betrayed and abandoned by those who initiated the strike.

The majority of the ex-air traffic controllers also felt sad and depressed that they were no longer able to practice a career for which they had trained long, hard hours and which most of them enjoyed. Unexpectedly, several days after they were fired for not returning to work, they discovered they were ineligible for any unemployment or federal assistance benefits in finding another job. In general, these ex-controllers blamed the bureaucracy of the Federal Aviation Administration and its negotiators for their unemployment and its impact on their careers and family lives. They felt caught in an untenable worker-management situation that proved to be a no-win situation for them.

Among the recovered alcoholics, initial feelings after making a commitment to stop drinking were unanimously ones of "being scared I couldn't do it," "fear, plain fear of what a nondrinking life would be like," and being "scared shitless, not knowing if I could really do it or not." For the recovered alcoholics, it was a minimum of six months before they began to feel optimistic and hopeful that a real change had occurred.

The Vacuum

There is one emotional experience that characterizes over three-quarters of all those I interviewed. The point in the process at which it occurred varied; some people experienced it before the turning point, during the process of weighing alternatives, and others after the turning point. Regardless of when it occurred, the majority of interviewees went through a period of feeling anxious, scared, at loose ends, that they didn't belong. The experience is best described as "the vacuum" in that people felt "in midair," "ungrounded," "neither here nor there," "nowhere." It is as though the individual takes one last glance backward to what he or she has been involved with in the past but knows is no longer viable. Yet the person isn't really sure at this point what the future holds. It seems that this last glance backward is necessary before actually taking the leap forward.

This period of anxiety and feeling in a vacuum occurred for some exiters just before they made a final decision, in that final stage of weighing pros and cons for one last time. It was as though the pros of exiting were clearly winning out but the person needed to take one nostalgic look backward to the things that were positive, pleasant, and familiar about the past role. In so doing, the prospect of the future became frightening in its uncertainty and unfamiliarity. The result was a feeling of "being nowhere," caught in a vacuum between the past which no longer existed and the unknown future.

An ex-nun who experienced the vacuum right before making a final decision to exit expressed it very succinctly:

> I requested an application from Rome to leave. The application came, I put it away in my desk drawer, and for three weeks was unable to look at it. It was not so much a process of intellectually weighing the pros and cons but of becoming comfortable with the idea of no longer being a nun. Those three weeks were a period of deep anxiety. For the first time in my life I found myself going among crowds and having tremors or feeling faint. I had not yet left the order; on the other hand, I had left it, in many ways. At that moment, I felt like a person without a country, without any footing, without any reason for being. I had no clear definition of who I was or what the future held. Intellectually, I could no longer justify my life as a nun . . . I was outwardly living the routines of religious life, yet I felt like a stranger. Yet, I was afraid of the unknown outside the order. Would I be happy outside the order? Would men find me desirable? Would I find a husband? What meaning and goals would my life have outside the order? What resulted from all this was the sense of living in a vacuum without any meaningful points of reference.

About half of the ex-nuns said they went through a vacuum period in which they felt like strangers in two worlds.

Divorced people tended to express the vacuum experience as one in which they no longer felt married but didn't identify as a single person either. As one interviewee said, "About two months before my divorce was finalized we were separated and I began to feel empty and at loose ends because I was married but not really. I felt caught between two worlds and it left me confused and feeling numb. I developed migraine headaches which disappeared once the divorce was settled and I was just plain single again."

The mothers who gave up custody of children tended to experience the vacuum in the days and months right after the divorce was finalized and formal papers were signed. Not only were they adjusting to being single again and having to be financially and emotionally independent, but they had to learn to live without the daily presence and responsibility of their children. Since most of them had been full-time homemakers, wrapped up in the daily care of their children, their adjustment was traumatic. The most frequent description of this early adjustment period was indicative of a vacuum experience: "in limbo," "numb," "dazed," "in shock." Most of the women reported going around in a daze, not able fully to comprehend what had happened. One woman was fired from her job because her boss thought she was on drugs. She said she was taking no medication but felt drugged by what had happened. Another mother without custody described her feelings as "being in limbo with no anchorings anywhere; feeling just plain numb and being caught in between two worlds and not really belonging in either one."

The vacuum experience is one in which taken-for-granted anchors of social and self-identity are suspended for the individual, leaving him or her feeling rootless and anxious. For some interviewees, this vacuum experience lasted only a short time (less than a week in several instances), while for others it extended into several years. The resolution of these feelings of worthlessness and anxiety were closely tied to successful efforts to begin to create and adapt to a new role in society.

Bridges

Among our interviewees, the process of adjustment and reestablishing a social identity was made easier and tended to occur more rapidly for those people who had built bridges while in their previous roles. In fact, there seems to be a direct relationship between the number and quality of bridges and the degree of role adjustment and happiness after the exit. Bridges tended to be in the areas of jobs, friends, family, and hobbies.

The occupational exiters who had a definite job or alternate career arranged before their exit had a far easier adjustment than individuals who quit one career with no definite plans for an alternate one. In fact, about a fourth of those who changed careers had begun retraining while still in their current jobs. For these individuals, retraining and, in some cases, actual jobs served as bridges which facilitated the exit process. For example, two ex-physicians had gone to law school and passed the bar examination before they officially gave up their medical practices. The transition from medicine to law was much easier than for the two physicians who left medicine for another career without knowing exactly what that might do and therefore with no anticipatory training.

Among all the interviewees, understanding and supportive family and friends were the primary factors influencing the adjustment process. Repeatedly, interviewees reported that supportive family members and friends were primary influences in their ability to get reestablished either in jobs, marital situations, retirement, or rehabilitation. In many instances, even one close friend or family member who was understanding served as a buttress for the individual. For example, one divorced woman said her sister was her "salvation" because "she stood behind me all the way even when other members of my family thought l was crazy. I never would have survived and had the courage to leave my awful situation without her." Another divorcée relied on the emotional support of a good friend "who held my hand the whole way." Throughout the interviews, many respondents mentioned a friend or family member who served as emotional support during and after the exit.

The five divorced people who established romantic relationships with other partners while still married had an easier adjustment than those who did not. The new partner tended to offer support during the divorce process as well as providing a relationship after the divorce.

Among those individuals who had most difficulty in leaving a role and adjusting to a new role there is one overriding pattern, namely, the absence of social support. Feelings of being isolated and alone and having no support are highly related to difficulty in making the exit.

While bridges in the form of job options and social support are central in the adjustment process, several interviewees expressed difficulty in establishing such bridges while still in a given role. An ex-physician put it bluntly when he said, "You can't really try out other possibilities before you leave. It's like being on a stone in the middle of a river. The next stone . . . You can't really straddle both of them. You've got to jump from one to the other. You've got to burn your bridge at the rock you're leaving before you get to the next stone." Another divorcé said that it was difficult to maintain old friends, most of whom were married, when you plan to become unmarried and single again. My data, however, show overwhelmingly that exiters who created bridges between the old role and the new tended to have greater coping resources than individuals who burned bridges before they moved on to creating a new social identity as an ex.

Summary

The following diagram depicts what happens during and after a turning point at which an individual actually decides to exit a role.

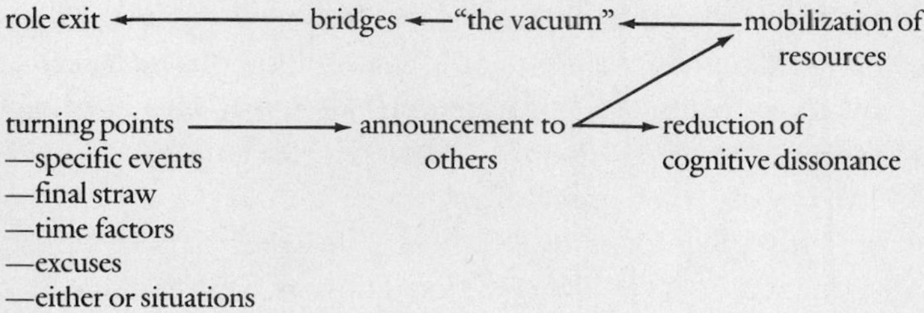

Turning points were of various types but the majority tended to fall into the following categories: (1) specific, usually traumatic events; (2) situations that were the culmination of a series of events or experiences and served as "the straw that broke the camel's back"; (3) time-related factors; (4) events that gave individuals excuses or justification for an exit; and (5) either/or situations in which a decision not to exit would have serious consequences. A decision to leave was usually followed by announcing that decision to other people. Making a decision public tended to reduce cognitive dissonance or mixed feelings in the exiter because in the process of announcing a decision individuals tended to justify or explain the reason behind the decision, thereby working through any doubts that may still have existed. Public announcement of a decision and the resolution of cognitive dissonance resulted in the mobilization of resources needed to make an exit such as emotional support, encouragement, and assurance of the viability of alternatives as well as more mundane help in the form of aid in a job hunt, introduction to new friends, or the offer of lodging or financial help.

Once individuals actually left, feelings varied for the groups studied, ranging from elation and euphoria to fear and anger. However, one emotional experience that characterized over three-fourths of the exiters was that of being in a vacuum, the feeling of being in midair and rootless. Those interviewees who had built bridges into a new role before actually leaving the old one (e.g., new job, friends, family, hobbies) were better able to move out of the vacuum stage and establish a new identity than exiters who lacked such bridges. Regardless of these differences, all of those who suddenly found themselves in an ex-status faced similar problems and challenges in establishing themselves in a new role identity which incorporated the fact that they were also an ex from a previous role.

5
Creating the Ex-Role

The final stage of the exit process is creating and adapting to an ex-role once one has actually left. The ex-role constitutes a unique sociological phenomenon in that the expectations, norms, and identity associated with it do not so much consist in what one is currently doing but rather stem from expectations, social obligations, and norms related to one's previous role. In a very real sense, the process of becoming an ex involves tension between one's past, present, and future. One's previous role identification has to be taken into account and incorporated into a future identity. To be an ex is different from never having been a member of a particular group or role-set. Nonmembers do not carry with them the "hangover identity" of a previous role and therefore do not face the challenge of incorporating a previous role identity into a current self-concept.

A person in the process of establishing him- or herself in a new role struggles to become emotionally distangled from the self-perceptions and normative expectations of a previous role while at the same time people in society are expecting certain role behavior based on a previous identity. Nowhere do individual self-identity and self-transformation intertwine more sensitively and centrally with societal expectations than in the area of ex-roles. A person who is establishing him- or herself in a new identity is engrossed in a number of social and psychological processes which are often painful and undetermined by role models. At the same time that the individual is going through this self-transformation, people in society are expecting certain role behaviors based on a previous identity. The essential dilemma involved in the ex-role is the incongruity and tension that exists between self-definition and social expectations. The individual going through the exit process is trying to shake off and deemphasize the previous identity. An important moment in the exit process occurs when one's friends, family, and co-workers begin to think of one as other than an ex. Goode (1956, 19), in his study of divorce, defines the process of adjustment as "one by which a disruption of role sets and patterns and of existing social relations is incorporated into the individual's life pattern such that the roles accepted and assigned do not take the prior divorce into account as the primary point of reference. In more common sense terms, the woman is no longer ex-wife or divorcée primarily, but first of all co-worker, date or bride."

While many variations existed among our interviewees with regard to disidentifying with a previous role and entering a new one, six areas stood out as issues with which the vast majority of interviewees struggled in becoming exes: presentation of self after the exit, social reactions, intimacies, shifting friendships, relating to group members and other exes, and role residual. Data on these areas of adjustment in creating the ex-role suggest ways in which the ex-role is sociologically unique.

Presentation of Self: Cuing Behavior

Once an individual has disengaged from a role and is beginning the process of entering a new role, he or she begins to emit cues that such a change has taken place. Like actors on a stage, exiters signal to audiences that they expect to be treated and reacted to differently than in the past. These presentations of self, or cues, are like masks that indicate a specific role change. Outward cues indicate to others inward identity and help others place the individual within the structure of a new social role with all of its normative expectations, values, and social interests.

The dramaturgical model, which views social life as actors on a stage, is emphasized and accentuated by Goffman's analysis of role behavior as the way we present ourselves to one another (Goffman 1959*a*). He stresses the role of impression management and social interaction and argues that people shape situations so as to convey symbolic meaning that will work to their benefit. He sees social situations as dramas in which people are actors who use "props" and "scenery" in creating impressions.

For most exiters that I interviewed, this presentation of self to others was a major factor in the adjustment process. Much time and attention was devoted to giving the kinds of cues that would portray a changed role identity. A dramatic example occurred in the case of ex-nuns who had left religious orders in the 1960s and early 1970s, for whom physical expressions of a change in identity were paramount. Clothes, for example, were a critical issue for most ex-nuns. While these nuns had been in modern habit for a short time, the habit was usually not the latest fashion. There was considerable anxiety and attention given to ways of dressing as a single woman in society as well as to hairstyles and makeup. As the identity of the ex-nun shifted in the direction of a new role, the shift was reflected in changes in appearance. When dating and relating as a laywoman became a central concern, clothes became one way of demonstrating a successful presentation of self. Many ex-nuns began reading fashion magazines or going to stores to see what was available. It was common immediately after leaving the convent to choose basic classic styles, such as a basic suit or simple skirt and blouse. To move from the clothes of even the modern nun to sexy bathing suits and low-cut dresses frequently took time for the ex-nun and indicated changes in her self-image. As ex-nuns came to define themselves more and more in terms of new roles, clothing styles tended to express these changes in self-perception.

One ex-nun who left in the early 1970s learned a very painful lesson in terms of the presentation of self. As she described,

> After I left I wore miniskirts and enjoyed showing my legs and getting male attention. I felt lost, everything was new. I met a man in a bar and was dancing and bumping and grinding with him and wearing a miniskirt. We went to the bar to have a drink and he started coming on to me. I got frightened and told him I was an ex-nun. He didn't believe me until I produced pictures. He then took me home, made me change into a longer skirt, and explained to me how men would interpret certain things and I feel he taught me a lot because I was so naive I didn't understand how people perceived things. I still say prayers for him.

Length of hair was frequently an indication that a nun was in the process of transition. When a nun began to let her hair grow and became concerned about its management this often signaled that she was in the process of leaving the convent. The ex-nun faced the task of learning how to wear her hair in such fashion that it did not signal her ex-nun status. For years nuns wore their hair cropped short underneath their coifs and bonnets. On leaving, these nuns usually let their hair grow and began to wear it stylishly in order not to signal the fact that they were ex-nuns.

In the traditional system of religious life, mannerisms and physical expressions were highly regulated. Nuns frequently received instructions in how to walk, how to speak softly and articulately, and even how to raise and lower their eyes in a way appropriate to religious women. Several nuns in the early sample had received instructions in "religious walk." After internalizing these physical mannerisms for years, ex-nuns were forced to relearn ways of carrying their bodies so that they would not be identified as "nunnish." Ex-nuns, therefore, had to relearn the whole world of feminine gestures in order not to be labeled as ex-nuns and in order to make their way in the world of single women.

In the early and mid-1970s, habits such as smoking were frequently taken up by ex-nuns. Smoking was absolutely forbidden in the traditional convent system; therefore, to take up smoking on leaving often became symbolic to the individual of a drastic change in behavior. In the early 1970s, it was still fashionable for professional women to be smokers. Many ex-nuns therefore took up smoking as a sign in making the transition to the world of single women and as a way of indicating a new social status.

For the ex-nuns who exited in the 1980s, the issue of the presentation of self by means of external cues was less dramatic since they had been wearing modern clothes, using makeup, and wearing more fashionable hairstyles while still nuns. Strangely enough, however, the issue of making the transition to an ex-status was in some ways more difficult for the recent leavers precisely because there was less dramatic change in external cues. There was less external manifestation of a role change, and fewer cues were available to indicate to significant others that a change had taken place.

In no instance is the presentation of self on the part of role exiters more dramatic than in the case of transsexuals. Learning not only to dress as a member of the opposite sex but how to wear makeup, walk, talk, and use gestures is a critical issue for transsexuals after sex-change surgery. Much time, attention, and effort is given to learning the ways of presenting oneself differently from the gender identity in which one was socialized as a child. To complicate the situation, men who have become women are often large-boned and have masculine characteristics which they are eager to compensate for and overcome in terms of gestures and mannerisms. The opposite is also true for women who become men and are faced with learning masculine gestures and mannerisms. To fully "pass" in society as a member of the opposite sex, however, it is important that the individual be able to cue correct gender identity. It is on this basis that others respond to the individual.

For divorced people who were returning to the single life, presentations of self also took on great importance. Eighty-five percent of the divorced people reported that external manifestation of their role change was a big issue for them upon exiting. Most invested in some kind of new wardrobe after the divorce, not only for a psychological lift but, more importantly for them, as a way of cuing to others that they were no longer married. Two women had breast augmentations and one woman had cosmetic surgery. In all three cases, the individuals said that this was something they had wanted to do for a long while and that they had decided that now, as they were beginning a new life, was the opportune time. Weight loss as a way of improving one's appearance was also a common technique after divorce. Taking off one's wedding ring or beginning to wear it on the opposite hand also had great symbolic importance as a way of cuing availability. As one woman said, "At first I felt naked when I took off my wedding ring; however, immediately men began to react differently to me when they didn't see a wedding ring on my left hand. I began to like their reactions." Another divorcée commented: "I went out and bought a new wardrobe. When I was married I took care of everybody else first. Now I take care of myself first. The children are taken care of too, but I definitely make sure I have nice clothes."

A mother who had given up custody of her children reported that she was eager to let people know that she was no longer married or in a mother role. Therefore, she took up smoking, drank heavily, and led a very active social life, except when her children were around when she again reverted to her old lifestyle so as not to give them the message that she no longer cared. However, the minute they left, she again took on the stance of a single woman available for a social life with men.

The ex-alcoholics were also concerned with presenting a different image to society once they felt they had really stopped drinking. The majority reported that they began to dress better, bought new clothes, began taking care of their hair, and began weight control and exercises in order both to improve their health and to present an image to society as one who had now decided to go straight. Many of them were reacting to the image of alcoholics as down and out bums or derelicts who did not care for themselves. They were eager to replace that image with one more acceptable to society and to themselves. An ex-alcoholic commented, "I was sloppy and wore the same outfit all the time. When I sobered up I bought new clothes. I have more care with my appearance now. I cut my hair, I am more polite and considerate, and try to conduct myself as an adult." Even the doctors who gave up medicine reported that they changed their presentations of self, usually by dressing less formally, giving up leather shoes and suits as everyday attire, and learning to be less formal and controlling.

Cuing to others that one has made a role change is a major area of concern for most role exiters. Mechanisms for the presentation of a "new self" range from changes in dress and mannerisms to taking up new habits as an indication that one has made a major role change. The major impact of the presentation of a new self is that other people pick up the cues and respond to them.

Social Reactions

One of the most important dynamics in being an ex and moving into an ex-role are the social reactions of other people. As an ex presents cues and indications that he or she is no longer in the role previously associated with him or her, people begin to react to the individual differently than before the exit. In many instances, however, ex-statuses are more salient to other people than current roles. For some ex-roles society has linguistic designations, such as divorcé, widow, alumnus. In other cases, however, the person is simply known as an "ex," (ex-physician, ex-nun, ex-alcoholic, ex-con). Those ex-roles that are more common and are more widely experienced in society carry less stigma and are more institutionalized in terms of expected behaviors. Those ex-roles that are less well defined institutionally tend to be what Glaser and Strauss call "emergent passages," that is, statuses which are created, discovered, and shaped by the parties as they go along (Glaser and Strauss 1971). In emergent passages there are few guidelines, precedents, or models to facilitate transfer between roles. Likewise, social reactions to such ex-roles are less well defined.

There are two types of role exits. First, there are those that are socially desirable, that is, role changes that society approves of such as the exit from alcoholic to ex-alcoholic, from convict to ex-convict, from prostitute to ex-prostitute. In these instances, society approves of the role change and tends to evaluate the individual more highly in his or her current status than in the previous one. However, in these instances, role residual, or the "hangover identity" from a previous status, often impacts current expectations and evaluations. Second, there are exits which are considered socially undesirable. These range from that of the transsexual to that of the ex-physician and also include such exits as those of the divorced person, mother without custody, and ex-nun. In each of these instances there is social stigma associated with the role change and often elements of status degradation (Garfinkel 1956).

In the case of socially desirable exits, while society lauds the exit itself, there is stigma attached to the role previously held by the individual (see Goffman 1963). Ex-convicts, for example, face the social stigma and labeling associated with having previously been in prison. There are numerous accounts of ex-cons who cannot find employment because of their previous records. The ex-con is in a continuous dilemma because not to admit the previous identity can be prosecuted as fraud; however, to admit a previous felony jeopardizes his or her chances at current employment.

A car mechanic in our study who had served three years in the penitentiary reported that customers who knew about his record didn't want him to work on their cars because they didn't trust him. Likewise, another mechanic at a radiator shop who was an ex-con reported that customers veered away from him and tried to keep their distance. Friends of his brother were also wary of his previous record and were reluctant to be seen with him in public. The man reported that any time he was in a group he attempted to stay out in the open because if the group were caught in illegal activities he would be the first person to be held suspect.

Ex-alcoholics also report that people who know about their previous alcoholic condition are often uncomfortable with them and do not understand that alcoholism is a disease and not a moral depravity. It is common for ex-alcoholics to associate primarily with other ex-alcoholics in order to avoid both the social reactions to their previous alcoholism as well as the temptations which society might offer in terms of a drinking environment. As one ex-alcoholic expressed it, "People often consider me a leper, a morally depraved individual, rather than someone with a disease. If they find out that I'm an ex-alcoholic, they often avoid me as if I would contaminate them." In addition to actually experiencing negative reactions, some ex-alcoholics were afraid of how people might react if they discovered their previous alcoholism. As one ex-alcoholic woman told us,

> Yeah, I felt rejected and once again it's my own perceptions. For a long time I was guarded about divulging the fact that I was a member of Alcoholics Anonymous and that I was alcoholic. In dealing with that openly with others I would not talk about it. I think what I have uncovered for me is that somehow there was a reservation in back of my mind that it was not a disease, but that it was a moral issue and that other people would be looking at me as if I were some kind of leper or some

> kind of weakling. I felt a necessity for a long time to kind of live in an AA ghetto.

An ex-prostitute we interviewed admitted that the primary reason she gave up prostitution was because of her six-year-old son and her fear that someday he would find out that she was a prostitute and condemn her for it. She also feared that society would punish her son and ridicule him because of her prostitution. She therefore decided to go straight not because she liked the straight life but out of fear of society's reaction.

Even though society approves of rehabilitation from what are considered deviant roles to nondiviant ones, individuals making this role change are still subject to negative societal reactions or social stigma based on their previous identities. In fact, the people making such socially desirable changes are often caught in "no man's land" because they lose the strong primary group association with their fellow deviants and find it hard to be accepted in mainstream society (Ray 1964). They are often caught in between the two worlds and find little acceptance from either world.

Of the socially undesirable role changes, that is, those which society stigmatizes in varying degrees, probably the most stigmatized and socially unacceptable at this point in time is that of the transsexual. The general social reaction to sex-change surgery for most people is still horror, shock, and disapproval of tampering with "God-given identity." Every transsexual interviewed struggled with negative social reactions on the part of various people to the sex change. In every instance some family member rejected the individual because of it. In only one case were parents accepting of the individual's decision. In the remaining cases, family, including parents, rejected the individual because of the decision to undergo sex-change surgery. Interestingly enough, parents became more accepting over time in all but one of the latter cases. Children were afraid to be accepting because of what their friends and others would think of them having a mother or father who used to be a person of the opposite sex. In the case of one woman who used to be a man, three of her four children ostracized her because of their fear of what their mother's reputation might do to their own.

Almost as stigmatized as transsexuals are the mothers who have given up custody of their children. Our society views these individuals as "weirdos" who are "totally irresponsible," "depraved and immoral," or "crazy." Undoubtedly the most difficult experiences that mothers without custody have to face are the negative social reactions of friends and acquaintances. This negative societal reaction often makes it difficult for the individual to gain a positive self-concept after having given up custody. One mother who had given up custody of her children commented about the reactions of others:

> It's kind of like people go *"oh"* when they find out. Like they're thinking, well, you know, "you're a bad mother." In fact, I had an incident around the corner from my house the other day. A lady was out there and she said, "Well, where's your little boy?" I said, "He's not here, he lives with his daddy." She said, "Oh," and then went on to something else like she was very uncomfortable with the idea. They don't want to discuss it, they don't want to probe it. Most of them say, "Oh," and then they just drop the subject, bury it someplace, will not discuss it. That's how ninety-five percent of the people react.

Another mother who had given up custody responded, "They think something must be wrong with you. They either think that you don't want the child or they think that the courts took them away from you and nobody bothers to ask why."

Most of the divorced people we interviewed also felt that society still considers divorce a stigmatized status and continues to value marriage over the single life in society. For these individuals, to be divorced carries more social stigma than having never been married. They felt divorce connotes failure, irresponsibility, and a threat to the basic social system.

Ex-nuns, especially in the 1960s and 1970s but even today in the 1980s, experience negative social reations. Even if the ex-nun is partially successful in deemphasizing her past identity in terms of her own self-image, she is frequently confronted by other people who remind her that she is an ex. People expect different things of the ex-nun. For Catholics, being an ex-nun usually means having certain religious qualities and values. To see her in lay clothes with makeup and feminine mannerisms and frequently in the company of a man is often shocking. For non-Catholics, the realization that a woman is an ex-nun frequently arouses bizarre ideas, or at least great curiosity about her former life. It is common for an ex-nun meeting non-Catholics who realize her status as an ex-nun to be barraged with questions about what her previous life was like. It is difficult for these ex-nuns to try to disengage from that previous status in the face of such attention and curiosity about who they used to be.

In the area of social reactions, there is little difference among ex-nuns between the early and the later leavers. It is as difficult for the later exiters to deal with the reactions of other people as it was for those who left earlier. Ex-nuns from both samples go through a series of stages in dealing with the issue of revealing their ex-status to others. Initially, while the individual is very sensitive to her recent identity, it is common to want to make sure that people know immediately whom she used to be. Then comes a period of wanting to hide that previous identity in an effort to deal with the new status herself. In time, ex-nuns seem to take their ex-status more naturally and allow it to come up in conversation only if it seems appropriate. As one ex-nun said, "Initially after I left I would blurt out right away the fact that I used to be a nun in the hopes that such initial disclosure would prevent future embarrassments. Then I moved to a stage where I switched completely and didn't reveal my ex-identity at all. Finally, I am now at a point where I take being an ex-nun as part of my life and my past. It is simply someone I used to be that has become incorporated in who I now am."

The ex-physicians also experienced varying social reactions. Some colleagues and social acquaintances admired the doctor for being able to make such a role change. Others, however, thought the ex-physician crazy to give up a privileged role in society. Most people tended to consider the ex-physician still part of the medical role and often continued to call him or her doctor even after he or she had left the role. It is as though it is "once a doctor, always a doctor" in society's image of the physician.

The combination of an exiter's presentation of self after a role exit and society's reaction to that exit makes the adaptation process either more difficult or easier for the individual. The kinds of feelings and coping mechanisms that exiters experience in the weeks and months after making the exit are highly dependent on how significant others react to the exit.

Related to the reactions of other people toward a role exiter is the process of labeling, that is, attaching names to categories of people that become self-fulfilling prophecies. Labeling theory was developed by sociologists interested in processes of social deviance (Kitsuse 1962; Lemert 1951, 1967; Scheff 1966; Schur 1971; Liska 1981). These theorists argue that society labels deviance and associates stereotypical behavior with these labels. In response, people so labeled tend to be true to that label. For example, a child who is labeled a troublemaker by a teacher is prone to make trouble because that's what people expect. Labels often become self-fulfilling prophecies whereby individuals live up to the expectations of the label. Likewise, drug addicts who are often labeled by nonaddicts as "bums" or "degenerates" find it difficult to have a positive self-regard in the face of such labels (Ray 1964).

Over the years there are labels that have been applied to various types of role exits. "Ex-convict," for example, conjures up images of dishonesty, nonreliability, aggressiveness, and danger. When a person is labeled an ex-convict, therefore, these stereotypes become associated with the given individual. As several ex-convicts explained, they faced the dilemma when filling out formal applications of whether or not to label themselves ex-convicts because of their fear of what effect these stereotypes would have. Employers are wary of trusting an ex-con. Many welfare agencies and social service agencies treat ex-convicts differently from other people eligible for assistance. It is as though the ex-convict gives up basic social rights and the right to be respected as an individual human being.

The term "mother without custody" has become a label in our society indicating irresponsibility, hard-heartedness, selfishness, and a lack of maternal instincts. The general stereotype of a mother without custody seems to be someone who doesn't care about her children and puts herself before them. Women who struggle with intense feelings of guilt after giving up custody struggle to regain self-confidence and self-esteem. One of the prohibitive factors is the constant labeling process that they face in society.

"Ex-nun" connotes images of naïveté, inexperience, innocence, noninvolvement in worldly affairs, modesty, and a sweet, caring personality. As an ex-nun struggles to learn the ways of the world, she is constantly challenged by the stereotypes associated with being an ex-nun. As she struggles to be accepted as an ordinary woman in society, she constantly has to disprove the label society gives her. In many instances the ex-nun goes overboard in trying to prove the label inaccurate in her regard. About half of the ex-nuns interviewed admitted that they went wild in regard to clothes, makeup, and behavior in order to prove that the stereotype of ex-nun was inaccurate in their particular cases. As one ex-nun expressed it, "When I left I went crazy in regard to clothes and makeup and how I acted. I didn't want people to label me as an ex-nun so I wanted to make sure I didn't fit the usual stereotype. Another ex-nun I was living with wanted to have sex immediately and was running around and picking up men. We moved from Cleveland so that no one would know we were ex-nuns and we would be treated as plain ordinary women."

Transsexuals also face the difficulty of living with a label. The general reaction in society toward transsexuals is still one not only of curiosity but of disapproval. Many people label transsexuals as unstable, crazy, mixed up, and immoral for trying to change nature. To be labeled a transsexual, therefore, carries these connotations. It is one of the difficulties that all of the transsexuals in our study constantly faced. Several of them commented that they struggled continually against the labels placed on them.

Intimacies

For three of the groups I interviewed, a primary area of social adjustment had to do with sexuality and intimate relationships. For most ex-nuns it had been five to twenty years since they had dated. Most nuns enter the convent either during or directly after high school. High school dating, especially in the 1950s and 1960s, was very different from the situation in which nuns found themselves after exiting the convent. The rules of the game had changed. As one interviewee put it, "Gee, men have become aggressive and permissive since I last dealt with them. To accept a dinner date almost inevitable meant sexual favors in return." Another said, "When I dated twenty years ago it was considered inappropriate for a man to expect a prolonged good night kiss at the door. Now men are offended if they are not invited into your apartment after a night out."

While nuns had been associating with men in educational and social situations prior to leaving, and while some had begun dating before they actually left, a major area of adjustment for them was learning to handle dating situations. This was true for both the early and the recent leavers. While recent ex-nuns had had more associations with men prior to exiting, the prescriptions of their religious roles influenced the nature of those relationships. Being a nun signaled sexual nonavailability. Ex-nuns, particularly those interested in marriage, realized that it was important to be successful in the area of relating to men. Ex-nuns reported feeling very insecure about sexual scripts, that is, what was expected of them in relating to a man in social life (Gagnon and Simon 1973). Part of sexual scripts involves cues which were strange to these ex-nuns since cues had changed over the years. Many ex-nuns reported misinterpreting cues, and frequently ex-nuns found themselves in embarrassing situations in which the man interpreted cues very differently from the way they had intended. For example, ex-nuns said they learned quickly that accepting an invitation to a date's apartment after going out to dinner or the theater indicated to him that she was interested in sexual involvement.

In the traditional system of religious life, "particular friendships" were forbidden. There were numerous structural mechanisms to discourage close personal relationships among nuns, such as drawing numbers to determine with whom a nun would walk or converse. This exercise reduced the probability that individual nuns would get too attached to one another. While fear of lesbian relationships may have been the covert rationale for forbidding particular friendships, the stated rationale was to encourage universal love among nuns for each other. Many ex-nuns wanted to develop close personal relationships with both males and females, but only gradually were the majority of them able to develop close friendships with lay people. In fact, the development of such friendships indicated successful adjustment to an identity other than that of ex-nun.

For the recent sample of leavers, issues of clothing, makeup, and hairstyles were significantly less traumatic than for the earlier sample since nuns in the renewed orders had more freedom to choose individual styles. In fact, most of the interviewees reported very little change necessary in physical appearance. It was in the area of intimacy and sexuality that the recent sample of ex-nuns found most difficulty. While they had been relating to men in many contexts before leaving, identity as a nun proscribed sexual behavior. On leaving, these ex-nuns reported difficulty in learning to relate to men in an available fashion. Most of them were eager to explore their sexuality and yet had to learn both the cues and the behavior appropriate to greater freedom in this area. As one ex-nun who left recently said, "I desperately wanted to date but I was not used to being available to men sexually. The freedom to respond emotionally was new. I didn't have it before since vows didn't allow that freedom. Now I had permission. I could go places and do things freely; however, I had to learn how to cue to men that I was available and interested and then I had a lot to learn about behavior with men once I was asked out. It was very scary at first. It was hard to make myself initiate relationships but I desperately wanted them."

Most ex-nuns soon discovered that eligible men had been previously married, at least men in their own age cohort. They then had to decide how they felt about dating a divorcé, or in some cases a married man who had not yet divorced. In some cases dating a divorcé also meant coming to know his children. Serious dating relationships brought forth the possibility of being a stepparent. In some instances, then, during the first year or so after leaving the order ex-nuns faced not only the issue of negotiating male-female relationships but also the possibility of becoming both wife and stepparent simultaneously.

One of the big issues for an ex-nun in a dating situation was whether to reveal to her date that she used to be a nun. Usually, people who are beginning to date discuss their pasts, where they were born, where they went to school, where they have been the past year. For the ex-nun, the question was always, Should I tell him or shouldn't I? To tell frequently caused embarrassment. Once a man realized that his date had been a nun, his reactions frequently depended on his own knowledge and experiences concerning nuns. Frequently, it was difficult for an ex-nun to explain where she had been and what she had done the past year without reference to her former identity. Most of the nuns we interviewed mentioned this dilemma as central when they began dating.

Another group that was especially concerned about dating in the adjustment process were divorced people. As with ex-nuns, it had been years since most of them were part of the dating game and they were scared and nervous. Eleven of the fifteen interviewees said dating was the hardest adjustment. They felt "awkward," "scared," "strange," "like a teenager again," "clumsy." In some instances they felt compelled to tell their dates immediately that they were divorced, as if to get that out front right away to see if it were important. Others were very hesitant to tell their dates they were divorced for fear he or she would not want to date them. The majority of interviewees felt that it was still a stigma to be divorced and that society still didn't consider divorce normal and acceptable. Several said the dating game had changed since they were last involved in it: women were more forward and aggressive; there was a freer attitude toward sex and more openness in discussing feelings. Several women were afraid that men wouldn't want to date them because of their children. They soon realized, however, that "everyone was in the same boat." As in the case of ex-nuns, people who were leaving marriages in which they had been a good number of years faced a world of new sexual stress in which the cues had changed. Like the ex-nuns, they had to relearn cues appropriate to the dating game.

For the transsexuals who had recently undergone sex-change surgery, dating and the area of sexual intimacy was also a critical area of adjustment. As one transsexual put it, "I could hardly wait to have sex after surgery. I knew it was going to be an interesting experience. All of a sudden I didn't have a penis to stand in the way of sexual pleasure. I did have sex with a friend of mine who worked with me. I didn't get too much from the first time. It felt good but I had no orgasm. In subsequent sex I did have orgasms. It is not easy to do. Sex, however, is more normal than it used to be."

All of the transsexuals we interviewed were both excited and scared anticipating their first sexual experience after surgery. It seemed to be a predominant concern in their first weeks after sex-change surgery. After all, these individuals had in most instances been having sex with people of the same sex before surgery, ostensibly a homosexual situation. After surgery, they were entering a heterosexual world. An interesting question posed by several of the transsexuals was whether sex previous to surgery had in effect been homosexual. Although they had sex with same-sex partners, they had heterosexual feelings. Most transsexuals had been involved in a gay life before surgery. In some instances transsexuals wanted to move out of the gay life and into a straight life after surgery. However, many of their close friends and acquaintances were part of the gay world. Most transsexuals that we interviewed continued some association with their gay friends even after sex-change surgery. As one transsexual said, "I don't see how you can get away completely from the gay life. I wouldn't want to cut away completely. These are my friends, people I've run around with. Even though I may not have sex with them, I have an understanding of them that most people in society don't. I want to have some gay friends and if I marry someday I want my husband to know there will be gay people in our lives. You can't run to straight people when you're in trouble and tell them your whole past history. They'll throw you out. Gays will understand better, especially friends."

Like the ex-nuns, the transsexuals were also faced with the dilemma of whether to reveal their past gender identity to dates and new acquaintances. Most of the transsexuals we interviewed did share their pasts with people they dated. In only one instance did a male-to-female transsexual ask me not to call her home because her fiancé did not know of her past. She intended to wait until after her wedding to tell him for fear of his reaction.

Reactions to knowledge of a partner's sex-change surgery varied and tended to determine the future of the relationship. In some instances, partners were horrified and eager to end the relationship. In other cases, partners were stunned, intrigued, and challenged to continue the relationship, frequently out of curiosity. In no instance did a transsexual report that a partner accepted the gender change as "normal." Rather, dealing with the knowledge of sex-change surgery became a major issue in each heterosexual relationship mentioned by interviewees.

The ways in which people labeled exiters and their reactions to knowledge of an individual's past identity was a major area of adjustment for interviewees. Related to this fact was the constant necessity of deciding whether or not to reveal their pasts. In addition to the impact of social reactions upon postexit adjustment, exiters also experienced shifts in their friendship networks.

Shifting Friendship Networks

The adjustment associated with role exiting also involves changes in the individual's friendship groups. Very rarely do exiters experience a role exit without some changes in the people they value and with whom they associate as friends. The most dramatic instance is probably the ex-alcoholics who tended to shift from other drinking alcoholics as friends to nondrinking alcoholics, often other members of Alcoholics Anonymous or some other self-support group. The majority of the alcoholics I interviewed indicated that prior to their rehabilitation they had associated primarily with people who were also alcoholics. One of the reasons for this is that in such friendship situations they didn't feel different or deviant; rather they were behaving as their friends behaved. Also, by having other alcoholic friends they were not challenged to change their behavior. However, at the point at which an alcoholic stopped drinking and became an ex-alcoholic, many considered it mandatory to stop associating with other alcoholics and to make friends with people who would discourage drinking. In the majority of cases, nondrinking alcoholics shifted friendship patterns to fellow members of self-help groups who understood their problem and also understood the necessity of supporting each other and not drinking. As a nondrinking alcoholic put it, "I was glad I was part of AA, that I belonged. At least I felt like I belonged. It felt good to be there. It was safe; therefore, I was inclined to associate with other AA members who knew my problem and would encourage me in nondrinking. In fact, I gave up all my old alcoholic friends and began to establish friends in the group."

Divorced people likewise tended to shift friendship patterns dramatically after divorce. (Vaughn [1986] found the same pattern for those uncoupling from intimate relationships.) They tended to be involved less with couples, especially those whom both they and their spouses knew previously, and to become closer friends with other single and divorced people. Almost every interviewee commented on being invited less frequently to couples affiars, such as dinners and parties, because of the awkwardness of being alone. Equally as common was being invited to every affair where someone needed an "extra" to complete a party. As one person said, "There is no room for uncouples. All invitations say Mr. and Mrs. and now there is no Mrs." It was also common for shifts to occur among friends of both husband and wife. It was as if former friends felt they had to take sides and wanted to avoid awkward conversations and situations. As one man explained, "Mutual friends were uncomfortable around me and avoided certain subjects."

After divorce, many people renewed friendships with old classmates whom their spouses didn't know well, people with whom they felt on common ground. Several people also became close to friends who were also divorced. Not only did they have more interests in common with these single friends but their life situations and social life were more in harmony. Nights and weekends were not tied up with family. One woman said she was no longer invited to friends' get-togethers because they felt funny with her around. She didn't invite people over because she didn't know what to do with the males.

Relating to Group Members and Other Exes

One characteristic unique to the ex-role is the fact that an ex once shared a role identity with other people, many of whom are still part of the previous role. Equally as important is the fact that usually there is a cohort or aggregate of other exes who have left the previous group. Therefore, exes are faced with the challenge of relating both to former group members as well as other exes. This is sociologically different from being a nonmember of a group. Nonmembers have never belonged in the role and, therefore, have not established in-group relationships with others in that role. People who have never been part of the previous group also do not share the common characteristics of being an ex of that particular group.

In the case of ex-nuns, many who left in the late 1960s and early 1970s felt hostile or angry about their years in the convent. Many of them felt they had wasted years that might have been devoted to marriage and a family. Some of them left at an age which prohibited having children, and in many instances the age factor also mitigated against entering certain professions. Among these nuns who were early leavers there was frequently little interest in maintaining a relationship with the former order; rather the desire was to start a new, independent life. At the same time, exiting was frequently considered a threat to those who remained in the order. In fact, in pre-Vatican II orders a member who was exiting was whisked away in the middle of the night so that other members of the group had no involvement with her. Nuns would wake up the next morning and realize that someone was missing from morning prayers or breakfast. It was usually indirectly that they realized the person was a defector. No correspondence or personal contact with ex-members was allowed. Even though ex-members were not publicly ridiculed, silence on the part of superiors often indicated disapproval. These was often little attempt on the part of the order to maintain relationships with those who left; rather, it was as though the former member were cut off from association with the group. No doubt, exiting was a threat to those who remained in the order.

In contemporary orders the situation has changed dramatically. The recent leavers all felt a close relationship both to the order in general and to individual members in particular and desired to continue some relationships with these people. However, the majority of them indicated that the quality of relationships with former members did change once they left. For many of them this was a sad experience. As one recent ex-nun put it,

> The hardest thing about leaving was to tell the other Sisters that I was close to. Especially those who didn't realize it was coming. There was a sense of loss on both parts. They lost part of the community they were committed to and I did, too. I lost community and they lost a person from the group. Especially now that median ages are increasing, to lose a young member is a tough thing. I still have many friends in the order and want to continue my relationship with them; however, for the most part these relationships changed once I left. It was difficult for me to deal with the fact that it had to be so.

Unlike the earlier leavers, therefore, recent ex-nuns on the whole want to maintain contact with the group. Simultaneously, contemporary orders are making attempts to maintain contact with former members. In the more open, modern system the philosophy of orders is that former members are who they are because of association with the group and, likewise, that the group has benefited from the contributions of former members. Many orders have established ex-member associations and invite ex-members to meetings, conventions, and social activities sponsored by the order.

A major difference between exiters in the previous system and those now exiting concerns the relationships that exist between ex-members themselves. In the previous system there were cohorts of exiters—nuns tended to leave in groups or at least in temporal proximity. Frequently, ex-nuns lived together in the first months after exiting as a way of maximizing financial resources as well as for mutual support. It was common in the 1970s to find two, three, or four ex-nuns living together. In many orders it was also common for ex-nuns to maintain an informal network among themselves and to socialize together. Finding ex-nuns to interview in the 1970s was a simple process because of the informal network that existed among leavers from a particular order. Today the exiting rate from orders has slowed down and nuns are no longer leaving in cohorts. It is therefore more common to find ex-nuns living alone in apartments. Networks among ex-nuns are also less common today. In the previous sytem, it was as though ex-nuns came together as a cohesive group ostracized by the former group. Theirs was frequently a "we against them" attitude. Today, such an attitude is no longer necessary since orders themselves are more open and positive toward ex-members. It is more common today, therefore, to find ex-members associating with former group members than with other exes. Ex-members today tend to be organized more formally by the orders themselves rather than through informal friendship networks.

Among the transsexual sample, there is much intellectual awareness of having previously been part of a social group of other transsexuals; however, the tendency is for transsexuals to move away emotionally from other transsexuals after sex-change surgery. The desire to become "normal" in society makes them reluctant to associate either with transsexuals who have not yet gone through the surgery or with other postsurgery transsexuals. As far as I am aware, there are no transsexual self-help groups organized for people who have been through the surgery.

In the past several years, self-help groups for mothers without custody of children have mushroomed in the United States. Increasing numbers of mothers without custody are joining together in an attempt to share problems and deal with feelings associated with this ex-role. The majority of interviewees in our sample belonged to such a self-help group and found it extremely helpful in adjusting to the ex-role. There is great camaraderie among women who have given up custody of their children and many of the interviewees commented on the therapeutic support such groups offer.

The entire basis of Alcoholics Anonymous is the mutual support that nondrinking alcoholics can give each other, and especially newcomers to the group. The philosophy of the group is to develop strong emotional ties among nondrinking alcoholics and to encourage the lack of association between members and drinking alcoholics. All of the nondrinking alcoholics I interviewed were fearful of maintaining association with previous group members, that is, drinking alcoholics.

Most of the exiters interviewed commented on having had to learn to deal with both members of the group they left and also other exes from the group. The nature of the kinds of relationships that were established depended on the type of group that was exited and also on the degree of "hangover identity" that a person maintained after the exit.

Role Residual

In the process of role exiting some individuals are better able to shake off their identification with a previous role than other individuals. As Turner puts it, "Some roles are put on and taken off like clothing without lasting effects. Other roles are difficult to put aside when a situation is changed and continue to color the way in which many of the individual's roles are performed" (1978, 1). Role residual is the identification that an individual maintains with a prior role such that the individual experiences certain aspects of the role after he or she has in fact exited from it. We can think about role residual as "hangover identity," that is, as aspects of self-identity that remain with an individual from a prior role even after exiting.

Role residual is analogous to the kind of nostalgia of which Davis (1979) speaks. He describes nostalgia as that "sometimes pedestrian, sometimes disjunctive and sometimes eerie sense we carry of our own past and its meaning for present and future."

Davis suggests that those who are more unhappy and dissatisfied with their present lives would show a considerable amount of nostalgia and be more likely to feel and speak favorably, and perhaps longingly, of the past. Whether the past in actuality was as satisfying and positive as one remembers it, to look back favorably on the past functions in maintaining a stronger self-identity. As Davis puts it, "In the clash of continuities and discontinuities with which life confronts us, nostalgia clearly attends more to the pleas for continuity, to the comforts of sameness and to the consolations of piety" (1979, 33).

Davis asserts that notalgia is experienced in a positive sense, whereby one looks back on the pleasurable events in one's past, pushing aside those negative experiences which occurred. This helps in coping with the fear and uncertainties that the future holds while believing that one's present self is the same as it was in the past. Since that self dealt successfully with life's complexities, it can and will continue to do so.

Role residual, then, is the continued identity an individual holds with aspects of a previous role. It consists of the remnants or leftovers from a previous identity that cloud and impact on one's current role. While some exiters leave a role with little continued identity, others maintain close identity with the previous role.

Analysis of occupational role exits shows that individuals exiting professional and semiprofessional roles tend to have more role residual than individuals exiting nonprofessional roles (see Phillips 1984). In the process of becoming a professional, changes occur in the self-identity of a person to the extent that identity and role expectations merge. As individuals internalize a professional role, they define themselves in terms of role expectations. The professionals in our study experienced more role residual than the semiprofessionals. The nonprofessional exiters had the least amount of role residual. Exceptions to the above findings, however, occurred in the cases of nonprofessional exiters who occupied highly visible roles in society, such as ex-opera singer, ex-astronauts, and ex-professional athlete. In all of these instances, role residual was as strong as it was for the professional exiters. One explanation for this finding has to do with the social visibility involved in these particular roles. Roles that are highly visible in society and which involve social support and social acceptability tend to be roles that are very difficult to exit from in a complete fashion. One reason is that the public keeps reminding the individual of exiting. As one ex-professional athlete in our sample put it,

> I think the first thing that happened to me when I left was that I kind of became shy. A little introverted because I didn't have my Samson hair real long. It had been cut short. I think one of the hardest things an athlete has that reaches that level is that so much of his life is made up of what he has done on Sunday and what people want to make you. It becomes a part of your life without your realizing it and once you realize that you don't have that to rely on anymore it gets kind of scary. People are always asking if you're going to go back and try out with the USFL. They want you to do it because they know you and they want you to be out there. So, they don't let go of it and you're always saying, no, no. And of course all that input you get all the time keeps working on your mind. It's like, well, maybe I should. As much as you try to consciously deal with it and work the things out yourself, then as soon as you do that you turn the corner and a guy says, "Hey, are you gonna try out next year"?

Another nonprofessional group that had a high degree of role residual was the group of air traffic controllers fired by President Reagan. The air traffic controllers resemble professionals in that their training is extensive and highly technical. They have tremendous responsibility for the safety of people and they constitute a highly organized group with strong ties of fellowship and solidarity. One ex-air traffic controller expressed his love for his previous occupation and how much he still thought about it and missed it when he said:

> I really enjoyed the job. I did not get up in the morning and say I hate going to work. I loved going to work. I really enjoyed what I was doing. I was learning. I've always been excited about aviation in general. I've always been aviation-oriented since college and I just like the whole field, I really do. It's fun to me. I really felt my reasons for going out on strike were valid and to be honest with you though if the job were offered back to me, I miss it, I would go back to it now. We have appeals pending in court and things like that but it's probably going to be forgotten. I still love aviation and some of the guys were there because it was a job and they couldn't understand where I was coming from sometimes because I took a pretty good interest in a lot of other things besides just the nine to five hour day so to speak. You know being that it was aviation-involved and I wanted to know more about the system I just took a better interest than most people I think.

The high idealism a professional generally carries into his or her role may also help in explaining why professionals experience role residual more often than semiprofessionals or nonprofessionals. Often an individual is attracted to the professional role at an early age and plans to enter a particular career for an extended period of time prior to beginning the training process. During this time, high expectations are formed and one becomes very idealistic concerning the role. For instance, one ex-surgeon who entered the medical field because his grandfather had been a doctor said, "I never thought of being anything else." Another former doctor had been practicing medicine for thirty years and had gone into practice because "It was always something I wanted to do. Medicine always intrigued me." He found his role very rewarding but was disappointed when patients became hostile when he could not cure them. Thinking there had to be more to life, he suddenly became responsible for managing some family money and decided after two years to leave medicine. He had no regret in leaving but constantly had the idea that at some point in time he might open an office by himself and see patients on a part-time basis.

Even though he is no longer actively practicing medicine, he said that he still always answers the phone, "This is Dr. ______" rather than "This is Mr. ______." He said, "I feel like a doctor. I still have my diploma." His sister once introduced him as an ex-doctor, and he told her, "They didn't take my diploma away. I still have my degree." He explained that at the present time "I feel I am not contributing too much to society. One thing about medicine, even if you are paid well, when you're practicing full-time, you feel you're performing a service that people need. Just managing my money is a kind of selfish thing to do. I think I am wasting my time. I ought to do something." Although the doctor had become disillusioned with several facets of the doctor role, he never regretted entering the medical field and never lost identification with his former role. As he said, "If I were eighteen years old, I would go to medical school again. I would be a doctor again."

All but one of the ex-physicians interviewed maintained affiliations with professional medical associations and still attended medical meetings. All of them still used their title "doctor" in specific circumstances. An interesting issue is when ex-physicians use the title "doctor" and when they use the title "mister." Most of them use "doctor" when speaking with other medical professionals or when the title will gain them entry into a particular social or business situation. At times when they want to deemphasize their previous role and be simply a business associate or a social acquaintance they use the title "mister."

Since all of the role exits included in this study deal with roles central to identity, there was some role residual present in almost all cases. Individuals were not only aware of a previous role but carried that awareness into aspects of their current role expectations and self-identity. It is safe to say that the more personal involvement and commitment an individual had in a former role, that is, the more self-identity was equated with role definitions, the more role residual tended to manifest itself after the exit. Time in a previous role was not as important as the amount of training and preparation for the role and the centrality of the role to a person's identity. Ex-professionals and ex-nuns manifested substantial role residual due in part to the extensive training involved for both roles and the identification of the person with the role. In the case of transsexuals there was almost constant role residual in that having experienced a sex change seemed to be a central part of the identity of all of the transsexuals interviewed. Likewise, ex-alcoholics were constantly aware of the fact that they are alcoholics, although now nondrinking alcoholics. Central to the identity of the ex-alcoholics was the idea that they are alcoholics, have been drinking alcoholics, and cannot allow themselves to fall back into that pattern.

For some ex-roles, role residual is not a constant attribute but is rather expressed circumstantially, that is, in certain instances in which one is reminded of a previous role. This was the case, for example, with several ex-schoolteachers and ex-police officers. The schoolteacher who coached football and then left teaching to join an oil company used to come back and sit in the athletic box for football games. Every game, however, would be a difficult emotional experience for him because he would miss teaching and coaching and especially the kids with whom he worked. As he said,

> Even after I quit coaching, I kept going up to the games and working. I kept coming home from those games and my wife could just tell it was tearing me up. Just ripping my heart out. But slowly and surely each year it's gotten a little easier and pretty soon I might quit messing with those games. I don't know the kids anymore. I don't

> know the kids' names. All they are are numbers now, so they don't mean as much to me. The personal contact isn't there anymore; however, the one thing that is missing in my life is helping people. I like to see those kids and how they've changed. That's why I kind of keep an eye on them now. I check on them when I can to see how they are growing. I'm alright most of the time. It's only when I go back to the school and sit in that box that I get real nostalgic and homesick.

An ex-police officer also said that circumstances could bring the nostalgia back to him. As he said, "After I left the police force it was kind of like a new world type of thing, but it was amazing how the five-and-a-half, almost six years of all the negatives and everything, how fast I got rid of it and got back into the mainstream. But there's still a little bit of it here and there. I still see a lot of the local crooks and the old feelings every time I see them still come back. I just now can go out and have a good time because my face hasn't been in that blue suit for about a year and a half and because of that a lot of them have forgotten me." The police officer experienced role residual in those instances in which he would see the local crooks and the people he used to deal with. Another police officer said, "It is very difficult to adjust to new friends. It had been easy to relate to other officers. Trying to have a conversation with someone who didn't know about police work was difficult and still is. I probably never got rid of feeling like an officer."

Another way in which role residual lingers after a person leaves a given role is in the form of dreams. Approximately one fifth of our interviewees indicated that they have recurrent dreams about still being part of the former role. In several cases, the dreams were painful nightmares centering around the struggle to make a decision whether to leave the role. As a former nun said, "About once a month I dream that I am still a nun and am agonizing over the decision to leave or not. Sometimes my husband and children are waiting for me to come home and I want to go home to them but have to struggle to make a firm decision to leave the convent. I think the dream shows what a painful decision it was to leave." All of those who said they have such dreams indicated that they never regretted leaving the former role. Dreams, therefore, do not appear to be related to ambivalent feelings about the decision but rather to deep-seated memories of the anguish involved in the decision-making process.

Summary

Being an ex is a unique role experience because identity as an ex rests not on one's current role but on who one was in the past. As exes struggle to disidentify with a previous role, others with whom they associate take their previous identities into account and frequently relate to them in terms of who they used to be. There are six major areas of adjustment that role exiters face as they begin to create a new identity as an ex: ways of presenting themselves and their ex-status; learning to deal with social reactions to their ex-status, including stereotypes associated with the labeling process; negotiating and establishing intimate relationships; shifting networks of friends; relating to members who are still part of the former group as well as fellow exes; and learning to deal with role residual that lingers after the exit. Successful adjustment to an ex-status required interviewees to find successful solutions to each of these challenges. To the extent that they were able to do so, exiters felt successful in having made a smooth transition in the role-exit process.

6
Summary and Conclusions

The Process of Role Exit

In analyzing the interview material, it became very clear that there is a unique social process of exiting a role that has characteristics different from that of socialization into a role. In the process of role exiting, socialization into a new role is an empirical issue. In some instances, exiters do engage in anticipatory socialization. However, there are some exiters who have little or no idea of what they will do after a major role exit. Rather, they focus exclusively on getting out of an unpleasant or undesirable present role. Even for those exiters who are looking toward new roles after exit, looking forward is simply one aspect of a much larger process of decision making, doubting, and disengaging from an array of obligations and expectations associated with present roles.

The dynamics of disengagement are very different from the dynamics of becoming socialized into a new role. Socialization literature has deemphasized the issue of disengagement and placed emphasis primarily on the new role that one is acquiring. Disengagement from old roles is a complex process that involves shifts in reference groups, friendship networks, relationships with former group members, and, most important, shifts in a person's own sense of self-identity. In the process of role exit, there tends to be mutual disengagement in that the individual moves away from the group while the former group simultaneously withdraws from the individual with regard to expectations and social obligations. This mutual disengagement has the consequence of reducing the exiter's sense of solidarity and commitment to the group and also of challenging the exiter to establish new ties and a new sense of self.

Socialization literature has also placed little emphasis on the impact of role residual or the holdover identity derived from a previous status. Role-exit theory, on the other hand, emphasizes the impact of previous role identification on current concepts of self. Also unique in the role-exiting process is the impact of social reactions to an individual that are based on a previous role. A major challenge to the exiter is learning to deal with the reactions of other people to who one used to be.

In addition to these characteristics of the role-exit process, what emerged throughout the interviews was the fact that a pattern exists in the sequence of events that exiters went through. Four "stages" in the role-exit process which emerged as a natural sequence for individuals exiting social roles enables us to describe a general pattern of exiting.

The first stage that exiters described was that time when they first began to doubt their role commitments. First doubts occur as a result of numerous kinds of events, the major ones including changes in the organizations with which they were affiliated, professional or job burnout, changes in relationships in which they were involved, and specific events. First doubts, regardless of the circumstances under which they happen, lead to cuing behavior which is initially unconscious but which indicates discontent with a current social role. These cues are picked up by others, especially people who are significant in the exiters' lives and serve as initial indicators of the fact that the individuals are dissatisfied or questioning role commitment. When others react negatively to such cues, exiters tend to reevaluate the costs and benefits of role performance. On the other hand, in some instances exiters will ignore negative reactions and seek out other individuals who will reinforce their doubts. Positive reactions of significant others to this cuing behavior leads to further reinforcement of doubts and to the negative interpretation of subsequent events that occur. Such events are interpreted as further evidence of how unbearable a given role is and how important it is to consider alternatives. As exiters begin to seek other options for role performance, those options that seem viable provide further reinforcement of the doubting process.

In the second stage of the exiting process, individuals begin to seek alternatives. Cuing tends to become conscious at this point and serves the function of reinforcing initial doubts, providing justification for the pursuit of alternatives, and indicating to others the degree of dissatisfaction in a current role. While negative reactions from others can interrupt or retard the process of alternative seeking, positive support enhances the seeking of role alternatives. Many individuals at this point also experience emotional relief as they realize that choice is possible and that they are not necessarily trapped in their present roles. As alternatives are narrowed and individuals begin to focus on one or several viable options, they begin to shift reference group orientations and to engage in imaginary and real role rehearsals that prepare them for making a definite choice. Such anticipatory behavior helps exiters imagine how they will fit into a new role and readies them for the turning point event which will lead to a final decision to exit.

The turning point, the third stage in the exiting process, is an event that mobilizes and focuses awareness on the fact that old roles are no longer desirable, combined with the realization that exiters have an opportunity to do something different with their lives. In some cases, turning points are major events in the exiters' lives; however, in many other cases the event itself is relatively insignificant but takes on great symbolic importance because of the time at which it occurs or the fact that it symbolizes role ambivalence and the culmination of dissatisfied feelings. Regardless of what constitutes the turning point, it serves three basic functions for individuals in the process of exiting: the reduction of cognitive dissonance, the opportunity to announce the decision to others, and the mobilization of the resources needed to exit.

Related to the turning point, and occurring either right before the decision to exit or in some cases shortly after the exit, was what exiters described as a "vacuum experience," that is, one last look back which results in anxiety and the feeling that one has one's feet in two worlds, both the past and the future. Exiters at this point feel in midair, ungrounded, nowhere. The future is unknown and yet they no longer belong to the past. The vacuum experience is one in which taken-for-granted anchors of self-identity are suspended, leaving exiters feeling rootless and anxious. The resolution of these feelings is closely tied to successful efforts to begin to adapt to a new role in society, one in which individuals are able to incorporate past identities within present roles.

The process of adjusting and establishing a social identity is made easier and occurs more rapidly for exiters who have built bridges while in their previous roles. Bridges tend to be in the areas of jobs, friends, family, and hobbies. Interviewees who had built such bridges were better able to move out of the vacuum stage and to establish a new identity than exiters who lacked such bridges.

The fourth stage in the exit process is that of creating an ex-role. Six areas stand out in considering the major issues with which exiters struggle. (1) Exiters are faced with the problem of signaling to others the fact that a change has taken place. This involves cuing behavior or, in Goffman's (1959*a*) sense, the presentation of self in a new identity. Exiters signal to others that a change has taken place and that they expect to be treated and reacted to differently than in the past. (2) As exes present cues that they are no longer in their previous roles, people begin to react to them both as ex-members of the previous role and as members of the current role. In many instances, ex-statuses are more salient to other people than current roles. Exiters have to adjust to the varied social reactions of other people. In some instances these reactions are positive and in other instances negative. Over time, many labels have been applied to various types of role exits, and exiters have to deal constantly with such stereotypes. (3) For some groups of exiters, learning to deal with intimate relationships, particularly in the area of friendship and sexuality, is a major challenge. Frequently sexual scripts or cues have changed over time and individuals are faced with an unfamiliar world. (4) In most instances, exiters experience changes in their friendship networks, that is, the people they value and with whom they associate as friends. (5) One characteristic unique to the ex-role is the fact that exes once shared a role identity with other people, many of whom are still part of the previous role. In addition, there is usually a cohort or aggregate of other exes who have left the previous group. Exes are faced with the challenge of relating to former group members as well as other exes. (6) Exes maintain an identification with the prior role such that the individual experiences certain aspects of the role after he or she has in fact exited from it. Some individuals are better able to shake off their identification with previous roles than other individuals. In all instances, however, dealing with role residual is a challenge to exiters.

Successful adjustment to being an ex required interviewees to find successful solutions to each of these challenges. To the extent that they were able to do so, exiters were successful in making a smooth transition through the role-exit process.

Properties of the Role-Exit Process

The variables associated with role exit outlined in chapter 1 have served as a means of analyzing data throughout the exit process. In a grounded theory sense, interview data have been used to determine the extent and the conditions under which each of the properties of role exit operate. It is now time to summarize the findings regarding each of the eleven properties.

Reversibility

Reversibility refers to whether or not the occupant of a role can return to the role he or she has exited. Some roles may be held numerous times by the same individual, such as a married or divorced person, or certain occupational roles (teacher, secretary, nurse), while other roles are held only once. In other words, once an incumbent abandons the role, he or she may not take on that role again. Such is the case with the ex-nun, the ex-priest, the ex-male or female, the ex-adolescent, or the individual who is past middle age. There are two conditions in my data under which roles are nonreverisble. The first is physical nonreversibility: in instances in which role change is associated with physical change, such as reversal of sex-related organs, it is impossible, at this point in time, to reverse the physical procedure. Therefore, it is impossible for individuals going through this procedure and thereby changing gender identity to again revert back to the previous identity. The second is organizationally defined nonreversibility: certain roles are defined by the organization in which they are embedded as nonreversible. While it would be feasible for an ex-nun to return to a convent, traditionally religious orders have been reluctant to accept ex-nuns back into the institution. So, too, judges who award custody of children to one spouse very seldom reverse that decision. In the vast majority of cases, judges reason that children who have done well enough with one parent should be left with that parent for reasons of stability and continuity. The mothers who gave up custody of children, hoping in later years to regain that custody, learned tragically that it is almost impossible to reverse that decision.

As Glaser and Strauss (1971) point out, roles are reversible under two conditions. The first concerns structural factors: if rules of an organization change over time, it is possible that someone who has exited may consider returning to the organization under changed conditions. Several physicians in the study decided to return to the practice of medicine under changed conditions, moving usually from clinic or group practices into private practice. The sudden emergence of a new role can take priority over current roles and cause an individual to move for the time being out of a given role to which he or she might later return. For example, sudden illness or a new job opportunity might cause someone to exit temporarily. The second condition concerns personal factors: a person who has exited a given role may experience changes in his or her personal and social life and decide to return to a previous role. Such is the case when divorced people find new mates and remarry or when mothers who have given up custody of their children get pregnant and have additional children.

Reversibility tends to impact the role exit process in the following ways: (1) Irreversible roles tend to be central to an individual's identity, that is, to be master roles that organize and order other roles, while reversible role exits are more commonly exits from roles less central to identity that are not all-encompassing. (2) Because irreversible role exits tend to involve central identities and master roles tend to be the organizing factor for multiple roles, irreversible role exits tend to upset and initiate change for an array of roles. Reversible role exits tend more frequently to be single exits that are more easily isolated from other aspects of an individual's life. (3) Because of the far-reaching consequences of irreversible role exits, individuals making irreversible role exits tend to be highly aware and conscious of the exiting process whereas individuals making reversible role exits tend to be less aware and less deliberate about the process. (4) Individuals making irreversible role exits tend to take longer to deliberate and weigh all the alternatives because they realize that their decision is irrevocable. (5) Individuals making irreversible role exits tend to participate in more role rehearsal and anticipatory socialization than individuals making reversible exits. (6) Individuals making irreversible role exits are more likely to actively set about reestablishing a new identity on exit than individuals making reversible role exits who tend to be less active in reestablishing their identity. (7) Individuals who have made irreversible role exits tend to have fewer regrets and doubts after the exit. This is due to the fact that such individuals have tended to be involved in a longer, more deliberate process prior to the exit and also to the fact that cognitive dissonance operates after the exit in such a way that these individuals feel a greater need to justify the irrevocable decision.

Duration

Duration refers to the length of time involved from first doubts to making the decision to exit as well as to the length of time in adapting to a new status. Data reveal the following characteristics and relationships related to duration of role exit. (1) Irreversible role exits are characterized by longer time spans in the deliberative stage. (2) Positive social support facilitates the process of role exiting whereas negative reactions halt or retard the process. Positive support functions in three ways to facilitate role exit. First there is reality testing, whereby significant others provide assurance that there are problems in the current role and that doubting concerning one's commitment is justified. Second, significant others suggest alternatives which the individual can then begin to consider seriously as possible opportunities. Entrapment in a role and feeling that the role is inevitable can be challenged by others. Third, making a private problem public can change social dynamics for the individual and can provide different definitions of events. (3) Exits in which individuals are aware and conscious of alternatives and consequences tend to extend over longer time periods than those in which individuals are less aware and deliberative. (4) Exiters who weigh alternatives carefully and go through a self-conscious process of decision making (a process that usually takes time) tend to have fewer regrets after leaving and to adjust to an ex-status more easily. (5) Up to a point, the longer the exit process, the easier the adjustment after exiting because length of time is positively associated with degree of deliberation; however, when deliberation extends over many years, it is as though the same material is reviewed and no new insights result. There seems to be a "ripe" time for exiting after all known alternatives and pros and cons are carefully weighed. Frequently, this "ripeness" corresponds to some situation or event that triggers the decision and serves as a turning point. (6) The duration of some exits is institutionalized and in such instances individuals have little or no personal choice. For example, transsexuals must cross-dress and accept psychiatric evaluation for six months prior to sex-change surgery. Nuns who apply for dispensation from vows are frequently advised to take a year's leave of absence before actually exiting. Most organizations specify a minimum and maximum retirement age. Frequently, states stipulate an amount of time during which a couple must live separately before applying for a legal divorce.

SINGLE VERSUS MULTIPLE EXITS

Some role exits necessarily or usually involve exits from related roles. Awarding custody of children usually occurs at the time that the divorce is finalized; sex change usually involves job change; divorce has ramifications for roles such as son-in-law and for kinship relationships. Other exits such as occupational or career changes may be single role exits in that they do not necessarily affect other role relationships.

When an individual begins doubting one role, especially if that role is central to his or her identity, these doubts often spread to other role involvements. For example, women who begin doubting the value of their marriages frequently doubt themselves as adequate parents. They can begin blaming their children for problems in their marriages and, as they reject commitment to marriage, they also reject commitment to ongoing care of children. Simultaneously, they might also be fed up with extended family involvements and desire to terminate those relationships as well. As individuals admit doubts about a central role, therefore, they may also begin to realize doubts in other related areas of their life.

Nuns who begin doubting their commitment to religious life frequently also admit doubts about their occupational commitments. This is especially true of nuns who have theological problems with their religious vows and are teaching in theologically related areas. Frequently, personal doubts carry over into doubts about one's desire to teach others what one does not necessarily believe in oneself. In most instances, these nuns give up teaching as well as their commitment to religious life.

While exit from a master role or one central to identity may be irreversible, exits from related roles may be reversible. For example, the nun who leaves religious life and gets out of teaching in parochial schools might well return to parochial school teaching at some point in the future. As ex-nuns work out their identity problems regarding being a nun, they are sometimes able to disassociate this role from the related role of teaching in church-related schools and to return to that teaching job after leaving the order and doing something else for a while. They are able to disassociate religious commitment from the occupation of parochial school teaching. Transsexuals are faced with an irreversible role exit once they have sex-change surgery. This surgery usually affects their jobs also; however, the latter exits may be reversible. Many transsexuals long for the day when society will accept their role change and allow them to continue in their careers. Several of them hope the day will come when they can return to their old jobs and once again be accepted.

An exit process that involves multiple exits is usually characterized by a longer deliberation period than a process involving a single role exit. This follows because of the more complicated process of weighing pros and cons when multiple exits are involved. Role exiters may have control over one exit but little or no control over related exits. For example, the transsexual can decide whether or not to have the sex-change surgery; however, that individual has little control over how others will respond to that role change in terms of job acceptance or social acceptance. Likewise, ex-nuns can decide whether to stay or leave a religious order; often the decision of continued employment, however, rests in the hands of a bishop or pastor of a parochial school.

Sometimes groups of individuals exit multiple roles together. A group of transsexuals underwent sex-change surgery at approximately the same time, left their previous jobs, and together began a new company involved in making signs and letterheads. Several groups of nuns exited religious life simultaneously and began careers in social work in the same city and for the same agency. Such multiple exits provide social support for those experiencing them. Individuals who experience multiple exits as part of a group tend to encounter less stress and easier adjustment than those who go through multiple exits alone.

Society has institutionalized some multiple exits, that is, it has regularized the pattern of several exits occurring simultaneously. For instance, several school systems have refused to allow transsexuals to teach in their school because of their fear of confusing children regarding sex-role identity. Transsexuals who had been schoolteachers before had to realize that to undergo sex-change surgery meant that they necessarily had to leave their school positions. Likewise, the archbishop of the diocese of Los Angeles in the early 1970s ruled that any Sister belonging to the Sisters of the Immaculate Heart of Mary who opted to defy Rome and enter a lay status would not be allowed to teach in parochial schools in the archdiocese. Nuns who made the choice to abandon canonical status as nuns therefore simultaneously made a choice not to teach in parochial schools in the archdiocese.

In some instances, exiters are aware of the interrelated multiple exits involved in their choices whereas in other instances there is minimal awareness of the interrelatedness of exits. After exiting a central role, some individuals realize for the first time the implications in terms of other role exits that will follow. The greater the awareness of multiple role exits during the deliberation process, the longer the process tends to take. This is the case because individuals have to take into account the advantages and disadvantages of several exits simultaneously.

The greater the awareness and anticipation of multiple exits, the better the adjustment after the exit process. Individuals who realize and are aware of the interrelatedness of several exits tend not to be overwhelmed and frightened at the point of exit. Rather, they tend to do more anticipatory socialization in preparation for the multiple exits.

Individual versus Group Exits

Exiters can leave as lone individuals, with one or more individuals, or as part of a cohort of exiters, a large group of similarly situated people who leave at approximately the same time. In addition, in either of the latter two cases the exiter may be aware or unaware of others experiencing the same process.

The fact that others are doubting frequently suggests doubts to the individual, who may not have been conscious of his or her own questions previously. Such was the case when the first nuns began leaving in the late 1960s. Many ex-nuns commented that they never even considered the possibility until the first nuns began leaving nationwide. In some cases, this was less important than having a friend or close acquaintance begin doubting. This was frequently the occasion of first doubts for the individual who later became an ex-nun herself.

Many exiters are similarly affected by a cohort effect, that is, by realizing that more and more like-situated individuals are relinquishing role commitments. Trends can be suggestive and challenging to one's own commitment. As large groups of nuns began leaving convents in the 1970s, nuns who never before doubted their commitment began to question religious life for themselves. Also, as more and more women give up custody of children to fathers the option is becoming more viable to women seeking divorces. Cohort effects can be both suggestive and supportive.

Experiencing the process of role exit along with others can facilitate the deliberative stage of the process in that others might present pros and cons of exiting as well as their own evaluations of the advantages and disadvantages. One of the purposes of the group therapy before sex-change surgery is for transsexuals to assist each other in anticipating the consequences of such surgery. Together, and with transsexuals who are already exiters, those in the deliberative stage of the process spend hours role rehearsing and trying to anticipate what it will be like to be a member of the opposite sex. Likewise, the two mothers in our sample who knew women who had given up custody of their children had an easier time anticipating what it would be like than those who left without such contact. In general, group exits tend to be shorter in duration than lone exits. This was evident in the case of the nuns in our sample who left during the 1980s, each of them alone. It took these nuns much longer to work through the decision process than it had the nuns who left earlier along with cohorts of fellow nuns.

As groups of individuals leave a given social role, it becomes easier for society to accept such an exit. Conversely, when lone individuals leave a given role they are often shunned and stigmatized by society. The first nuns to leave religious life were often ostracized by their families and local parishes as well as the Catholic church in general. They were seen as traitors and fickle women who were denying their sacred calling; at that point, however, it was also an oddity to meet a woman who had been a nun. As more and more nuns left their religious orders, people began to realize the difficulties that must be involved in maintaining such a commitment. In the last fifteen years, therefore, society has become more accepting of ex-nuns. Nuns in the process of deciding whether or not to leave religious life take into account the social values and evaluations placed on the role of ex-nun. In earlier years the nun had to weigh stigmatization by society as a factor in her decision. Today, social attitudes have changed and therefore count as less of a disadvantage in considering the option of leaving. Likewise, after exiting, the ex-nun today faces much less social stigma than was previously the case. The role of the ex-nun is becoming more acceptable in society.

Society institutionalizes certain role exits as group exits. For example, individuals graduate from high school, college, and trade school as the graduates of 1986 or 1988. Likewise, physicians become ex-medical students as a group at the time of their graduation from medical school. Other exits such as that of the transsexual or the convict being released from prison or the alcoholic giving up alcohol are individual exits without such societal institutionalization. It is usually more difficult to experience an individual exit without the companionship of others or the ritual of an institutionalized role passage. Lone exiters must themselves define to society that they are no longer who society thinks they are without the rituals that assist in such expression.

One way society institutionalizes group exits is through the vast array of support groups that are available to people leaving various roles. Alcoholics Anonymous (AA) is probably the oldest and best-known of such support groups; however, today there are such groups as Parents without Partners, Mothers Without Custody, Stepfamily Association, groups for divorced and widowed people, Forty Plus for the unemployed executive, etc. The function of these self-help groups is to offer mutual support and encouragement for people who share an ex-status.

Degree of Control

The degree of control an individual has over various aspects of the exit process varies. The divorced person, for example, may be able to decide whether or not to remain in a marriage; however, he or she is constantly interacting with a spouse whose behavior and attitudes affect the quality of the marriage. Someone exiting a career or occupation likewise has bosses and co-workers to contend with. The ex-air traffic controllers had the choice of going on strike or not; however, once they decided to go on strike their futures depended on the actions of the president of the United States.

Group exits frequently give the impression of greater control than lone exits. It is as though there is power in numbers. The air traffic controllers who decided to go on strike felt that their sheer numbers would put pressure upon the administration to allow them to return to work. In this case, their sense of control was mistaken, as the president ruled that they were not to be allowed to return to work. Until that decree, however, the ex-air traffic controllers had great faith that they would put pressure upon the administration to call them back. Likewise, when large numbers of people experience an exit such as divorce or leaving the convent, a cohort effect may suggest to others in the role that they have control over the decision to stay or leave.

Exits that are socially desirable and have the approval of society also give the impression of being more under the control of individuals than exits that are socially disapproved. For example, convicts on their good behavior in order to gain early parole have a sense of being able to control this factor with society's support for good behavior and early dismissal.

In instances in which society institutionalizes an exit (e.g., graduations, retirement parties), it often appears that individuals have little control over the turning point event: at a specified date the role exit will occur. This time-related dimension frequently creates crisis points for the individuals undergoing the exit and puts pressure on them to make certain decisions related to the institutionalized exits. There is a sense of little control over the sequential nature of the exit.

In some instances, closed awareness contexts (Glaser and Strauss 1966) created by the structure of the organization in which roles are embedded give the impression of a lack of control over the exit process. Individuals are led to believe they have no choice in the role commitment. Such is the case of the nun in the cloistered convent or of transsexuals before sex-change surgery became a possibility. This is also the case with many alcoholics who feel they are physically trapped in their alcoholism. As people become more aware of their freedom of choice, they realize they do have control over the process.

Sequentiality of events can also create the impression of lack of control. The medical student knows that at a certain point in time he will graduate from medical school and be expected to take his medical boards. He then knows that his residency program follows. The same is true for the novice who has fulfilled her time of probation and faces pronouncement of final vows. This sequentiality gives the impression that the individual has no control over the process whereas in fact he does have the choice of proceeding in the process or dropping out.

Social Desirability

Social desirability is the degree of social approval or disapproval of the exit. Some exits, such as those of the ex-prostitute and the ex-alcoholic, carry social approval, whereas other exits, such as those of the divorced person, mother without custody, transsexual, and ex-nun, frequently are socially less desirable and carry social stigma. The degree of social desirability impacts various aspects of the exiting process.

While some role exits such as remarriage, taking on responsibility for children again, and returning to a professional career are reversible, society frequently defines how often such reversibility is acceptable. For example, except in the cases of certain movie stars, divorce and remarriage five or six times is defined as instability. Leaving and reentering a career three or four times is defined as fickleness and lack of commitment. Thus while exits may be reversible, in fact societal attitudes can taint them as irreversible.

The degree of social desirability of an exit is a major factor that enters into the formula when individuals weigh advantages and disadvantages of exiting. Social desirability frequently accelerates and encourages the process whereas social undesirability or social stigma becomes a cost that the individual must pay in exiting.

Social desirability is one of the major factors impacting the process of creating an ex-identity. Exiters tend to hide the fact of their previous role when such ex-roles carry stigma as in the instance of the ex-nun, the mother without custody, or the divorced person. The degree of social desirability highly impacts the kinds of cues the individual presents after the exit as well as the adaptability of the individual to the ex-role.

Lone exits, especially those that are infrequent, usually carry more social undesirability than group exits. When groups of people begin exiting a given role, it is as though society must take note of such numbers and begin to reevaluate the meaning and significance of these exits. In the cases of the ex-nun and the transsexual, and also of mothers without custody, the sheer numbers of people exiting within the last few years is beginning to affect society's definition of the ex-role.

When a single exit has ramifications for related exits in an individual's role set, it is possible that one exit may be socially desirable while others may be socially undesirable. For example, a mother seeking divorce may face less stigma as a divorcée than as a mother giving up custody of her children in the process. Likewise, the ex-minister in our study faced less stigma in giving up his ministerial post than he did in simultaneously leaving the church with which he was affiliated.

Role exits that are seen as socially desirable frequently are associated with rites of passages such as retirement parties, giving individuals gold watches, or graduation ceremonies which recognize the individuals moving from one social role into another. However, role exits that are not socially desirable such as those of divorced people, mothers without custody, and ex-nuns are not associated with institutionalized rites of passages. In fact, in some instances role exits involve degradation ceremonies (Garfinkel 1956) whose purpose is to lower the status of the individual.

In most instances, individuals undergoing role exits are aware of the degree of social desirability of the exits. There are some cases, however, in which the individuals are less aware of what awaits them next. Many divorced people commented that there was more social stimga involved in being divorced than they imagined. Many of the mothers without custody also commented that society stigmatizes them significantly more than they anticipated. Many of these mothers were so guilt-ridden at the time they made their decision that they sublimated their awareness of what awaited them from society after they gave up custody.

Degree of Institutionalization

Degree of institutionalization is the degree to which society associates expectations and rituals with any aspect of the role-exit process. For instance, La Gaipa (1982) argues that cultural rituals are associated with the breakdown of intimate relationships. While the rituals themselves are a form of behavior, the cultural beliefs about close relationships underlie such actions. The degree to which role exits are institutionalized and ritualized impacts various aspects of the exiting process.

Some role exits are considered irreversible because of physical limitations, as in sex-change surgery. Other role exits, however, are irreversible because society makes them so. Some states, for example, put a limitation on how frequently a convict can receive a probated sentence. After *x* number of reconvictions, he is denied probation.

Some role exits are institutionalized in terms of time factors. Such exits are one case of what Merton (1984) calls "socially expected durations" (SED), that is, socially patterned expectations about temporal durations. For example, most companies either specify a retirement age or at least expect employees to retire at a given time. A nun who has requested a leave of absence is expected either to exit her religious role after the leave is over or to return to the order as a fully committed member.

There are societal expectations as to how much time after an exit an individual is allowed to adjust. The widow, for example, who wears black and is in mourning five years after the death of her husband is considered to be behaving inappropriately, as is the divorcée who takes several years to adjust to a divorce. There is a socially acceptable time frame in which exiters are expected to adjust.

Institutionalization frequently gives the impression of lack of control over an exit. Even though a student may feel that he or she can acquire sufficient training in two rather than three years, the institution may forbid graduation until the specified time has elapsed. So, too, an individual wanting a divorce must meet the specified time of separation before a legal divorce is possible. Institutionalization, therefore, jeopardizes individual control over an exit.

Society defines certain exits as group exits and others as individual exits. Graduating classes, for example, are institutionalized as group exits, whereas divorces are institutionalized as lone exits, that is, decisions made by the individuals involved.

Awareness contexts are related to degree of institutionalization since some institutions prohibit open awareness contexts. Cloistered, closed systems deliberately keep incumbents from being aware of options so that doubts are less likely than in open contexts in which individuals are allowed to examine other options.

Degree of Awareness

Degree of awareness refers to the extent that a role exit is a conscious and deliberate act. In most exits, exiters are more aware of some factors affecting the process than others. Part of the deliberation process is becoming aware of and anticipating as many consequences as possible.

As we have seen in previous sections, individuals who are aware of the irreversibility of an exit tend to take longer to ponder the decision and weigh alternatives. They also tend to adapt to an ex-role more successfully than individuals who were not conscious of or did not focus on the irreversibility of the exit.

Organizations, as well as social institutions, create awareness contexts for their members, that is, structures that allow or inhibit the free flow of information among members themselves and especially between members and outsiders (Glaser and Strauss 1966). In general, the more open the awareness context, the easier it is for members to seek and evaluate role alternatives. Closed awareness contexts, on the other hand, tend to inhibit and discourage doubts regarding role commitment by providing a taken-for-granted ideology or worldview that integrates role commitment into a totalistic system. When closed systems undergo change and experience a challenge to their taken-for-granted worldview, individuals are highly likely to question and doubt their continued commitment.

The greater the awareness in the role-exit process, the longer the doubting and deliberation process tends to take. This is due to the greater number of factors that must be considered in making the decision.

Awareness is also associated with realizing which factors are within one's control and which are not. Frequently, deliberation before and adaptation after exiting are facilitated when an individual sorts out what he or she can control and what cannot be controlled. This realization allows the person to then focus on what is within his or her control and not worry about managing the rest.

Even though an exit may be a group exit in that two or more individuals are leaving the same role at approximately the same time, exiters may or may not be conscious of fellow travelers.

The more aware they are of a group exit, the more likely they are to feel support both in the deliberation stages of considering alternatives and in the postexit stage of establishing a new role identity. It is easier to make a role change when one is not unique and realizes the company of others.

While single role exits tend to take less time in the deliberation stage than multiple exits, this relationship depends on the degree of awareness the exiter has of the single/multiple nature of the exit. It is highly possible that what one sees as a single exit may in fact be related to multiple exits which are unanticipated. The hardest exits to handle in terms of adaptation are those that are viewed as single exits in the deliberation process but turn out, after the fact, to be multiple exits. Such was the case with a number of divorced people who were well aware of alterations in their role relationships with their spouses but failed to realize the impact the divorce would have on their extended family relationships or friendship roles.

The awareness of social approval or disapproval is an important factor both in weighing pros and cons and in adjusting to being an ex. Most exiters were quite aware of and able to judge the degree of social approval associated in general with a given exit. Level of approval seemed to be embedded in the cultural norms and quite well internalized by those making an exit. These norms of approval or disapproval loomed large in considering the consequences of a role-exit decision.

SEQUENTIALITY

Sequentiality refers to the specified progression of some exits. Sequential roles often create doubts in people and sometimes serve as the turning point event as they realize they must move to the next step at a specified time or drop out of the role progression. Medical students sometimes get cold feet just before medical boards. Nuns with temporary vows frequently decide to leave the convent as they approach the time when they must make final vows for life.

Multiple role exits may be such that one is a sequential exit which triggers related exits. For example, the medical student who decides not to finish medical school and become a doctor is involved in a role exit of a sequential nature. However, this exit has ramifications for other roles he plays such as husband or boyfriend, citizen of a given city, member of a medical community, friend of fellow students, all roles which are nonsequential in nature.

Some role sequences are highly valued by society and to begin the sequence and then drop out is considered dishonorable or a failure. In the traditional Catholic church, it was somewhat dishonorable for novices not to proceed to the status of nun and for seminarians, especially those near ordination, to exit the seminary. Many engaged couples, especially those who have set a wedding date and sent out invitations, suffer social stigma if they decide not to proceed to marriage. Social expectations regarding role sequences often become an important factor in whether to exit the sequence. Most sequences are institutionalized by society in terms of norms and role expectations. Such is the case with engagement and marriage, medical school and being a physician, movement from one grade to another. Other sequences, however, like rookie junkie to drug pusher, classroom teacher to master teacher, or vice president to president may be less institutionalized. The less institutionalized the role-exit sequence, the less social pressure is placed on the individual to exit a given role in order to move on to another.

The nine variables described above are important in describing the dynamics of the role-exit process. In addition, there are two variables that served as criteria in selecting the sample described in this book: centrality of the role to identity and voluntariness in exiting a role. While these two variables were relatively constant in our sample, an adequate and complete analysis of the role-exit process must take them into account. What follows are insights derived from the study regarding these two variables and how they might be incorporated in future research on role exit.

CENTRALITY OF THE ROLE

This variable refers to the saliency and importance of a given role to an individual's self-identity. Some roles serve to organize and prioritize a sense of self. They are what we call "master roles." Other roles that we have play a relatively minor part in defining who we are. It is possible to move in and out of these minor roles with little shift in our identity. On the other hand, when individuals exit a master role, they usually experience a radical transformation in self-identity, a fact that makes the exit process a major decision in life with repercussions in terms of adjustment and adaptation to a new self.

In this book I have described role exit for individuals who exited a role which they considered central to their identity. One reason for doing this was to describe the strong cases, that is, instances in which the dimensions of role exit would be highlighted and underscored. Since very little research has been done on role exit, I felt I should begin with cases that would put the process in bold relief. It is my contention, however, that the process described in this book characterizes all role exits to a greater or lesser extent and that the same variables will describe the process regardless of how central the role is to the exiter. Whether this hypothesis is true awaits further studies of role exit, especially studies in which centrality of the role is indeed conceptualized as a variable and samples are selected in which exiters vary in how important the role is to self-identity.

VOLUNTARINESS

Voluntariness refers to the amount of choice an individual has in whether or not to exit a role. It is not a dichotomous variable but one which can vary in degree of choice. Many unemployed people, for instance, have been fired from their jobs for factors totally out of their control such as the oil crisis. These exits are involuntary. On the other hand there are individuals, such as many of the physicians in our sample, who decided to exit their jobs for a variety of reasons. In between these two extremes are people who are not exactly forced out of their jobs but who are encouraged by means of various incentive systems (or the lack of them) to consider exiting. Voluntariness, therefore, is a variable that must be considered in describing the role-exit process even though, in our sample, we selected individuals who had a choice in whether to exit.

In the study described in this book we restricted ourselves to samples of voluntary exiters in order to simplify the study and focus more sharply on the process of exiting. However, it is impossible a priori to hold voluntariness completely constant and have a sample with no variation in this regard. In some instances of occupational exits, such as the ex-air traffic controllers I interviewed, there is less control over the exit than in other cases. So, too, with the divorced people and mothers who gave up custody of children. In some instances, less pressure was put on individuals to exit than in others. What resulted were samples of exiters who, on the whole, did have a choice in whether to exit but for whom the degree of choice varied because of factors in the situation from which they were exiting.

Throughout the analysis of data, there were clues which indicated that exits which were less voluntary differed from voluntary exits in the stages of the process proceding the actual exit. First doubts, for example, as well as unconscious cuing behavior that usually accompanies first doubts, would not occur because the decision to exit was made by someone other than the exiter. Likewise, the process of weighing pros and cons of a current role as compared to viable alternative roles is inappropriate because the current role is no longer a possibility. The turning point event is the fact that one is fired. What data I did have on involuntary exits indicates that many variables that occur prior to exiting for the voluntary exiters occur after the exit for those who leave a role involuntarily. What seems to happen is that the involuntary exiters experience events as positive and negative social reactions to their exit; these influence how they proceed in interpreting their exit and in weighing role alternatives in the weeks after they leave a role. Significant others both suggest and reinforce role possibilities at this point in a way similar to the dynamics that occur prior to the exit for those who leave voluntarily. The vacuum experience tends to occur for involuntary exiters at the point at which they accept the fact that they no longer occupy a previous role and have not yet generated new role possibilities. The issues which face exiters after the exit, such as presentation of self, dealing with societal reactions, shifting friendship networks, relating to group members and other exes, etc., seem to be similar to the challenges faced by individuals who left voluntarily. Given the fact that involuntary exits were excluded from our study, the preceding remarks are simply suggestive of what occurs when an role exit is involuntary. Systematic comparative research is needed to specify similarities and differences between voluntary and involuntary exiting.

The original purpose of the research reported throughout this book was to describe a process that has become very widespread in modern soceity but which has been studied very little. By necessity, the research was exploratory. The major goal of the project was to delineate characteristics of the ex-role, to describe the process of exiting, and to specify variables that influence aspects of the role-exit process. In order to test the ideas and develop the theory of role exit more extensively, there are several areas in which future research is needed. First, the variables associated with each stage of the process need to be tested with larger samples of role exiters. I hope that the present study is suggestive of the variables which characterize the role-exit process and which need to be operationalized in a systematic fashion in future studies. Second, in order to be able to predict the conditions under which role exit occurs, it is important to compare individuals in the same situations who exit with those who opt to remain in the role. Third, as indicated above, further studies are needed which compare both voluntary and involuntary exits as well as those which describe exits from roles less central to a person's identity. The contention throughout this book is that role exit is a process that is generalizable to all types of exits. And, finally, role exit and what we know about it as a basic social process must be incorporated into the broader sociological literature on role theory. In order to develop a comprehensive and adequate explanation of social roles, the notion of role exit must be as pressing and central as the traditional concept of socialization into new roles. Only then will we understand the process whereby we both learn and unlearn, engage and disengage, from the social roles that define who we are, especially in this rapidly changing world in which role exit is becoming commonplace.

Epilogue: Applied Settings

The purpose of this book was to describe the role-exit process and what is involved in creating an ex-role identity. While the primary reason for writing the book was to explicate and elaborate the process theoretically and thereby add to what we know about social life, the insights gained about role exiting will, I hope, be helpful to professionals working with individuals who are in the process of exiting various roles or who are already exes. The descriptions presented of the role-exit process are potentially useful for therapists and counselors involved with people who are struggling to come to terms with a role-exit decision or its aftermath. Likewise, anyone involved in the numerous self-help groups established to provide support for exes from various roles will, no doubt, relate to the material presented and perhaps gain insight into the general patterns that exist across role exits. In addition, agencies and organizations are continually dealing with issues of turnover rates and their impact on organizational structure. Knowledge of the process of making an exit decision could assist administrators with intervention techniques in the cases of employees whom they want to keep or in developing structures that generate greater worker commitment and reduce the "pushes" that might lead to doubts regarding role commitment.

Ideas in this section were developed in collaboration with a psychiatrist, Albert L. Ebaugh, M.D.

As examples of ways in which knowledge of the role-exit process might have applied implications, I briefly turn attention to application of the findings to therapeutic settings—first to those involving a counseling professional, and, second, to self-help groups. Whether the counseling professional be a psychiatrist, psychologist, social worker, or other mental health professional, most counselors in the course of their routine practice deal with clients who are undergoing a decision regarding a major role change. Because role exit is intricately intertwined with issues of self-identity, such a decision usually creates anxiety and is experienced as a major life decision.

A major role of the therapist is to help the individual to become aware of options and to be able to evaluate these options in the light of their personal needs, values, and interests. Frequently, clients approach a therapist at the stage of first doubts when they are generally and vaguely discontented with their lives but have not clarified the cause of their discontent. Or, equally as likely, the presenting symptom may be unrelated on the surface to unhappiness in a specific role. The function of the therapist is to help the individual clarify the problem and then begin to deal with its resolution through a nondirective approach. Once the issue is labeled as a role-decision problem, it is helpful for the therapist to be aware of the stages and influences that constitute a routine role-exit decision for individuals.

Labeling the problem can itself be therapeutic both in clarifying what is going on and, equally as important, in helping the person realize that the problem is not unique to him or her but that many other people go through a similar process. Appendix B describes how helpful it is to people to realize that they are not alone in what they are experiencing but that others share their fate.

Once the issue is labeled as a major role decision, both the therapist and the client can benefit from knowing the issues that routinely confront individuals making decisions about role commitment and exit. Awareness of timing, in terms of stages in the process, is important because it can help the therapist know when to raise issues that might influence the decision and can also help the client anticipate factors that need to be considered.

The therapist him- or herself may well become a significant other in the process, one whose opinions and reactions are important in determining outcomes. No doubt, therapists themselves can be either retarding or accelerating influences in the role-exit process for individuals under their care.

Frequently, therapists first encounter role exiters who are going through the vacuum stage of the process, described in chapter 4. Since this period is one of extreme anxiety and creates a sense of normlessness, it is quite common for people to seek therapeutic help at this stage of the process. If the therapist is aware that most role exiters go through a similar experience, he or she can create a context and definition of the situation for the individual such that feelings and anxieties are seen as "normal" and to be expected rather than indicative of deeper psychological problems. Sometimes the greatest help a therapist can give an individual "caught" in the vacuum stage is to help him or her begin to identify as an ex and move on to the creation of a new role.

Similarly, the therapist who is aware of the issues and challenges that most exes experience in creating and adapting to an ex-identity can help the person negotiate these challenges and find ways to deal with them effectively rather than muddle through each one as it occurs. In general, the more aware the individual is of what is happening and what to expect, the easier is adaptation to becoming an ex. Therapists who are themselves aware of the process can aid such awareness and can offer coping strategies.

In the past ten years, numerous self-help groups have arisen to provide material and emotional support to people who are or have exited various roles. Alcoholics Anonymous (AA) is one of the oldest and best-established of such groups and has provided a blueprint for other groups such as drug rehabilitation groups (e.g., Palmer Drug Abuse Program, PDAP) and Over Eaters

Anonymous (OA). Divorced people have the advantage of all kinds of mutual support groups, ranging from such nonsectarian groups as Parents without Partners to numerous church-related groups (e.g., First Beginnings, a nondenominational religious group for divorced people). Mothers-Without-Custody is now a nationally organized group with regional divisions and groups in major cities. Stepfamilies is also a national group organized to provide mutual support for families whose members stem from more than one marriage. The purpose of all such "self-help groups" is to gather together people who have exited a major role and provide mutual support for dealing with the problems and challenges that usually accompany such an exit. One of the primary benefits reported by members in such groups is the realization that others have similar problems and the sharing of successful solutions some have found to handle them. For exes who have participated in self-help groups, identifying with others who are also exes and realizing that one is not unique and alone in one's life situations is the single most important benefit.

This book, I hope, can further expand awareness beyond any particular group of exes to the realization that all exes, regardless of the role they have exited, share a similar life experience and that being an ex is a unique challenge in terms of establishing a role identity.

Appendix A: Demographic Characteristics of the Sample

Table A.1 Characteristics of the 1971 Ex-nun Sample

	Age	Time since exit	Time in order
Range	23–50	6 months–7 years	1 year–28 years
Median	33	1 year, 3 months	9 years

	Highest degree			Marital Status	
High school	4	7 (%)	Married	15	26 (%)
B.A. or B.S.	26	46	Single	40	70
M.A.	22	38	Engaged	2	4
Ph.D.	1	2			
No data	4	7			

Table A.2 Characteristics of the 1984 Sample

Types of exits			
Occupational		Divorced people	15
Physicians and dentists	10	Mothers without custody	10
Police Officers	8	Retirees	9
Teachers	8	Ex-ideological	10
Mental health workers	5	Recovered alcoholics	12
Air traffic controllers	7	Ex-convicts	7
Miscellaneous occupational	2	Miscellaneous	3
		Total	106

	Age	Time since exit	Time in role
Range	21–80	1½ weeks–2 years	1–63 years
Median	40	3 years	10 years

	Highest degree			Marital Status	
No high school	7	6 (%)	Married	48	42 (%)
High school	22	18	Divorced	35	30
Some college	17	15	Remarried	13	11
B.A. or B.S.	40	34	Widowed	7	6
M.A.	12	10	Single	13	11
Ph.D.	7	6		Income	
M.D.	9	8	Less than $15,000	19	16 (%)
J.D.	4	3	$15,000–$25,000	19	16
	Sex		$25,000–$40,000	21	20
Male	72	62 (%)	Over $40,000	57	49
Female	44	38			

Appendix B: The Therapeutic Impact of the Information Interview

The interview may be defined as a two-person encounter in which one participant directs conversation with a specific purpose and program in mind. Social scientists have traditionally distinguished two types of interviews: the therapeutic interview (also called the clinical interview) whose outcome is the modification of behavior of the respondent, and the information interview which is directed toward gathering data regarding specific issues of interest to the interrogator. The different goals of the two types of interviews lead to emphasis on diverse techniques in structuring the interview experience.

While a wealth of literature exists on each type of interview, with emphasis placed on the importance of distinguishing them, relatively little has been written on the interface of the two. This is due to the fact that they are abstractly differentiated on the basis of goals set by the interviewer as well as by their use in various professional settings. However, actual studies show that numerous instances exist in which, during the course of an interview, information-seeking questions and therapeutic consequences often coexist. Caplow (1956), in his frequently quoted article on the information interview, suggests that participants are sometimes motivated to cooperate for therapeutic reasons. However, he does not elaborate the implications of such a motivation for the interview situation or the interviewer. Merton, in his early study of Craftown (1947), indicates that a proportion of people interviewed perceived the interview situation as cathartic. Roethlisberger and Dickson in the Western Electric studies (1950) also suggest a therapeutic motivation for employees to volunteer to be interviewed. There is also mention of the cathartic or therapeutic effect on participants in such studies as Schneider and Conrad's (1980) analysis of people with epilepsy and Rubin's (1969) study of white working-class families. Despite these suggestions that elements of the therapeutic interview might be present while an interviewer is conducting an information interview, very little literature analyzes the relationship between the two types of interviews in terms of implications for the interview process.

A review of a dozen textbooks on interviewing shows no systematic discussion of how to deal with catharsis on the part of the interviewee. Likewise, an extensive review of psychological and sociological articles dealing with interviewing that have appeared over the past fifteen years also demonstrates an almost total lack of attention to this issue. The one exception is the work Rubin has been doing with couples research (Rubin 1974, Rubin and Mitchell 1976). In the course of administering questionnaires to student couples, he and his team of researchers realized that participating in the study had an impact on the relationships of the couples involved. In fact, one year after the study began, they sent a follow-up questionnaire to the original couples asking whether they thought the study had had an impact on their relationship. About half of the respondents answered affirmatively. Rubin then became interested in and concerned about the unintended effects of studying close relationships (Rubin 1976). Rubin's work is based primarily on paper and pencil questionnaires; however, it raises issues that are also pertinent for interview studies, especially face-to-face interviews.

In studies of a sensitive nature that explore feelings and/or events that are or have been painful or emotionally laden for the respondent, the information interview may take on characteristics of the therapeutic interview. Since data-gathering interviewers are usually not trained to handle such therapeutic situations, a number of problematic issues arise, including validity of data, interviewer training, and ethical responsibility both to interviewer and the interviewee.

The Therapeutic Interview and the Information Interview

In addition to many books written by psychiatrists on techniques of interviewing, most general textbooks of psychiatry devote a substantial section to describing the process of the therapeutic interview. The *Comprehensive Textbook of Psychiatry* (Kaplan et al., eds., 1980) summarizes characteristics of the therapeutic interview and the role of the interviewer. It puts the psychiatric interview into perspective by stating that "one person is suffering and desires relief; the other person is expected to provide the relief. It is the patient's hope of obtaining relief from his suffering that motivates him to expose himself and to tell all" (MacKinnon 1980). The confidentiality of the doctor-patient relationship and the fact that the psychiatrist is seen as an expert in the field of interpersonal relations facilitates openness and communication.

The most important role of the interviewer is to listen and understand the patient in order to establish rapport and develop a treatment plan. The interviewer uses his own empathic responses to facilitate the development of rapport. This means that the interviewer is "nonjudgmental, interested, concerned, and kind" (MacKinnon 1980).

The interviewer also makes suggestions to the interviewee either implicitly or explicitly. He or she may suggest ways to explore feelings or practical suggestions regarding life. Many of the interviewer's activities at this point serve to gratify the patient's emotional need to feel protected or loved. The interviewer also helps build the patient's self-esteem by focusing on successful achievements and talents. The interviewer offers interpretations that both clarify issues for the patient and confront him or her with unconscious feelings he or she might be avoiding.

Since the purpose of the therapeutic interview is to explore conscious and unconscious feelings in order to effect changes in the respondent's emotional life, frequently the respondent displays intense emotional reactions to material being discussed. Crying, screaming, anger, intense embarrassment, or profound relief are common occurrences in the course of such interviews. Psychiatrists and mental health professionals are trained to respond appropriately and in a therapeutic manner to such outbursts. They are taught to display concern and interest in the patient's moods without losing the objectivity necessary to help the patient deal successfully with the situation.

While the information interview shares a few of these characteristics of the therapeutic interview, such as techniques of establishing rapport, basically the nature of the information interview is very different (Whyte 1960). First and foremost, since the purpose of the interview is to maximize the validity of data, the interviewer is trained not to express value judgments or personal opinions or attitudes but rather to remain as objective and nonintrusive as possible while asking questions. When forced to offer attitudes or experiences as a means of preserving rapport, interviewers are trained to be as neutral and impersonal as possible. The skilled interviewer is constantly on guard against displaying any reaction which might modify or influence the respondent's answer to a question. In effect, the interviewer learns as much as possible about the respondent while revealing as little about him- or herself as is necessary to maintain the appearance of a conversation (Gordan 1980, Johnson 1975).

Most information interviews proceed by means of a schedule or set of questions asked of each respondent, thereby guaranteeing uniformity of questions and completeness of data. Idiosyncratic experiences are important only if they relate directly to the problem being studied. In fact, the trained interviewer is skilled at focusing conversation on the issues at hand and redirecting responses back to pertinent questions.

Open-ended and less structured questions often require probing by the interviewer into areas not at first obvious to the respondent or into areas that touch on more sensitive emotional issues. Feelings and emotional responses are frequently data of interest to the researcher as part of the study. However, rather than allow a respondent to explore an emotional issue until he or she arrives at some insight or resolution, interviewers are trained to proceed just as far as necessary to obtain pertinent information.

While conducting an information interview, it is not unusual for the questions asked to arouse deep emotions within the interviewee. In some cases, the individual is reminded of painful past experiences or feelings that have not yet been resolved. In other instances, questions may focus on issues that are deeply meaningful, arousing strong positive or negative feelings. How are interviewers to handle such situations in a way that preserves objectivity of data while maintaining an ethical and human responsibility to the participant?

Emotional Reactions to Information Interviews

Part of the role-exit data presented in this book was collected by five graduate students enrolled in a research practicum which I ran in conjunction with the study. The students were involved in developing the interview guide, pretesting it, envolving a snowball sample of respondents, and conducting the actual interviews. Each student interviewed approximately twenty people, each interview lasting about two hours. Responses were recorded on the guide as well as taped whenever possible.

None of the students had previous interview training or experience so I spent considerable time lecturing on interview techniques, conducting a sample interview before the group, and requiring each student to conduct and tape three sample interviews which I carefully critiqued and discussed with each of them. As in most training for the information interview, I emphasized techniques of introducing the interview, establishing rapport, skillfully probing responses, assuring that every question be asked and adequately answered, maintaining objectivity and nonintrusiveness of personal opinions and attitudes, and, finally, accurately recording and transcribing responses. On the basis of the initial pretest interviews, I felt my students were quite well prepared and skillful in the art of interviewing.

The research seminar met weekly to discuss progress and problems. Within the first week, students reported instances of respondents wanting to prolong the interview to three to four hours and expecting the interviewer to enter into lengthy conversations regarding the emotional impact of the role exit experience on the person. In many instances, interviewees were still working through conflicts and emotional reactions to previous role involvements. They saw the interview as an opportunity to discuss their feelings with an interested but objective outsider whom they assumed had training in understanding human emotions. To many of the interviewees, sociology was synonymous with psychology and both were seen as mental health fields related to counseling and understanding people. As a result, the interviewers were frequently confronted with highly emotional responses: crying, expressions of anger and frustration, and, most frequent of all, a drive to talk incessantly and in minute detail about the emotional impact of exiting a previous role and reestablishing a new one.

Early in the project, I faced the problem of teaching the interviewers to allow enough free expression of emotion to tap areas of central interest to the study without losing control of the interview and discouraging respondents from giving the responses we needed to understand important dimensions of the role-exit process. At this point I realized the reality of the often-quoted description of interviewing as an art. By means of frequent seminar meetings and ongoing discussions, we managed to collect some very rich data, often at the expense of long interviews and more emotional involvement with respondents than textbooks on interviewing allow. In the process I was challenged to rethink the kinds of training we traditionally give interviewers before we send them into the field.

While the interviewing was going on, I received several calls from respondents thanking me for the study and for selecting them to participate because of the emotional and therapeutic impact the interview had on them. As one recovered alcoholic commented, "As we talked, we touched on some things I had not really dealt with previously and I needed to work out. While the interview was very painful for me, there were things I needed to deal with, talk about, and work out. It was vital to my continued recovery."

The interviewers were also reporting repeated instances of interviewees commenting on the helpfulness of the interview in challenging them to think about aspects of their exit they hadn't considered before and working through emotional conflicts and feelings that still lingered from their previous exit process. While other respondents did not articulate what they experienced personally during the interview, episodes of crying and other expressions of strong emotion indicated that the interview aroused strong feelings.

During the four months of interviewing, I became increasingly aware that the interview experience was having an emotional impact on a significant number of respondents. I became interested in exploring this serendipitous finding—not only how many respondents were personally affected by the interview but also the types of impact it had, aspects of the interview situation that encouraged such personal response, and whether the impact occurred during the interview or at some later time. I sent a short questionnaire to each respondent with a cover letter expressing my appreciation for their participation in the study and requesting that they answer the enclosed few questions. I asked whether being interviewed had any impact on them personally during the interview, one to three days after the interview, and a week or more later. If they answered yes, I asked what kind of impact it had at each time period. Then I asked what about the interview led to its having an impact and whether they viewed that impact as helpful or harmful. About half of the respondents returned the questionnaire (fifty-three of the 106) with no follow-up. Of these fifty-three individuals, twenty-seven replied the interview did affect them emotionally and the remaining twenty-six said it had no personal impact. Obviously, the N's are not large enough to conduct a systematic statistical analysis; however, the responses are indicative of a range of reactions to the interview process.

The strongest reactions came from six individuals who said the interview had an impact on them at all three time periods. It was obvious that these repondents thought a lot about the interview and that they were personally affected by the questions. One divorcée replied, "The interview method was a very different approach to my feelings compared to introspection or attempted explanation because in the latter two I'm always trying to formulate a point or conclusion before even beginning, rather than dealing with raw feelings in themselves. I realized I still had a lot of feelings I had never worked through and really needed to face."

Another person, a recovered alcoholic, said she went through an agonizing week after the interview trying to piece together all the feelings it had aroused. She said the interview "made me nervous and uncomfortable thinking about my addiction to alcohol." Several days after the interview she reported that "I realized I was the main person I hurt." About a week later she began to reassess her whole situation and reflect on her life history as she had reviewed it during the interview. Her conclusion was "I felt I could maintain my freedom from addiction if I chose to." In her case, the interview challenged her to rethink her life history of addiction and reconfirmed her determination to stay sober.

Another alcoholic who was struggling to get his life together and remain sober said several questions during the interview upset him greatly and "caught him off guard." He thought he was progressing beautifully in overcoming alcoholism; however, the fact that the questions bothered him so much suggested to him that he still "didn't have it all together." He was very tempted to start drinking again and forget it all; instead, however, he's been "working on things that were difficult during the interview."

A mother who had given up custody during divorce proceedings was very eager to do the interview because she "really needs to get some things together." She entered the interview situation expecting to obtain help. After the interview, she appeared more relaxed and said she had gained some real insights.

Eleven of the respondents said the interview had an impact only during the experience itself. For about a third of these people, the interview gave them a sense of having made a right decision and reconfirmed the course their present lives were taking. As one ex-executive put it, "The interview had a very positive impact on me. It made me realize that my decision to leave my previous career to pursue another one had been a very good decision. It also made me remember my future career goals and reassess them." Another respondent indicated that the interview brought a lot of old emotions to the fore again and raised some "second thoughts" about the decision. However, he said as the interview progressed "talking about it made me realize I was doing the right thing. It confirmed things." Another person commented, "The most prominent effect the interview had upon myself was affirmation of my choice or ability to choose again if I feel the need."

Throughout the questionnaires, two themes emerged repeatedly. Almost half the respondents commented that they were flattered that someone was interested enough in their life to take the time and effort to talk with them. The following response was typical of many comments: "I felt relieved and happy that someone cared how I felt." This corroborates the often-made contention that basically most people like to be interviewed because of the attention and esteem it affords the respondent.

A second recurring theme expressed in the questionnaires is the realization that there are many other people who have gone through similar life experiences and that one's own problems are not so unique after all. The act of labeling a major change in life as "role exit" helped many respondents realize their life experiences are part of a larger phenomenon which is happening to many people today. As one person expressed it, "The interview made me realize that my changes of life-style weren't so different and this gave me confidence in myself." Another said "The topic itself, role exit, had an effect on me. I had never labeled the changes in my life. Mainly, I have never given myself credit for surviving the drastic changes or exits. Looking at these was painful. But just realizing other people go through similar exits made me proud that at least I have survived." Another said, "The interview was very helpful by letting me know that there are lots of people who are dealing with similar feelings. Now I am eager to meet other role exiters and share experiences. This would help me a lot, I feel."

When asked why the interview seemed to have an impact on them, there were two major reasons given. The most frequently mentioned was the interest, concern, and insightfulness displayed by the interviewer. As one respondent said, "Although the nature of the questions had a moderate impact, I feel the interviewer was responsible for putting me at ease, allowing my true feelings to surface. The interviewer's questions were well organized and she was pleasantly inquisitive about my ex-career." Likewise, another said, "My interviewer elicited, through her empathy, the desire to be as honest as possible."

Equally as important to respondents was the neutrality and objectivity of the interview situation itself. As one ex-executive put it, "Discussing and explaining the whole situation in depth, for the first time, to someone who was not personally involved in my case was a tremendous help because now I can look upon the whole situation from an observer's viewpoint." An ex-professional athlete said, "Besides asking dynamite questions, talking to someone with an understanding already, allows you to deal with thoughts and feelings under a controlled situation. Not feeling whether they are judging you right or wrong is important."

In addition to the questionnaire data, another indication that the interviews had an impact on respondents' personal lives was the fact that a significant number of them made contact with the interviewer after the interview itself. In most instances, they wanted to talk further about their lives and get feedback and help from the interviewer in dealing with their situations. Several said they had thought further about some of the questions and wanted to discuss their ideas and feelings.

Implications for Interviewer Training

A review of the major texts and handbooks focused on interviewing makes it clear that there is a commonly assumed array of knowledge and skills considered necessary for the adequate training of interviewers before sending them into the field. These include areas such as initial introduction of the interview, sponsorship, gaining rapport, verbal and nonverbal communication skills, probing to obtain more complete data, dealing with problems of resistance and reticence, and the accurate recording of information. Virtually none of the texts deal systematically with how to handle emotional outbursts or pain experienced by the respondent or situations in which the interviewer is expected to help the participant deal with problems. While there are recorded instances of such occurrences during particular interview studies, we social scientists seem to have neglected formal training of interviewers with regard to appropriate and humane responses to such situations.

A theme that recurs in training manuals is the importance of the interviewer's remaining neutral, objective, and in control of the interview in order to assure valid and reliable data. While it is true that the interviewer is essentially a data gatherer, the fact remains that in some instances participants are hurting and reaching out to the interviewer as a fellow human being. Skilled interviewers are frequently people who are sensitive to emotional nuances and social situations. Strong emotional outbursts on the part of the respondent can present a dilemma to the interviewer who is caught between cannons of objectivity and normal human empathy.

It is not only impossible but also dysfunctional to expect interviewers to be trained mental health counselors. Nevertheless, there are several things we might do to prepare interviewers for such situations. Warning interviewers such outbursts might occur is a first step in preparing them to anticipate emotional implications of questions. Second, they can be trained to redirect questions and reword them in ways that elicit less painful responses. Strong emotional responses can frequently be ameliorated by asking a factual question which requires the respondent to give a rational response. Interviewers can also be taught to sympathize with participants by suggesting ways of getting professional help such as therapists and counseling services. To make such suggestions indicates care and concern without drawing the interviewer personally into the situation and jeopardizing research results.

References

This list includes references cited in the text as well as other works that are relevant to the topic of role exit.

Abbot, Walter M., S. J. 1966. Decree on the Appropriate Renewal of the Religious life. *Documents of Vatican II*. New York: America Press.

Adler, Patricia. 1985. *Wheeling and Dealing: An Ethnography of An Upper-level Drug Dealing*. New York: Columbia University Press.

Allen, Vernon L., and Evert van de Vliert. 1984. *Role Transitions: Explorations and Explanations*. New York: Plenum Press.

Allport, Gordon W. 1961. *Pattern and Growth in Personality*. New York: Holt, Rinehart and Winston.

Alutto, J. A., L. G. Hrebiniak, and R. C. Alonso. 1973. On Operationalizing the Concept of Commitment. *Social Forces* 51:448–54.

American Psychological Association. 1973. Ethical Principles in the Conduct of Research with Human Participants. *American Psychologist* 28:79–80.

Anderson, N. 1923. *The Hobo*. Chicago: University of Chicago Press.

Babbie, Earl. 1983. *Sociology: An Introduction*. Belmont, Calif.: Wadsworth.

Banton, Michael. 1965. *Roles: An Introduction to the Study of Social Relations*. New York: Basic Books.

Barker, Eileen. 1984. *The Making of a Moonie: Choice or Brainwashing?* Basil Blackwell.

Becker, Howard S. 1953. Becoming a Marijuana User. *American Journal of Sociology* 59:235–42.

———. 1960. Notes on the Concept of Commitment. *American Journal of Sociology* 66:32–40.

———. 1963. *Outsiders: Studies in the Sociology of Deviance*. New York: The Free Press.

———. 1966. Introduction to Clifford Shaw, *The Jack Roller*. Chicago: University of Chicago Press.

Becker, Howard S., Blanche Geer, Everett Hughes, and Anselm L. Strauss. 1961. *Boys in White*. Chicago: University of Chicago Press.

Beckford, James A. 1985. *Cult Controversies*. London: Tavistock Publications.

Biddle, Bruce J., and Edwin J. Thomas. 1966. *Role Theory: Concepts and Research*. New York: John Wiley.

Blau, Zena Smith. 1972. Role Exit and Identity. Paper presented at the American Sociological Association Meetings, New Orleans.

———. 1973. *Old Age in a Changing Society*. New York: Franklin Watts.

Blumer, Herbert. 1969. *Symbolic Interaction, Perspective and Method*. Englewood Cliffs, N.J.: Prentice-Hall.

Blumstein, Philip, and Pepper Schwartz. 1983. *American Couples*. New York: William Morrow.

Bridges, William. 1980. *Transitions: Making Sense of Life's Changes*. Reading, Mass.: Addison-Wesley.

Brim, Orville G. 1968. Adult Socialization. In J. A. Clausen, ed., *Socialization and Society,* pp. 183–226. Boston: Little, Brown.

———. Theories of Male Mid-life Crisis. In Nancy K. Schlossberg and Alan D. Entive, eds., *Counseling Adults,* pp. 1–18. Monterey, Calif.: Brooks/Cole.

Brim, Orville G., and Carol D. Ryff. 1980. On the Properties of Life Events. In Paul B. Baltes and Brim, eds., *Life-span Development and Behavior,* 3:386–88. New York: Academic Press.

Brim, Orville, and Stanton Wheeler. 1966. *Socialization After Childhood: Two Essays*. New York: John Wiley.

Brinkerhoff, Merlin B., and Kathryn L. Burke. 1980. Disaffiliation: Some Notes on "Falling From the Faith." *Sociological Analysis* 41:41–54.

Bromley, David A., and Anson D. Shupe. 1979. Just a Few Years Seem Like a Lifetime: Role Theory Approach to Participation in New Religious Movements. In Louis Krisberg, ed., *Research in Social Movements, Conflicts and Change*. pp. 159–85. Greenwich, Conn.: JAI Press.

———. 1984. Affiliation and Disaffiliation: A Role Theory Interpretation of Joining and Leaving New Religious Movements. Paper presented at the Association for the Sociology of Religion Meetings, October, San Antonio, Tex.

Burr, Wesley R. 1972. Role Transitions: A Reformulation of Theory. *Journal of Marriage and the Family* 34:407–16.

Caplow, Theodore. 1956. The Dynamics of Information Interviewing. *American Journal of Sociology* 62:165–71.

Chambliss, William J. 1975. *Box Man: A Professional Thief's Journal* (by Harry King as told to and edited by Bill Chambliss). New York: Harper and Row.

Charmaz, Kathy. 1983. The Grounded Theory Method: An Explication and Interpretation. In Robert M. Emerson, ed., *Contemporary Field Research: A Collection of Readings,* pp. 109–26. Boston: Little, Brown.

Cherniss, Cary. 1980. *Professional Burnout in Human Service Organizations*. New York: Praeger.

Cicourel, Aaron V. 1970. Basic and Normative Rules in the Negotiation of Status and Role. In Hass P. Dreitzel, ed., *Recent Sociology No. 2: Patterns of Communicative Behavior,* pp. 4–45. New York: Macmillan.

Converse, Jean M., and Howard Schuman. 1974. *Conversations at Random: Survey Research as Interviewers See It*. New York: John Wiley.

Cressey, P. 1932. *The Taxi-Dance Hall*. Chicago: University of Chicago Press.

Cumming, Elaine, and William E. Henry. 1961. *Growing Old: The Process of Disengagement*. New York: Basic Books.

Dannefer, Dale. 1984. Adult Development and Social Theory: A Paradigmatic Reappraisal. *American Sociological Review* 49:100–116.

Davis, Fred. 1979. *Yearning for Yesterday: A Sociology of Nostalgia*. New York: The Free Press.

DeFleur, Melvin L., William V. D'Antonio, and Lois B. DeFleur. 1984. *Sociology: Human Society*. 4th ed. New York: Random House.

Denzin, Norman K. 1969. Symbolic Interactionism and Ethnomethodology: A Proposed Synthesis. *American Sociological Review* 34:922–34.

______.1978. *The Research Act: A Theoretical Introduction to Sociological Methods*. New York: McGraw-Hill.

Douglas, Jack. D. 1985. *Creative Interviewing*. Beverly Hills, Calif. Sage.

Duch, Steve, ed. 1982. *Personal Relationships. 4: Dissolving Personal Relationships*. New York: Academic Press.

Dworkin, Anthony Gary. 1986. *Teacher Burnout in the Public Schools: Structural Causes and Consequences for Children*. Albany: SUNY Press.

Dworkin, Anthony Gary, Janet S. Chafetz, and Rosalind J. Dworkin. 1986. The Effects of Tokenism on Work Alienation Among Urban Public School Teachers. *Work and Occupations* 13, no. 3, 399–420.

Ebaugh, Helen Rose Fuchs. 1977. *Out of the Cloister: A Study of Organizational Dilemmas.* Austin: The University of Texas Press.

______. 1984. Leaving the Convent: The Experience of Role Exit and Self Transformation. In Joseph A. Kotarba and Andrea Fontana, eds., *The Existential Self in Society,* pp. 156–76. Chicago: University of Chicago Press.

Elder, Glen H., Jr. 1975. Age Differentiation and the Life Course. In Alex Inkeles, ed., *Annual Review of Sociology,* 1:165–90. Palo Alto, Calif.: Annual Reviews.

______. 1980. Adolescence in Historical Perspective. In Joseph Adelson, ed., *Handbook of Adolescent Psychology,* chap. 1. New York: Wiley.

Erikson, Erik H. 1959. Identity and the Life Cycle: Selected Papers. *Psychological Issues* 1:5–173.

______. 1963. *Childhood and Society.* New York: W. W. Norton.

______. 1968. *Identity, Youth, and Crisis.* New York: Norton.

Erickson, Rosemary J., Wayman J. Crow, Louis A. Zurcher, and Archie V. Connett. 1973. *Paroled But Not Free.* New York: Behavior Publications.

Etzioni, Amitai. 1969. *The Semi-Professionals in Their Organization.* New York: The Free Press.

Featherman, David L., and Robert M. Hauser. 1978. *Opportunity and Change.* New York: Academic Press.

Ferraro, Kathleen J. 1979. Hard Love: Letting Go of an Abusive Husband. *Frontiers* 4, no. 2, 16–18.

Festinger, Leon. 1957. *A Theory of Cognitive Dissonance.* Stanford, Calif.: Stanford University Press.

Fitzpatrick, Joseph. 1971. *Puerto Rican Americans: The Meaning of Migration to the Mainland.* Englewood Cliffs, N.J.: Prentice-Hall.

Foner, Anne. 1974. Age Stratification and Age Conflict in Political Life. *American Sociological Review* 39:187–96.

Freudenberger, H. J. 1974. Staff Burn-Out. *Journal of Social Issues* 30:159–65.

Gagnon, J., and William Simon. 1973. *Sexual Conduct: The Social Sources of Human Sexuality.* Chicago: Aldine.

Garfinkel, Harold. 1956. Conditions of Successful Degradation Ceremonies. *American Journal of Sociology* 61:420–24.

Gennep, Arnold Van. 1960. *The Rites of Passage*. Chicago: University of Chicago Press.

Gist, Noel P., and Anthony Gary Dworkin. 1972. *The Blending of Races: Marginality and Identity in World Perspective*. New York: Wiley-Interscience.

Glaser, Barney G. 1978. *Theoretical Sensitivity*. San Francisco: University of California Press.

Glaser, Barney G., and Anselm L. Strauss. 1966. *Awareness of Dying*. Chicago: Aldine.

______. 1967. *Discovery of Grounded Theory*. Chicago: Aldine.

______. 1971. *Status Passage: A Formal Theory*. New York: Aldine-Atherton.

Glick, Paul C., and Arthur J. Norton. 1977. Marrying, Divorcing, and Living Together in the U.S. Today. In *Population Bulletin*, 32, no. 5, pp. 36–37. Washington, D.C.: Population Reference Review, Inc., October.

Goffman, Erving. 1959*a*. *The Presentation of Self in Everyday Life*. Garden City, N.Y.: Doubleday.

______. 1959*b*. *Encounters: Two Studies in the Sociology of Interaction*. Indianapolis: Bobbs-Merrill.

______. 1961. On the Characteristics of Total Institutions. In *Asylums: Essays on the Social Situation of Mental Patients and Other Inmates*. Garden City, N.Y.: Doubleday.

______. 1963. *Stigma: Notes on the Management of Spoiled Identity*. Englewood Cliffs, N.J.: Prentice-Hall.

______. 1967. *Interaction Ritual: Essays on Face-to-Face Behavior*. Garden City, N.Y.: Doubleday.

Goldner, Fred H., R. Richard Ritti, and Thomas P. Ference. 1977. The Production of Cynical Knowledge in Organizations. *American Sociological Review* 42:539–51.

Goode, William J. 1956. *After Divorce*. New York: The Free Press.

______. 1960. A Theory of Role Strain. *American Sociological Review* 25:483–96.

Goodman, Ellen. 1979. *Turning Points*. New York: Fawcett Crest.

Gordan, Raymond L. 1980. *Interviewing: Strategy, Techniques and Tactics*. Homewood, Ill.: The Dorsey Press.

Goslin, David A., ed. 1969. *Handbook of Socialization Theory and Research*. Chicago: Rand McNally.

Gross, Harriet, and Marvin B. Sussman. 1982. *Alternatives to Traditional Family Living*. New York: The Haworth Press.

Gross, Neal, Ward Mason, and Alexander McEachern. 1958. *Explorations in Role Analysis*. New York: John Wiley.

Hage, Jerald, and Gerald Marwell. 1968. Toward the Development of an Empirically Based Theory of Role Relationships. *Sociometry* 31, no. 2, 200–212.

Handel, Warren. 1979. Normative Expectations and the Emergence of Meaning as Solutions to Problems: Convergence of Structural and Interactionist Views. *American Journal of Sociology* 84:855–81.

Heiss, Jerrold. 1968. *Family Roles and Interaction.* Chicago: Rand McNally.

———. 1981. Social Roles. In Morris Rosenberg and Ralph H. Turner, eds., *Social Psychology: Sociological Perspectives,* pp. 94–132. New York: Basic Books.

Hochschild, Arlie R. 1975. Disengagement Theory: A Critique and Proposal. *American Sociological Review* 40:553–69.

Hogan, Dennis P. 1981. *Transitions and Social Change.* New York: Academic Press.

Hughes, Everett. 1928. *A Study of a Secular Institution: The Chicago Real Estate Board.* Ph.D. diss., University of Chicago.

———. 1958. *Men and Their Work.* New York: The Free Press.

Jacobs, Janet. 1984. The Economy of Love in Religious Commitment: The Deconversion of Women from Nontraditional Religious Movements. *Journal for the Scientific Study of Religion* 23, no. 2, 155–71.

Jacobs, Jerry. 1967. A Phenomenological Study of Suicide Notes. *Social Problems* 15:60–72.

———. 1969. *The Search for Help: A Study of the Retarded Child in the Community.* New York: Brunner/Mazel.

Jacobson, Gerald F. 1983. *The Multiple Crises of Marital Separation and Divorce.* New York: Grune and Stratton.

Janis, I. L., and L. Mann. 1977. *Decision Making: A Psychological Analysis of Conflict, Choice, and Commitment.* New York: The Free Press.

Johnson, Davis G., and Edwin B. Hutchins. 1966. Doctor or Dropout? A Study of Medical School Attribution. *Journal of Medical Education* 41:1098–1269.

Johnson, John M. 1975. *Doing Field Research.* New York: The Free Press.

Johnson, John M., and Kathleen J. Ferraro. 1984. The Victimized Self: The Case of Battered Women. In Joseph Kotarba and Andrea Fontana, eds., *The Existential Self in Society,* pp. 119–30. Chicago, Ill.: University of Chicago Press.

Jones, Landon Y. 1980. *Great Expectations: America and the Baby Boom Generation.* New York: Ballantine Books.

Joseph, N., and N. Alex. 1972. The Uniform: A Sociological Perspective, *American Journal of Sociology* 77:719–30.

Kadushin, Alfred. 1972. *The Social Work Interview.* New York: Columbia University Press.

Kahn, Robert L., Donald M. Wolf, Robert P. Quinn, Jr., Diedrick Snoek, and Robert A. Rosenthal. 1964. *Organizational Stress: Studies in Role Conflict and Ambiguity.* New York: John Wiley.

Kanter, Rosabeth Moss. 1968. Commitment and Social Organization: A Study of Commitment Mechanisms in Utopian Communities. *American Sociological Review* 33:499–517.

———. 1972. *Commitment and Community: Community and Utopia in Sociological Perspective.* Cambridge, Mass.: Harvard University Press.

———. 1977*a*. *Men and Women of the Corporation.* New York: Basic Books.

———. 1977*b*. Some Effects of Proportions on Group Life: Skewed Sex Ratios and Responses to Token Women. *American Journal of Sociology* 82:965–90.

Kaplan, Harold I., M.D., Alfred M. Freedman, M.D., and Benjamin J. Sadock, M.D. 1980. *Comprehensive Textbook of Psychiatry.* Vol. 1. London: Williams and Wilkins.

Kearl, M. 1988. *Endings: A Sociology of the Dying and the Dead.* London: Oxford University Press.

Kelley, Harold H. 1952. Two Functions of Reference Groups. In G. E. Swanson, T. M. Newcomb, and E. L. Hartley, eds., *Readings in Social Psychology,* pp. 410–14. New York: Henry Holt.

Kelman, Herbert C. 1972. The Rights of the Subject in Social Research: An Analysis in Terms of Relative Power and Legitimacy. *American Psychologist* 27:989–1015.

Kemper, Theodore D. 1968. Reference Groups, Socialization and Achievement. *American Sociological Review* 33:31–45.

Kessler, Suzanne J., and Wendy McKenna. 1978. *Gender: An Ethnomethodological Approach.* New York: John Wiley.

Kimmel, Douglas C. 1974. *Adulthood and Aging: An Interdisciplinary and Developmental View.* New York: John Wiley.

King, Stanley H. 1962. *Perceptions of Illness and Medical Practice.* New York: Russell Sage Foundation.

Kitsuse, John I. 1962. Societal Reactions to Deviant Behavior: Problems of Theory and Method. *Social Problems* 9:247–56.

Kohlberg, Lawrence. 1969. Stage and Sequence: The Cognitive-Developmental Approach to Socialization. Chap. 6 in *Handbook of Socialization Theory and Research.* Chicago: Rand McNally.

Kuhn, Manford H. 1954. Factors in Personality: Socio-Cultural Determinants as Seen Through the Amish. In Francis L. K. Hsu, ed., *Aspects of Culture and Personality,* pp. 43–60. New York: Abelard Schuman.

La Gaipa, J. J. 1982. Rules and Rituals in Disengaging from Relationships. In Steve Duch, ed., *Personal Relationships. 4: Dissolving Personal Relationships,* pp. 189–210. New York: Academic Press.

Lawrence, Barbara S. 1980. The Myth of the Midlife Crisis. *Sloan Management Review* 21, no. 4, 35–49.

Lemert, Edwin. 1951. *Social Pathology.* New York: McGraw-Hill.

———. 1967. The Concept of Secondary Deviance. In Lemert, ed., *Human Deviance, Social Problems and Social Control,* pp. 40–64. Englewood Cliffs, N.J.: Prentice-Hall.

Levinson, Daniel J. 1978. *The Seasons of a Man's Life.* New York: Ballatine Books.

Linton, Ralph. 1936. *The Study of Man.* New York: Appleton-Century-Crofts.

Liska, Allen E. 1981. *Perspectives on Deviance.* Englewood Cliffs, N.J.: Prentice-Hall.

Lofland, John. 1966. *Doomsday Cult.* Englewood Cliffs, N.J.: Prentice-Hall.

———. 1976. *Doing Social Life: The Qualitative Study of Human Interaction in Natural Settings.* New York: John Wiley.

Lofland, John, and Rodney Stark. 1965. Becoming a World-Saver: A Theory of Conversion to a Deviant Perspective. *American Sociological Review* 30:862–75.

Louis, Meryl Reiss. 1980. Career Transitions: Varieties and Commonalities. *Academy of Management Review* 5, no. 3, 329–40.

McCall, George J., and J. L. Simmons. 1978. *Identities and Interactions: An Examination of Human Associations in Everyday Life.* New York: The Free Press.

McHugh, Peter. 1966. Social Disintegration as a Requisite of Resocialization. *Social Forces* 44:355–63.

MacKinnon, Roger A. 1980. Psychiatric Interview. In Harold I. Kaplan, M.D., Alfred M. Freedman, M.D., and Benjamin J. Sadock, M.D., eds., *Comprehensive Textbook of Psychiatry,* 1:895–905. London: Williams and Wilkins.

Maines, David R. 1977. Social Organization and Social Structure in Symbolic Interactionist Thought. *Annual Review of Sociology* 3:235–59.

Manis, Jerome G., and Bernard N. Meltzer, eds. 1972. *Symbolic Interaction: A Reader in Social Psychology.* Boston: Allyn and Bacon.

Marshall, Victor W. 1980. *Last Chapters: A Sociology of Aging and Dying*. Belmont, Calif.: Wadsworth.

Maslach, Christina. 1976. Burned-Out. *Human Behavior* 5:16–22.

———. 1978. The Client Role in Staff Burnout. *Journal of Social Issues* 34, no. 4, 111–24.

———. 1982*a*. Understanding Burnout: Definitional Issues in Analyzing a Complex Phenomenon. In W. S. Paine, ed., *Job Stress and Burnout: Research, Theory and Intervention Perspective*, pp. 29–40. Beverly Hills, Calif.: Sage.

———. 1982*b*. *Burnout: The Cost of Caring*. Englewood Cliffs, N.J.: Prentice-Hall.

Mead, George Herbert. 1934. Selected Writings. Edited by Andrew Beck. Indianapolis: Bobbs-Merrill.

Meltzer, Bernard N., John W. Petras, and Larry T. Reynolds. 1975. *Symbolic Interactionism: Genesis, Varieties and Criticism*. London: Routledge and Kegan Paul.

Merton, Robert K. 1947. Selected Problems of Field Work in the Planned Community. *American Sociological Review* 12:304–12.

———. 1957*a*. *Social Theory and Social Structure*. New York: The Free Press.

———. 1957*b*. The Role Set: Problems in Sociological Theory. *British Journal of Sociology* 8:106–20.

———. 1963. Sociological Ambivalence. In E. A. Tyriakian, ed., *Continuities in Social Research: Essays in Honor of Pitirim Sorokin*, pp. 91–102. New York: Macmillan.

———. 1984. Socially Expected Durations: A Case Study of Concept Formation in Sociology. In Walter W. Powell and Richard Robbins, eds., *Conflict and Consensus: A Festschrift in Honor of Lewis A. Coser*, pp. 262–83. New York: The Free Press.

Merton, Robert K., and A. S. Kitt. 1950. Contributions to the Theory of Reference Group Behavior. In R. K. Merton and P. S. Lazarsfeld, eds., *Continuities in Social Research Studies in the Scope and Method of "The American Soldier."* Glencoe, IL: The Free Press.

Merton, Robert K., and Alice S. Rossi. 1957. Contributions to the Theory of Reference Group Behavior. *Social Theory and Social Structure*. New York: The Free Press.

Sr. Bertrand Meyers, D. C. 1965. *Sisters for the Twenty-first Century*. New York: Sheed and Ward.

Milgram, Stanley. 1969. *Obedience to Authority*. New York: Harper and Row.

Mills, Trudy. 1985. The Assault on the Self: Stages in Coping with Battering Husbands. *Qualitative Sociology* 8:36–48.

Mobley, W. H., R. W. Griffith, H. H. Hand, and B. M. Meglino. 1979. Review and Conceptual Analysis of the Employee Turnover Process. *Psychological Bulletin* 86:493–522.

Money, John, and Patricia Tucker. 1975. *Sexual Signatures: On Being a Man or a Woman*. Boston: Little, Brown.

Moore, Joan W. 1970. Internal Colonialism: The Case of the Mexican Americans. *Social Problems* 17:463–71.

Morris, Peter. 1974. *Loss and Change*. London: Routledge and Kegan Paul.

Neal, Marie Augusta. 1984. *Catholic Sisters in Transition: From the 1960s to the 1980s*. Wilmington, Del.: Michael Glazier.

Olesen, Virginia, and Elvi Whittaker. 1968. *The Silent Dialog: A Study in the Social Psychology of Professional Socialization*. San Francisco: Jossey-Bass.

O'Neill, Nena, and George O'Neill. 1974. *Shifting Gears: Finding Security in a Changing World*. New York: M. Evans.

Park, Robert E. 1928. Human Migration and the Marginal Man. *American Journal of Sociology* 33:881–93.

______. 1931. The Sociological Methods of William Graham Summer, William I. Thomas and Florian Znanieki. In Stewart A. Rice, ed., *Methods of Social Science: A Case Book*, pp. 154–175. Chicago: University of Chicago Press.

______. 1952. *Human Communities*. Vol. 2 of *The Collected Papers of Robert Park*. Edited by E. Hughes, C. S. Johnson, J. Masuoha, R. Redford, and L. Wirth. Glencoe, Ill.: Free Press.

______. 1955. *Society*. Vol. 3 of *The Collected Papers of Robert Park*. Edited by E. Hughes, C. S. Johnson, J. Masuoha, R. Redford, and L. Wirth. Glencoe, Ill.: Free Press.

Parsons, Talcott. 1961. *The Social System*. London: Routledge and Kegan Paul.

Pfuhl, Edwin H., Jr. 1980. *The Deviance Process*. New York: D. Van Nostrand.

Phillips, Deena J. 1984. *Role Residual and the Role Exit Process*. M.A. thesis, University of Houston.

Pines, Ayola, and Elliot Aronson. 1981. *Burnout: From Tedium to Personal Growth*. New York: The Free Press.

Press, Robert C. 1975. Labeling Theory: A Reconceptualization and a Propositional Statement on Typing. *Sociological Focus* 8:79–96.

Price, James L. 1977. *The Study of Turnover*. Ames: Iowa State University Press.

Prus, Robert C. 1978. From Barrooms to Bedrooms: Towards a Theory of Interpersonal Violence. In M. A. Beyer Gammon, ed., *Violence in Canada*, pp. 51–73. Toronto: Methuen (Carswell).

———. 1987. Generic Social Processes: Maximizing Conceptual Development in Ethnographic Research. Forthcoming in *Journal of Contemporary Ethnography*.

Rasmussen, Paul K., and Kathleen J. Ferraro. 1979. The Divorce Process. *Alternative Lifestyles* 2:443–60.

Ray, Marsh B. 1964. The Cycle of Abstinence and Relapse Among Heroin Addicts. In Howard S. Becker, ed., *The Other Side: Perspectives on Deviance,* pp. 163–77. New York: The Free Press.

Reynolds, Janice M., and Larry T. Reynolds. 1973. Interactionism, Complicity, and the Astructural Bias. *Catalyst* 7:76–85.

Richardson, James T. 1978. *Conversion Careers: In and Out of New Religions*. Beverly Hills, Calif.: Sage.

Richardson, James T., Jan van der Lans, and Frans Derks. 1986. Leaving and Labeling: Voluntary and Coerced Disaffiliation From Religious Social Movements. In Kurt Lang, ed., *Research in Social Movements, Conflicts and Change,* 9:97–126. Greenwich, Conn.: JAI Press.

Riley, Matilda W. 1978. Aging, Social Change and the Power of Ideas. *Daedalus* 107:39–52.

Riley, Matilda W., Marilyn Johnson, and Anne Foner. 1972. *Aging and Society*. Vol. 3, *A Sociology of Age Stratification*. New York: Russell Sage.

Rodriguez, Nestor. 1987. Undocumented Central Americans in Houston: Diverse Populations. *International Migration Review* 21, no. 1, 4–26.

Roethlisberger, F. J., and W. J. Dickson. 1950. *Management and the Worker*. Cambridge, Mass.: Harvard University Press.

Rosenbaum, James. 1983. *Careers in a Corporate Hierarchy: Structural Timetables and Historical Data*. New York: Academic Press.

Rosenberg, Morris. 1979. *Conceiving the Self*. New York: Basic Books.

Rossi, Alice. 1980. Life Span Theory and Women's Times. *Signs: Journal of Women in Culture and Society* 6:4–32.

Rubin, Lillian B. 1969. *Worlds of Pain: Life in the Working Class Family*. New York: Basic Books.

———. 1979. *Women of a Certain Age*. New York: Harper.

Rubin, Zick. 1974. Lovers and Other Strangers: The Development of Intimacy in Encounters and Relationships. *American Scientist* 62:182–90.

Rubin, Zick, and Cynthia Mitchell. 1976. Couples Research as Couples Counseling: Some Unintended Effects of Studying Close Relationships. *American Psychologist* 31:17–25.

San Giovanni, Lucinda. 1978. *Ex-Nuns: A Study of Emergent Role Passage*. Norwood, N.J.: Ablex.

Sarason, Seymore B. 1977. *Work, Aging, and Social Change:*

Professionals and the One Life-One Career Imperative. New York: The Free Press.

Sarbin, T. R. 1954. Role Theory. In G. Lindzey, ed., *Handbook of Social Psychology*, pp. 223–58. Cambridge, Mass.: Addison-Wesley.

Sarbin, T. R., and K. E. Scheibe. 1980. The Transvaluation of Social Identity. In C. J. Bellone, ed., *The Normative Dimension in Public Administration*, pp. 219–45. Boston: Allyn and Bacon.

Sarbin, Theodore R., and Vernon L. Allen. 1968. Role Theory. In Gardner Lindsey and Elliot Aronson, eds., *The Handbook of Social Psychology*, 2d ed., Reading, Mass.: Addison-Wesley.

Scheff, Thomas J. 1966. *Being Mentally Ill: A Sociological Theory*. Chicago: Aldine.

Schneider, Joseph W., and Peter Conrad. 1980. In the Closet with Illness: Epilepsy, Stigma Potential and Information Control. *Social Problems* 28:32–43.

Schur, Edwin. 1971. *Labeling Deviant Behavior: Its Sociological Implications*. New York: Harper and Row.

Schwartz, Howard, and Jerry Jacobs. 1979. *Qualitative Sociology: A Method to the Madness*. New York: The Free Press.

Shaw, Clifford R. 1931. *The Jack Roller: The Natural History of a Delinquent Career*. Chicago: University of Chicago Press.

Shaw, Marvin E., and Philp F. Costanzo. 1970. *Theories of Social Psychology*. New York: McGraw Hill.

Sheehy, Gail. 1976. *Passages: Predictable Crises of Adult Life*. New York: Dutton.

______. 1981. *Pathfinders*. New York: Bantam Books.

Shibutani, Tamotsu. 1955. Reference Groups as Perspectives. *American Journal of Sociology* 60:562–69.

Shover, Neal. 1985. *Aging Criminals*. Beverly Hills, Calif.: Sage.

Shupe, Anson D., and David G. Bromley. *The New Vigilantes*. Beverly Hills, Calif.: Sage Publications.

Simmel, George. 1950. *The Sociology of George Simmel*. Edited and translated by K. Wolff. New York: The Free Press.

______. 1955. Conflict and the Web of Group Affiliations. Edited and translated by K. Wolff. New York: The Free Press.

Skolnick, Arlene. 1975. The Limits of Childhood: Conceptions of Child Development and Social Context. *Law and Contemporary Problems* 39:38–77.

Snow, David A., and Cynthia L. Phillips. 1980. The Lofland-Stark Conversion Model: A Critical Reassessment. *Social Problems* 27:430–47.

Spangler, E., M. Gordon, and R. Pipkin. 1978. Token Woman: An

Empirical Test of Kanter's Hypothesis. *American Journal of Sociology* 84:160–70.

Spilerman, Seymour. 1977. Careers, Labor Market Structure, and Socio-economic Achievement. *American Journal of Sociology* 83:551–93.

Spitzer, Stephan, Carl Couch, and John Stratton. 1970. *The Assessment of Self.* Iowa City: Effective Communications.

Stanley, David T. 1976. *Prisoners Among Us: The Problems of Parole.* Washington, D.C.: Brookings Institute.

Stevens, John M., Janice M. Beyer, and Harrison M. Trice. 1978. Assessing Personal, Role, and Organizational Predictors of Managerial Commitment. *Academy of Management Journal* 21:380–96.

Stoller, Robert J. 1968. *Sex and Gender: On the Development of Masculinity and Femininity.* New York: Science House.

Stonequist, Everett V. 1937. *The Marginal Man: A Study in Personality and Culture Conflict.* New York: Charles Scribner's Sons.

Stouffer, Samuel A., Edward A. Suchman, Lelan C. DeVinney, Shirley A. Star, and Robin M. Williams. 1949. *The American Soldier.* Princeton, N.J.: Princeton University Press.

Strauss, Anselm L. 1959. *Mirrors and Masks: The Search for Identity.* Glencoe, Ill.: Free Press.

Stryker, Sheldon. 1968. Identity Salience and Role Performance: The Relevance of Symbolic Interaction Theory for Family Research. *Journal of Marriage and the Family* 30:558–64.

———. 1980. *Symbolic Interactionism.* Menlo Park, Calif.: Benjamin Cummings.

Sutherland, E. 1937. *The Professional Thief.* Chicago: University of Chicago Press.

Tannenbaum, Frank. 1938. *Crime and Community.* New York: Columbia University Press.

Thibaut, J. W., and Kelley, H. H. 1959. *The Social Psychology of Groups.* New York: John Wiley.

Thomas, W. I., and Florian Znaniecki. 1927. *The Polish Peasant in Europe and America.* Boston: R. G. Badger.

Thompson, Wayne E. 1958. Pre-Retirement Anticipation and Adjustment to Retirement. *Journal of Social Issues* 14, no. 2, 35–45.

Thornton, Russell, and Peter N. Nardi. 1975. The Dynamics of Role Acquisition. *American Journal of Sociology* 80:870–85.

Toch, Hans. 1965. *The Social Psychology of Social Movements.* Indianapolis: Bobbs-Merrill.

Turner, Jonathan H. 1978. *The Structure of Sociological Theory.* Homewood, Ill.: The Dorsey Press.

Turner, Ralph H. 1976. The Real Self: From Institution to Impulse. *American Journal of Sociology* 81:989–1016.

———. 1978. The Role and the Person. *American Journal of Sociology* 84:1–23.

———. 1985. Unanswered Questions in the Convergence Between Structuralist and Interactionist Role Theories. In H. J. Hille and S. N. Eisenstadt, eds., *Micro-Sociological Theory: Perspectives on Sociological Theory,* Sage Studies in International Sociology, 2:22–36.

Vaughn, Diana. 1986. *Uncoupling: Turning Points in Intimate Relationships.* New York: Oxford University Press.

Waller, Willard. 1930. *The Old Love and the New: Divorce and Readjustment.* New York: Liveright.

Weiss, Robert S. 1975. *Marital Separation.* New York: Basic Books.

Wheeler, Stanton. 1961. Socialization in Correctional Communities. *American Sociological Review* 26:697–719.

Whyte, William Foote. 1960. Interviewing in Field Research. In Richard N. Adams and Jack J. Preiss, eds., *Human Organization Research: Field Relations and Techniques,* pp. 352–74. Homewood, Ill.: Dorsey.

Wright, Charles. 1967. Changes in Occupational Commitment of Graduate Sociology Students: A Research Note. *Sociological Inquiry* 37 (Winter): 55–62.

Wright, Stuart A. 1984. Post-involvement Attitudes of Voluntary Defectors from Controversial New Religious Movements. *Journal for the Scientific Study of Religion* 23, no. 2, 172–82.

Yankelovich, Daniel. 1981. *New Rules: Searching for Self-Fulfillment in a World Turned Upside Down.* New York: Bantam Books.

Zablocki, Benjamin. 1980. *Alienation and Charisma: A Study of Contemporary American Communes.* New York: The Free Press.

Zurcher, Louis A., Jr. 1977. *The Mutable Self: A Self-Concept for Social Change.* Beverly Hills, Calif.: Sage Publications.

———. 1979. Role Selection: The Influence of Internalized Vocabularies of Motive. *Symbolic Interaction* 2 (Fall): 45–62.

———. 1983. *Social Roles: Conformity, Conflict, and Creativity.* Beverly Hills, Calif.: Sage.

Zygmunt, Joseph F. 1972. Movements and Motives: Some Unresolved Issues in the Psychology of Social Movements. *Human Relations* 25:449–67.

Name Index

Subject Index

For headings beginning with "Ex-," see special profession or role, e.g., for ex-nuns, see nuns